KU-258-529

THE
PAUL HAMLYN
LIBRARY

TRANSFERRED FROM

THE
CENTRAL LIBRARY
OF THE
BRITISH MUSEUM

2010

Palestinian Costume

PUBLISHED FOR THE TRUSTEES OF THE BRITISH MUSEUM

BY BRITISH MUSEUM PUBLICATIONS

Palestinian Costume

SHELAGH WEIR

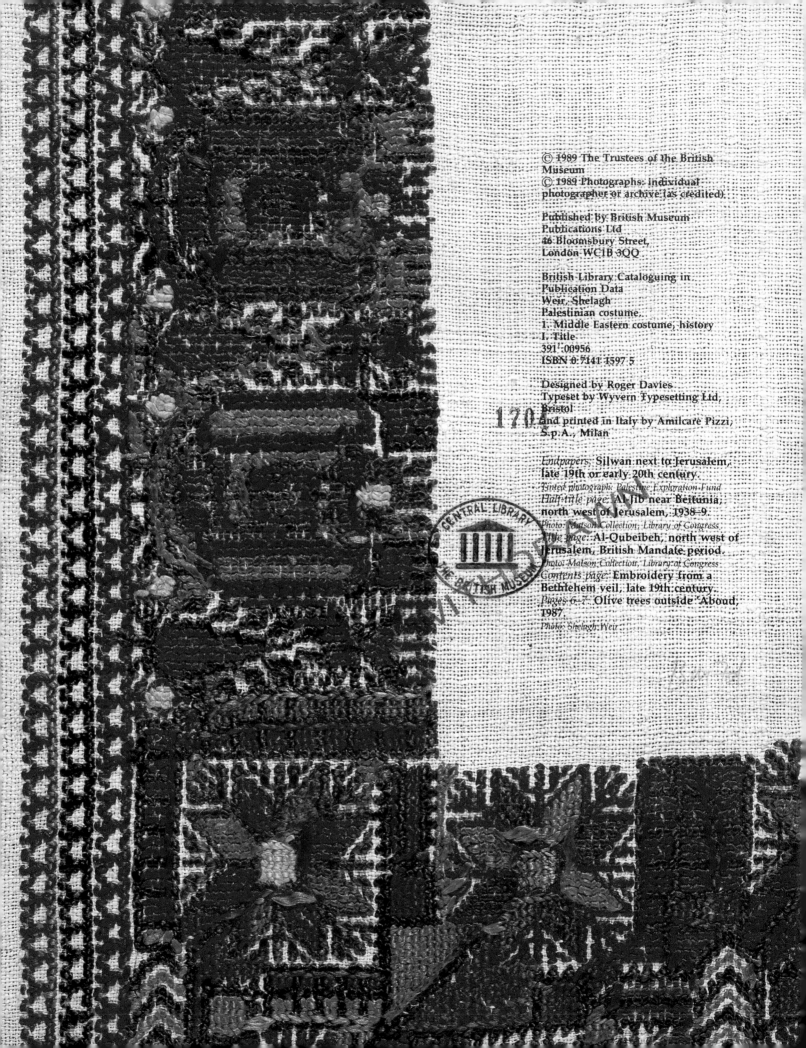

© 1989 The Trustees of the British Museum
© 1989 Photographs: individual photographer or archive (as credited).

Published by British Museum Publications Ltd
46 Bloomsbury Street,
London WC1B 3QQ

British Library Cataloguing in Publication Data
Weir, Shelagh
Palestinian costume.
1. Middle Eastern costume, history
I. Title
391'.00956
ISBN 0 7141 1597 5

Designed by Roger Davies
Typeset by Wyvern Typesetting Ltd, Bristol
and printed in Italy by Amilcare Pizzi, S.p.A., Milan

170

Endpapers: Silwan next to Jerusalem, late 19th or early 20th century.
Tinted photograph: Palestine Exploration Fund
Half-title page: Al-Jib near Beitunia, north west of Jerusalem, 1938-9.
Photo: Matson Collection, Library of Congress
Title page: Al-Qubeibeh, north west of Jerusalem, British Mandate period.
Photo: Matson Collection, Library of Congress
Contents page: Embroidery from a Bethlehem veil, late 19th century.
Pages 6-7: Olive trees outside 'Aboud, 1987.
Photo: Shelagh Weir

Contents

The Trustees of the British Museum wish to acknowledge with gratitude the generous support of the following individuals and institutions towards the publication of this book.

Sami Alami

Soraya Antonius

The Arab Ambassadors Council

The Arab-British Chamber of Commerce

Tharwat al-Barghouti

Mary Barrow

The Council of Saudi Chambers of Commerce

Sir James Craig

Ramzi Dalloul

Rafiq Hariri

Nizar Jardaneh

Suad and Ahmed Juffali

Walid Kattan

Salwa Khuri-Otaqui

Munib al-Masri

Zein Mayassi

Zaki Nusseibeh

Hani Jameel Al-Qaddumi

Abdul-Muhsin al-Qattan

Jehan Rajab

Haseeb Sabbagh

The Diana Tamari Sabbagh Foundation

Mahdi Saifi

Fuad Es-Said

Abdul-Majeed Shoman

Munzer Wehbe

The Welfare Association

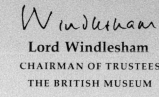

Lord Windlesham
CHAIRMAN OF TRUSTEES
THE BRITISH MUSEUM

PALESTINE
before 1948
showing Arab villages

Arab village
market village
TOWN

200–400 metres
over 400 metres

kms
0   10   20

Hunin
Qeitiya
Al-Na'ima
Al-Salihiya
Mallaha
Lake Huleh

LAKE TIBERIAS
TIBERIAS

Ja'una
SAFED
Salha
Jish
Deir al-Qasi
Sa'sa'
Safsaf
Suhmata
Al-Buquei'a
Beit Jann
Nahf
Upper Galilee
Majd al-Kurum
Yirka
Sha'ab
Sakhnin
Tamra
'Ibillin
Shafa 'Amr

Hittin
Lubya
Saffuriyeh
Kefr Kenna
NAZARETH
Dabburiyeh
Yafa
Lower Galilee

Sirin
BEISAN
uep.

Al-Bussah
Kafr Yasif
Abu Sinan
ACRE
HAIFA

Al-Tireh
Isfia
Mount Carmel
Daliyat al-Karmil
Jaba'
Ijzim
'Ain Ghazel
Umm al-Zinat
Tantura

Plain of Esdraelon
Abu Shusheh
Afula

Sabbarin
Al-Sindyana
Baqa

Umm al-Fahm
JENIN
Burqin
Qabatiyeh
'Araba

'Attil
Shuweika
Tulkarm

Tammun
Tubas
Meithalun
'Attara
'Jaba'
Anabta
Burqa

MEDITERRANEAN

DEAD SEA

Desert

Negev

TEL AVIV
JAFFA

JERUSALEM
Al-'Aizeriyeh
Abu Dis
Silwan
Surbahar
BETHLEHEM
Beit Sahur
Artas

RAMALLAH
El-Bireh

JERICHO

Nabi Musa

Sayidna Ali

Qalqilya

Kafr Qasim

Huwwara
'Awarta
Beita
'Aqraba
'Qabalan

Thulth
Deir Istia
Jamma'in

Sinjil
Salfit
Jiljiliyeh
Bir Zeit
Silwad
Beitin
Taybeh
Deir Dibwan

Kafr
Thulth
Bidya

'Aboud
Deir Qadis
Na'lin
Ain Arik
Beitunia
Beit Nuba
Abu Ghosh

Zakariyeh
Al-Qubab

Kafr 'Ana
Deir Terif
Beit Naba'a
Qibya
Zakariyeh

Selameh
Kheriyeh
Saqiyeh

Beit Dajan
Safriyeh
LYDDA
Nabi Salih
RAMLEH

Yazur

Sarafand

Nabi Rubin

Yibna
'Aqir
Al-Na'ani

Qatra

Masmiyyeh

Berqosia

Sumeil

Kudna
Deir al-Nakhas

Beit Jibrin

Falujeh

Beit Daras
Tell al-Saffi

Kaukaba

Huleiqat

Qubeibeh ibn 'Awadh

Dawaimeh

Ashdod
(Isdud)

Al-Jura
Mejdel

Hirbya

Bureir

Beit Lahiyah

Jabaliya

GAZA

Deir Al-Balah

KHAN YUNIS
Bani Suheila

Rafah

Lifta
Deir Yasin
'Ain Karim
Al-Malha
Beit Safafa
Beit Jala

Bureij

Kharas
Beit 'Ula
Idna
Tarqomiyah

Beit 'Ummar
Si'ir
Halhul
HEBRON
Dura
Yatta
Samu'ah

Bani Na'im

Dhahariyeh

BEERSHEBA

Acknowledgements

This book is based primarily on field research among Palestinians in Israel, the Occupied Territories and Jordan, and also on research in libraries, museums and private collections. In the course of this work, which has been conducted at long intervals and spanned many years, I have been helped by many people to all of whom I wish to express my gratitude.

My interest in Palestinian costume began in late 1965, soon after I joined the British Museum, when I was required to select Palestinian costumes from the Church Missionary Society (CMS) collections then being disposed of. In this I was helped by Violet Barbour who had collected costumes in the 1930s for the Palestine Folk Museum in Jerusalem, of which she was a founder member.[1] Violet passed on both her knowledge and enthusiasm for the subject which, combined with the beauty and variety of the costumes, stimulated me to do research. I therefore owe Violet special thanks for her early influence and also for her help and friendship over the ensuing years.

During my first two research visits of several months to Israel and the Israeli-occupied West Bank and Gaza in 1967 and 1968, in addition to collecting and

Bethlehem market, British Mandate period.
Photo: American Colony

documenting more garments and other artefacts for the British Museum, I was mainly concerned with learning the large vocabulary of costume and with identifying the main regional styles. The latter process was facilitated by gaining access in 1968, through Yusef Saad, to the former Palestine Folk Museum Collection, then in storage.

During short visits in 1969 and 1970, I extended my research and collecting to Palestinian refugees living in Jordan, and first worked with Widad Kawar in Amman, with whom I also visited weaving centres in Syria. This early work resulted in two exhibitions which opened at the Museum of Mankind in 1970: *Costumes of Palestine* and *Spinning and Weaving in Palestine*, and two pamphlets published to accompany them (*see* Weir, 1970a & b).

In the 1970s the focus of my research narrowed to Beit Dajan, and on several short visits to Jordan, the West Bank and the Gaza Strip I worked with former inhabitants of the village (all refugees), concentrating on the significance of costume in the context of marriage. Much of the research on Beit Dajan was done in collaboration with Widad Kawar, and a joint article on our findings was published in 1975. It was a special pleasure to work with someone who shared enthusiasm for the same subject, and who has a superb collection of Palestinian costumes (*see* Kawar, 1982 and Kawar and Hackstein, 1988). I am also very grateful to Mrs Kawar and her family for their generous hospitality on many occasions.

During my field work in Jordan, the West Bank and Gaza I received valuable help in interviewing informants and translating tapes from Louba Breen, Nadia Bseiso, Afaf Ibrahim, Vera Tamari and Emily Zabaneh. I am also grateful to officials of the United Nations Relief and Works Agency (UNRWA) for their help. My work was enriched by discussions with the late Ziva Amir whose artistic insights and exuberant friendship are sorely missed.

My greatest debt is to the many Palestinians who welcomed me so warmly into their homes and answered my questions so patiently, especially the people of Beit Dajan who painstakingly explained their costume language, and vividly evoked their former wedding customs. It is impossible to name everyone who gave me information, but I would like to mention my main Beit Dajan informants in Amman: the late Imm Sa'id and her daughter Ruqiyeh Abbas (Imm Ibrahim), Imm Ibrahim, Halimeh and Ruqiyeh (the daughters of Sheikh Yusef), Imm Muhammad and the late Abu Subuh.

I would like to thank the International Folk Museum, Santa Fe, for allowing me to study the John Whiting

11

Collection, and the Royal Ontario Museum, Toronto, for access to the Holman Hunt collection.

I am grateful to a number of photographic archives for permission to publish pictures from their collections, and to their archivists for their help: Gillian Grant of the Middle East Centre, Oxford, Rupert Chapman of the Palestine Exploration Fund, Michael Willis of the Imperial War Museum, the staff of the Harvard Semitic Museum, and especially George Hobart of the Library of Congress for his help during two weeks studying the rich Matson Collection. I would also like to thank Bryony Llewellyn and Charles Newton for their help in consulting the Searight Collection in the Department of Prints at the Victoria and Albert Museum, Judith Bronkhurst for advice on the work of Holman Hunt, and Manchester City Art Galleries for permission to reproduce Hunt's 'Shadow of Death'.

Many of the most engaging and well-documented photographs in the book were taken by women, all sadly now deceased, who did research of various kinds in Palestine during the British Mandate period: Grace Crowfoot, Hilma Granqvist, Jan Macdonald and Olga Tufnell. I am grateful to them and their families for making the pictures available, and to Olga Tufnell and Elizabeth Crowfoot for donating photographs to the Museum of Mankind. Klaus-Otto Hundt, Nabil Anani and Sliman Mansur also kindly lent photographs. I have made extensive use of the unique collection of photographs taken by Hilma Granqvist in Artas between 1925 and 1931, and relied heavily on the valuable information provided in the book edited by Karen Seger (1982) in which many were published.

Most of the above research was conducted under the auspices of the British Museum, and I am grateful to the Trustees for their support and for special leave of absence. Important help and support was also given at various stages by colleagues at the Museum: the late Richard Barnett, Celia Clear, William Fagg and Jean Rankine.

Most of the costumes illustrated are from the collections of the Museum of Mankind; most were purchased in the Middle East or in London, and the rest have been generously donated to the Museum over the years. The remainder of illustrations are of costumes lent to the Museum especially for the exhibition *Palestinian Costume* which opened in late 1989. I would like to thank the following people and institutions for their generous loans which have greatly enriched both the book and the exhibition: Violet Barbour, Philip Meader of The Church's Ministry Among the Jews, Hind Husseini of The Dar al-Tifl Museum, Jerusalem, Julia Dabdoub, Widad Kawar, Schuyler Jones and the Trustees of The Pitt Rivers Museum, Oxford, Ivy and Sari Nasir and Val Vester. I am also grateful to Karin v. Welck and Gisela Volger at the Rautenstrauch-Joests-Museums in Cologne and Annie Montigny, Sophie Caratini and Jean Hannoyer of the Institut du Monde Arabe, Paris, for their help in arranging photography of pieces from the Kawar collection. In Cologne Katharina Hackstein kindly provided hospitality and stimulating discussion.

I am most grateful to the following friends and colleagues for their constructive comments on drafts of the final two chapters of this book: Frederik Barth, Edmund Leach, Ioan Lewis, Serene Shahid, Nancy Tapper and Richard Tapper. I am especially grateful to Stace Birks for his detailed and helpful comments on the final manuscript and for his encouragement. The support of Elizabeth Fernea, Michelle Gernand, Serene Shahid and Walid Khalidi has also been greatly appreciated.

Various colleagues at the British Museum have made valuable contributions to the book: Rebecca Jewell drew the diagrams and maps, Helen Wolfe helped with maps, Margaret McCord and Alison Rae of the Department of Conservation supervised the conservation of the costumes, Henry Brewer and other members of the British Museum Photographic Service did the initial studio photography, and Rachel Rogers and Julie Young of British Museum Publications shepherded the book through the editorial and production processes.

The impact of a richly illustrated book such as this depends heavily on the quality of photographs and design. I would therefore like to express special thanks to Jane Beamish, Principal Photographer in the Museum of Mankind, who took most of the studio photographs, and to Roger Davies who designed the book. Their creative contributions have greatly enhanced the final result, and it has been a pleasure to work with them

Last but by no means least, I would like to express my warm personal thanks to the people and institutions, named on page seven, whose generous donations have enabled us to do justice to this rich and colourful aspect of the Palestinian cultural heritage.

Note on Arabic terms
Arabic terms have been transcribed with diacritical signs in the Index.

Right **Village women at the well, location unknown, British Mandate period.**
Photo: Matson Collection, Library of Congress

This book describes the costumes of the villagers and bedouin who formed the majority of the population of Palestine prior to 1948. My main aims have been to illustrate the great variety and beauty of Palestinian garments, and to interpret their meanings in the context of Palestinian society and culture. The main historical focus of the study is the thirty-year period of British rule from the end of the First World War to 1948; reference is also made to the costumes of the nineteenth century, and those worn up to the present day.

First it is necessary to provide the social and historical background to the study, and to describe the approach which has been taken to its subject.

Historical background[1]

For the four centuries preceding the First World War, Palestine was part of the Ottoman Empire. In the early nineteenth century, Ottoman control over Palestine was weak, and the country was divided into several relatively autonomous petty chiefdoms. In 1831 Palestine was invaded by Ibrahim Pasha, whose occupation until 1840 was punctuated by revolts against his successful suppressing of independent chiefdoms.

During and after Ibrahim Pasha's rule, increasing numbers of European travellers, churchmen, scholars and artists visited Palestine, many of whom produced books, paintings, drawings and photographs of their observations and experiences. Some information about costume can be gleaned from these sources, but most provide remarkably little information on the contemporary society and culture of Palestine, though they contain abundant information on the country's antiquities, settlements, topography and natural history. This is odd considering the mainly Biblical focus of most of the journeys, and the prevailing (though erroneous) assumption that the customs of the Palestinian villagers and bedouin were relatively intact survivals from Biblical times. The imbalance probably reflects the sex, experience and attitudes of the writers, who were almost entirely male, had limited contact with the rural population, especially the women, and were often disdainful towards a people whose life-style seemed primitive. Women's costumes tend to be described more sketchily than men's, mainly the relatively plain garments of peasants seen toiling in the fields or visiting markets, or the finer costumes of the better-off, mainly Christian villages of Bethlehem and Ramallah whose inhabitants were encountered socially and professionally.

When the Ottoman Empire was apportioned between the European Powers after the First World War, the Mandate for Palestine was awarded to Britain. During the 1920s and early 1930s, there was a marked improvement in economic conditions and communications which was directly reflected in costume. There are more pictorial and written sources on costume and village life for the Mandate period, but they are not abundant, and the accounts of older villagers are by far the richest source of available information.

Prior to the end of the British Mandate in 1948, the majority of the Arab population of Palestine lived in over eight hundred villages

Detail from a painting by William Hole representing Martha and Mary with Jesus in Bethany (Al-'Aizeriyeh) next to Jerusalem. The women are portrayed in Bethlehem costumes, including the 'green' dress (*thob ikhdari*), the embroidered veil (*khirkah*) and the coat (*bisht*) of handwoven wool. The male figure is wearing a typical blue and white striped coat (*qumbaz*), probably of cotton (*dima*), brown overcoat ('*abayeh*), red *tarbush* and striped turban (*laffeh*). The authenticity of the costumes (for the late 19th century, but certainly not for Biblical times) is due to the fact that Hole was advised by David Whiting, a collector of, and expert on, Palestinian village costume. *From: Hole, 1906 plate 47*

Above right **Detail from 'The Shadow of Death' by Holman Hunt, 1873.**
The costume of this figure, representing Mary the mother of Jesus, is remarkably well observed, partly due, perhaps, to the fact that Hunt collected costumes during his visits to Palestine (now housed in the Royal Ontario Museum); but the way the costume is worn can only be attributed to careful observation on the spot. The dress, which is the type worn in southern Palestine not Nazareth where this scene is set, is of handwoven indigo-dyed cotton or linen, and its pointed sleeves (*irdan*) are tied at the back, as Palestinian women did when working. Other details of the dress are also authentic: the patterned silk or cotton lining of the sleeves, the position and stitching of the seams, and the brown hem-binding. The head veil could be a silk *zurband*, a veil worn in the Nablus area and Galilee; as here, it was secured with a headband, and formed a long train down the back. The silver bracelets are a common southern Palestinian type (*haydari*), and were often worn in pairs as here. The bangle above the elbow appears to be of blue glass, also common in southern Palestine, and made in the glass factories in Hebron. *City of Manchester Art Galleries*

Lower right **Painting of Palestinian villagers at a well by R. J. Grunwald.**
The date and title of this painting are unknown, though from the style and costume it is probably late 19th or early 20th century. It contrasts with earlier paintings in showing villagers as recognisably real people engaged in normal, everyday activities, and not idealistically or as Biblical survivals. The women are wearing the light blue indigo-dyed dresses more common in the last century, and Bethlehem-style jackets (*taqsireh*). Both the men are wearing striped woollen overcoats ('*abayeh*). *National Gallery, Amman*

scattered along the coastal plain of the Mediterranean in the west and the hill regions in the north and centre of the country. The map on pages 8–9 shows the distribution of these villages, and names a selection of the largest of them, and most of those mentioned in this book.[2] The villagers, or 'people of the land' (*fellahin*), depended mainly on agriculture for their livelihood, though from the late nineteenth century and especially during the British Mandate period an increasing number engaged in wage labour and many migrated to the towns. The nomadic or semi-nomadic bedouin, who formed between five and ten per cent of the Arab population, depended mainly on animal herding and lived in the northern hills of Galilee, the hills west of the Dead Sea, and in the southern Negev desert.

The remainder of the Arab population lived in the towns, the commercial, administrative centres of Palestine where a variety of urban trades and professions were pursued, and the wealthier, educated class was mainly concentrated.

The majority of Palestinian Arabs are Sunni Muslims, with small minorities of Shi'ah Muslims and adherents of the Druze religion in Galilee. There is also a large minority of Christian Arabs (about ten per cent), mainly of the Orthodox or Greek Catholic Churches. Most Christians were and are town-dwellers or inhabitants of the large semi-urban villages of Ramallah, Bethlehem and Beit Jala.

Up to 1880 roughly six per cent of the population of Palestine were Jews, who also lived in the towns. Following the birth of political Zionism in the 1880s, dedicated to creating a national home in Palestine for the Jewish people, many thousands of Jews migrated to Palestine from Europe, swelling the urban Jewish communities, and establishing new settlements in the rural districts of northern and western Palestine. Jewish immigration, land purchase and settlement further increased after the First World War, and accelerated from the 1930s as Jews fled persecution in Europe, so that by 1948 Jews constituted nearly a third of the population of Palestine.

Throughout the British Mandate period the Zionist goal, at first implicit, later explicit, of creating a Jewish state in Palestine provoked a series of protests and hostilities from the Arab population, threatened economically and politically by Jewish colonisation, and with their own growing nationalistic aspirations.

In late 1947 the British handed the Palestine problem over to the United Nations, announcing their intention of terminating their Mandate in May 1948, and the UN General Assembly endorsed a plan to divide Palestine into two states. This was rejected by the Arabs, and war broke out between the two communities in which the superior Jewish forces were victorious. Following the declaration of the establishment of the Jewish State of Israel on May 14 1948, Israel was invaded by Arab armies of the surrounding countries, which were also defeated.

During the 1948 war Jewish forces captured territory on the Arab side of the proposed partition line, and by the time of the armistice

Photograph entitled 'Sword ceremony, wedding, Ramallah', circa 1900.
This stiffly posed picture, typical of 19th and early 20th-century photographs, nevertheless depicts authentic costumes of the period. The 'bride' is wearing a number of articles illustrated in this book: a coin headdress (*saffeh*); a choker (*bughmeh*) with pendant chains and coins; silver *haydari* and *habbiyat* bracelets (often worn together in this way); a Bethlehem-style jacket (*taqsireh*) with couched embroidery; a black crepe veil (*shambar*) with

coloured silk fringe; and a red silk sash (*kashmir* or *ishdad*) with red silk fringe (*dikkeh*), tied at the front. The 'groom' is wearing a turban (*laffeh*), a striped waistcoat (*sidriyeh*) and a striped woollen overcoat (*'abayeh*). This couple could be a real bride and groom, but the 'sword ceremony' at weddings usually consisted of the removal of the sword carried by brides by another woman at the entrance to the bridegroom's house, and did not involve the bridegroom, whose first encounter with the bride was inside his home. *Photo: Library of Congress*

in 1949 they controlled three-quarters of the former area of Palestine. The rest of Palestine came under Arab rule. The West Bank (so called because it is west of the river Jordan) was annexed by the Hashemite Kingdom of Jordan (formally created in 1950), and the Gaza Strip in south west Palestine fell under Egyptian administration.

During the hostilities which took place between December 1947 and September 1949, it is estimated that between 600,000 and 760,000 Arabs fled or were driven from their homes in the territory which became Israel. During this mass exodus over 350 Arab villages were abandoned (most in the coastal plain), and these and others were subsequently demolished by the Israeli government.[3] The village refugees have since lived in camps in the West Bank, Gaza, Lebanon, Jordan and Syria, while the wealthier, better educated refugees from the towns are more widely dispersed throughout the Arab world and in Africa, Europe and the Americas.

A second major wave of Palestinian refugees was created by the Six-Day War of 1967 between Israel and the neighbouring Arab states, in which Israel was again victorious and captured the Golan Heights from Syria, the West Bank from Jordan, and the Gaza Strip from Egypt. These Occupied Territories, as they are generally known, have remained under Israeli military administration, so that since 1967 the entire territory of former Palestine has been under Israeli rule. The total number of Palestinians in the world was estimated to have increased to nearly five million by 1986, of which 650,000 live in Israel, and about 1,400,000 in the West Bank and Gaza Strip. About one million of the latter are refugees.[4]

The study

Up to 1948, and to an extent still today, styles of dress reflected the major social divisions of Palestinian society. Male and female costume differed primarily according to whether the wearer was a towndweller, villager or bedouin, and secondarily according to the region they came from. Within each region there were also finer distinctions between the costumes worn by the women of different villages and bedouin tribes, though less so that of men.

At the outset of my research I shared common assumptions about 'folk costume': that each village or region had only one main style of female dress ('*the* Bethelehem dress' and so on), and that village attire fell into two main categories – 'traditional', that is relatively static and totally indigenous, and 'modern', that is transformed and corrupted by outside, mainly European, influences. The simplistic model of 'traditional' costume, as timeless, changeless and neatly arranged by regions and villages, was eroded by the discovery that village women's costume was a far more diverse and constantly changing phenomenon than assumed. Several distinctly different styles of dress could and did co-exist in each village or region at any one time; some elements of costume did indeed vary regionally, but others were common to several regions and some to the entire country; and although

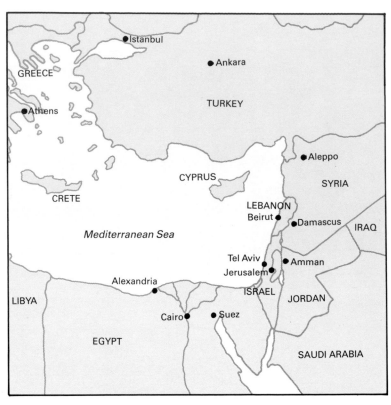

The village of Al-'Aizeriyeh near Jerusalem, British Mandate period.
The stone houses are typical of the hilly areas of Palestine. *Photo: Matson Collection, Library of Congress*

MAP 1 *Above right* **The countries of the eastern Mediterranean, 1989.**

MAP 2 *Right* **Palestine under the British, 1918–48.**

MAP 3 *Far right* **Israel and the Occupied Territories (in the darker shade), 1989.**

Above left **Village men ploughing and sowing, British Mandate period.**
Photo: Matson Collection, Library of Congress

Above **Village women sifting wheat, British Mandate period.**
Photo: Matson Collection, Library of Congress

Above right **Street scene in Ashdod, circa 1914–18.**
The thatched houses of mud brick are typical of the villages and small towns of the coastal plain. *Photo: Imperial War Museum*

Above **Interior of a village house in Silwan, 1886.**
Watercolour by James Clark RA, Palestine Exploration Fund

certain costume features had persisted for generations, others had been subject to many changes in fashion.

It was evident that this complicated and dynamic reality could only be grasped by focusing on the costumes of single villages, perhaps one in each region, and tracing the evolution of their fashions. The village of Beit Dajan was chosen to start with because of its beautiful costumes, and because it had been a leader of fashion in the Jaffa region. In the event, the study of Beit Dajan costumes became so absorbing that the original intention of doing similar research on other villages was not pursued.

The shift in focus to the costumes of one village transformed the emphasis of the research. Whereas hitherto it had seemed sufficient to amass ethnographic 'facts' (nomenclature, materials, provenances), as is required of museum anthropologists, now the role and meaning of costume in Beit Dajan society and culture became of prime interest. It was soon clear that the wedding was the key event for illuminating the social and symbolic significance of costume, and I therefore began collecting information on wedding trousseaus and bridal costume, concentrating on the period from around 1920 to the 1940s – the starting point being determined by the date the oldest people interviewed had married, the end point by the exodus of 1948 when the entire population of Beit Dajan evacuated their village.

All research based on oral history must take account of the possibility that informants are creating a nostalgic, golden-age picture of their youth, especially if they have lost their homes and lands as well as their past. However, though Beit Dajan people idealised their village and its customs in a general way, their descriptions of the specific matters being investigated were, I think, relatively reliable, for the following reasons. Firstly, they distinguished (often spontaneously) between the ideal or 'normal' and what had actually taken place. For example, they would describe the ideal wedding, then explain why in their case this custom or that article of clothing had differed from the ideal. Women's descriptions of their trousseaus were similarly objective; they would readily recite the contents (usually in hierarchical order), then explain why certain items had not been included. Secondly, there was great consistency between the accounts of Beit Dajan people interviewed in Jordan, the West Bank and Gaza, most of whom had not met since 1948. If a substantial amount of mythologising had taken place, such convergence would be remarkable.

The Beit Dajan research revealed that Palestinian costume, women's far more than men's, is an extraordinarily rich medium of visual communication. This led to the emphasis of this book on costume as a language, and the attempt to elucidate its structure and meanings. When organising the material I decided that these interpretative aims were better served by describing each category of garment in turn than by the more conventional, regional approach of primarily descriptive costume books.

Some Palestinian costumes and their constituent elements have

Below **Bedouin woman, Negev desert, probably British Mandate period.**
Photographer unknown

Facing page, above left **A family picnic, British Mandate period.**
The photograph is entitled 'The reapers' repast'. *Photo: Matson Collection, Library of Congress*

Facing page, above right **Village women crushing olives, British Mandate period.**
Olives were the chief crop of many hill villages. *Photo: M Collection, Library of Congress*

Facing page, below **Silwan near Jerusalem, 1979.**
Photo: Shelagh Weir

meaning because of some intrinsic and obvious quality; for example, red is associated with blood and silver with wealth. Such symbols are often explicit, and easily interpreted. But most costumes derive meaning from their position in a set of contrasted elements in a specific cultural context, such as a ritual; to take a western example, white wedding dresses take part of their significance from their contrast with black widows' weeds. This symbolism is often implicit, and can only be interpreted by contextual analysis and by reference to often oblique poetical allusions. This type of linguistic or structural analysis has been attempted in the concluding two chapters.[5]

1 Materials and Merchants

Right **Mejdel market, 1939/40.**
Photo: Matson Collection, Library of Congress

The merchant has cut the cloth!
The merchant has cut the cloth!
A piece of good life
We are in your home Abd
Laying our mattresses for sleep
The merchant has cut the cloth!
The merchant has cut the cloth!
A silver coin dress!
We are in your home Abd
Life is so sweet!

*Beit Dajan song to celebrate
buying the trousseau*

Jewish cotton cleaner with teasing bow (*qos al-nadaf*), Jerusalem, pre-1880.
Both locally produced and imported cotton balls were cleaned in this way. This trade existed in several towns in association with cotton weaving and mattress making. In Jerusalem it was a Jewish specialization.
From Wilson, 1880–84, I:44

Palestinian costumes are made from a variety of materials: relatively simple cottons, linens and woollens, some woven in Palestine, the rest imported from Egypt and Europe; and finer, intricately woven silks, satins and brocades, mostly imported from the large textile-producing centres of Syria.

Fabrics were differentiated and classified according to their weave, colour, pattern and texture, not only by producers and traders whose livelihood depended on them, but also by the Palestinian consumers for whom they were important as the visual, material and financial basis of an elaborate costume language. Obviously textiles have the basic function of covering and protecting the body, but their transformation into garments with distinctive shapes and decorative embellishments is a cultural phenomenon. For Palestinians the particular fabrics used, and the way they were deployed in the garment, were filled with significance.

One aim of this chapter is to describe and name the main clothing textiles referred to in the remainder of the book. The villagers had a name for every fabric (*qmash*), as they did for every other component of their clothing down to the smallest detail, such rich nomenclature being itself an important, verbal, component of the language of costume. Most terms were identical to those used by merchants, but some differed – especially from those used outside Palestine, for example by Syrian producers. The names given here are those used by the Palestinian villagers, and mostly shared by the local merchants who directly served them.[1]

The other aim is to indicate the sources of the various textiles, how they were marketed, and something of the relationship between the merchant-shopkeepers in the towns and their customers in the villages.

Local raw materials

From the mid-nineteenth century most textiles woven in Palestine were made from cotton, linen and silk yarns imported from Egypt, Syria and England. However locally-produced cotton and wool were also used for making costume fabrics, and must have been a major source of textile yarns historically, especially for the poorer members of the population who could not afford imported fabrics.

Cotton was cultivated in Palestine until the beginning of this century, mainly in Galilee, the Merj ibn Omar (Plain of Esdraelon), the Nablus hills, and the coastal plain.[2] Palestinian cotton was an important commercial crop from the mid-seventeenth century, when it was imported by French factors in Ramleh through Jaffa, Acre and Sidon.[3] In 1697 Maundrell observed 'the country people' north of Jerusalem 'now everywhere at plough in the fields, in order to sow cotton',[4] and in the following century Volney observed locally-spun cotton being sold at Lydda market for export from Jaffa.[5] In the first half of the nineteenth century raw cotton from Safad and Nablus supplied the cotton-weaving industry in Zahleh (in present day Lebanon),[6] and cotton was cultivated throughout the coastal plain as far as Gaza.[7] At this period European demand increased, and French and British merchants competed for Galilee cotton.[8]

In the 1850s and 1860s cotton prices rose sharply due to the Crimean and American Civil Wars, and Palestinian production expanded.[9] During this boom, Tristram observed cotton cultivation near Lake Huleh and, near Nablus, 'camels, in long file, laden with cotton-bales ... mingling with asses bearing ... baskets of cotton-husks to the city'. The importance of cotton in the city was evident:

Among the low Oriental domes and the tall palms which here and there wave over the courtyards of Nablous, rises a large modern structure of yesterday – neither more nor less than a cotton mill! The chimney is absent, for it is merely a great warehouse and place for cleaning the cotton for exportation ... The busy hum of the cotton-gins greeted us on all sides, and heaps of cotton-husks lay about the streets. Cotton has this year [1863–4], in consequence of the war in America, become the staple of the place; and though we had seen everywhere the signs of a nascent cotton-trade, yet in no place was it so developed as here.[10]

Production decreased with falling prices after the end of the American Civil War in 1866. From the 1870s cotton was increasingly imported from Egypt, yet Palestinian cultivation survived into the early twentieth century in Jericho, Beisan, Lake Tiberias (the Sea of Galilee), the Plain of Jezreal, the Acre district, the coastal plain and around Nablus where its quality was especially prized. About seventy-five per cent of Palestinian cotton was exported at this period, the rest being used for rugs and clothing fabrics.[11]

After the First World War, most cotton used in Palestinian costumes was imported as yarn or cloth from Egypt, Syria or Europe.[12]

Wool was handspun by men, women and boys, and left its natural colours (white and shades of brown), or dyed red or blue in the yarn. Several important articles of dress were made from local wool: men's overcoats, women's jackets, men's and women's belts, and women's hair bands. Wool was sold to male weavers in the towns and villages by the bedouin, the main sheep herders of Palestine. (The bedouin wove only rugs, saddle bags and tent-cloth on their own looms, not clothing.[13]) Grant tells how a weaver in Ramallah refused to sell his land to a well-to-do neighbour 'because it is on the outskirts where he is a position to get first chance at those who come into the village from that direction to sell fleeces'.[14]

Dyes

Before chemical dyes were available, by far the most important dye for Palestinian costumes was indigo (*nileh*).[15] Some plain cotton and linen fabrics were left their natural colour, for example those used for men's undershirts, women's headveils, and some women's dresses. But most was dyed different shades of indigo blue, the dominant colour of women's main garments (coats in Galilee, dresses in southern Palestine).

Indigo was cultivated in the Beisan area south of Lake Tiberias, and had been an important crop along the Jordan valley (the Ghor) for centuries. In 1811–12 Burckhardt observed that 'Indigo is a very

A Ta'amreh bedouin woman spinning wool, Artas south of Bethlehem, 1925–31.
Photo: Hilma Granqvist

Woman in Abu Dis near Jerusalem, 1926–35.
She is displaying the wool she has spun for making a hammock cradle. *Photo: Grace Crowfoot*

common production of the Ghor; the Ghowarene sell it to the merchants of Jerusalem and Hebron, where it is worth twenty per cent more than Egyptian indigo',[16] and it was still a 'conspicuous' crop in the mid-nineteenth century, and was stored in underground silos like grain.[17] During the late nineteenth century local indigo was increasingly supplemented with imports from India, and from this century was mixed with synthetic indigo. This was much easier to use, and eventually supplanted the natural dye.

Most main towns, especially those which were weaving centres, had dyeing establishments; they included Safad, Nablus, Jerusalem, Hebron, Beersheba, Ramleh, Lydda, Mejdel and Gaza. Often customers bought their materials undyed, and took them to the dyers themselves.

Warren describes indigo dyeing in Jerusalem in the early 1870s:

This trade is carried on about the Murestan, the vacant spaces within being taken advantage of for dyeing, and exposing the articles dyed. On a fine day may be seen hundreds of yards of ground covered with blue stuff. There are about ten dyeing establishments, in each of which there are ten men required to carry on the work, and a boy assistant learning the trade.[18]

Most indigo dyeing was for the dresses of 'coarse calico', as Warren calls it, of village and bedouin women. Cloth was soaked in several vats to get the strongest tints; light blue cloth was therefore cheaper, because it involved less work, and dark blue cloth was more expensive and prestigious.

Red was the next most important colour for Palestinian costumes; women's coats, headdresses and embroidery threads were dyed red, some locally using madder, kermes and cochineal.[19] Madder was the cheapest and most available of these, being widely cultivated in the area, and was often used by women for home wool-dyeing. Kermes and cochineal were also cultivated in Palestine, though most supplies were imported. Cochineal was cultivated around Nablus[20] where, in the 1860s, Tristram observed that 'the hum of the cotton-bow murmured on every side, and walls were dripping with the juices of cochineal and indigo, as the webs of silk or cotton were hung out to dry'.[21] Yellow and orange, other colours combined with red in early Palestinian embroidery, could also have been obtained from local dye-plants and substances.[22]

Synthetic (anilin) dyes, developed in Germany from the 1880s, were probably not introduced into Palestine until early this century, but were widely adopted after the First World War, almost entirely supplanting the use of natural dyes.

Dyes are a problematic basis for dating Palestinian costumes and embroidery, because articles dyed entirely with natural materials can postdate the introduction of anilin dyes. Also, some anilin-dyed embroidery threads and fabrics were probably imported from Syria and Europe before the dyes themselves were used locally. Articles with anilin-dyed fabrics or silks, such as brilliant green or pink embroidery threads, must, however, date from the late nineteenth century onwards.

Palestinian textiles

The Palestinian textile industry was tiny compared with those of Egypt and Syria, and its products were relatively simple; weaving was not highly developed technically or artistically, as it was in Syria. Nevertheless, despite the competition from Egyptian, Syrian and (from the second half of the nineteenth century) European textiles, a variety of materials for village garments were hand-woven in Palestine from local and imported yarns: thick woollen cloth for men's and women's coats, silk, cotton and linen fabrics for women's dresses, veils and headdresses, and more luxurious fabrics with silk stripes for festive and trousseau dresses.

Although the Palestinian weaving industry declined sharply after the First World War, with the influx of mass-produced, machine-made textiles from Europe and later Asia, some hand-woven clothing fabrics were still being made in the 1930s and 1940s, and some as late as the 1960s. The local weaving industry survived as long as it did because it was in close touch with village requirements and changing local fashions, in some cases producing materials not made elsewhere.

Now, however, Palestinian weaving has declined to relative insignificance, the main clothing materials still made being striped fabrics for schoolchildren's uniforms, woven in the Gaza Strip. At least one weaver, Abu Adnan in Jerusalem, makes an open-weave cotton fabric for the use of welfare centres in Ramallah, Jerusalem

Below **Weaver in Ramallah, pre-1900.**
The fabric being woven appears to have a woollen weft and a cotton warp, so may be for a man's overcoat (*'abayeh*). Twelve weavers are reported to have been working in Ramallah in about 1907 (Grant, 1907:194). *Photo: Library of Congress*

Below right **Weaver in Mejdel, British Mandate period.**
He is clearly weaving material with broad contrasting bands for a man's overcoat (*'abayeh*). *Photo: American Colony, Jerusalem*

Weavers in Mejdel, 1939/40.
They are weaving a broad cotton or silk
material. *Photo: Matson Collection, Library of Congress*

and the Hebron area, which sell locally-embroidered articles such
as table-cloths and cushions, mainly to foreigners.

Garment fabrics were woven on simple treadle looms by professional male weavers who worked in a number of towns and
small villages, mainly Safad, Nazareth, Nablus, Ramallah, Beit Jala,
Bethlehem, Hebron, Gaza and Mejdel. The greatest variety of local
fabrics, and the finest, were produced in Gaza, Mejdel and Bethlehem using yarns imported from Egypt, Syria and Britain.

Gaza and Mejdel were the largest weaving centres in Palestine.
Fifty looms were operating in Gaza before the First World War, and
five hundred looms in Mejdel in 1909, of which only two hundred
remained only a few years later.[23] Weaving continued in both
places, albeit on a smaller scale, through the Mandate period; in
1927 there were 119 weaving establishments (employing 440
people) in the Southern Subdistrict of Palestine, the great majority
of which were in Gaza and Mejdel.[24]

The history of Mejdel as a centre for textile production has yet to
be written, but according to oral tradition its development was
closely bound up with Egypt. Not only were the cotton, linen and
silk yarns for its fabrics imported from or through Egypt, but it may
also have been established as a weaving centre by Egyptians. In any
case, weavers probably migrated periodically from Egypt to Mejdel
for economic and political reasons. In 1948, most of the population
of Mejdel fled to the Gaza Strip, where a few weavers continued
their trade.

In 1943 Abd al-Aziz Daud of Mejdel started a weaving establishment in the Jaffa area, employing Mejdel weavers on hand looms
and producing fabrics for local villages. However the venture was a
repeated casualty of the subsequent political upheavals. In 1948 he
and his weavers fled to Jericho, where they continued to weave
Mejdel fabrics for refugees from the Gaza-Mejdel area living in the

Jericho camps (who wanted to maintain their distinctive dress). Business flourished, and around 1960 they installed machine looms.

In addition to clothing materials, they produced an open-weave cotton fabric for the Mennonite and YWCA embroidery projects established after 1948 to help refugees. During the 1967 war Abd al-Aziz fled once more, this time to Amman. He bought new looms and started again, only to have all his equipment destroyed during the 'Black September' strife between the Palestinians and Jordanians in 1970; the tragedy of the Palestinian refugees in microcosm.

Mejdel produced the greatest variety of fabrics in Palestine. Several grades and colours of plain cotton were woven there: *shash*, white muslin for women's veils, *burak* and *bayt al-sham*, plain white cottons used for underdresses; *karnaysh*, white cotton with crinkled stripes; *bazayl*, a flannelette for men's nightgowns and women's dresses; *durzi*, indigo-blue dyed cotton used for women's everyday dresses, and for lining headdresses; and *dendeki*, a rusty-red cotton similar to *durzi*, used for women's headdresses and hairbands, cushion covers and hem-binding.

Three of Mejdel's most famous products were luxury dress fabrics of linen or cotton with variously-coloured silk warp stripes.[25] Like all dress fabrics, these were sold in dress lengths (*maqta'*) of about eight metres, and sometimes had a panel of silver (*qasab*) thread woven into the end of the length which was positioned at the back of the skirt in the completed dress.

The most expensive fabric, containing the greatest quantity of silk and requiring the most labour, was the *malak* or 'royal' fabric. Later versions of this fabric, called the 'royal with flowers' (*malak abu wardeh*[26]), have a red floral pattern which required a man to raise and lower the selected warp threads while the material was woven. The next in this hierarchy of fabrics is the *ikhdari*, meaning 'green', with narrower red and green bands, and, in some versions, a floral pattern like the *malak* fabric. The third fabric is the *jiljileh*,[27] with plain dark red bands at each edge.

The *malak*, *ikhdari* and *jiljileh* fabrics were used for festive dresses throughout southern Palestine up to the 1940s, and were important components of wedding trousseaus. Around 1940, copies of the *malak* fabric, both in similar materials and in velvet, were imported from Germany; whatever impact this might have had on local production was overtaken by the events of 1948.

Mejdel weavers also produced several fabrics similar to the above, but narrower – about 35cm wide. These were of navy or white cotton, with narrow silk (or artificial silk) selvedge stripes in different combinations of red or pink, green, white, black and orange. One of the fabrics, which comes in both blue and white, is called 'heaven and hell' (*jinneh u nar*) because it has a green silk stripe at one selvedge and red at the other. Another white fabric (*tubsi*) has two plain red silk or cotton stripes; another of similar description, used for underdresses in the southern plain, went by the romantic name of 'breath of the soul' (*nasheq rohoh*). The white

Samples of Mejdel dress fabrics, 1960s.
From top to bottom: *jiljileh*; *abu mitayn* ('father of two hundred'); *jinneh u nar* ('heaven and hell'); and *biltajeh*. All navy cotton with silk (warp) borders. The fabrics are 33–34cms wide, and were sold in dress lengths of 8–8.5m. Similar fabrics, and cheaper versions with cotton stripes, were used throughout the southern coastal plain of Palestine up to the 1940s, and were still being woven for the refugee women in the camps of the Gaza Strip in the late 1960s. *Museum of Mankind: 1971 AS1 123*

Right **Dress fabrics woven in Mejdel and Bethlehem.**
From top to bottom: *jiljileh*; *ikhdari* ('green'); *ikhdari* with flowers (*wardeh*) replacing the narrow stripes; early *malak* ('royal') fabric; *malak abu wardeh* ('royal with flowers'), showing the edge of the silver (*qasab*) panel ('*alam*) woven into the end of the dress length. These are the most luxurious dress fabrics which were woven in Palestine, being a mixture of linen with silk stripes. The most expensive was the *malak* because it used the most silk. The woven flowers also added to the cost because of the extra labour involved. The fabrics range from 44 to 48cms in width.

Left **Weaver from Mejdel, working in Jabaliyah refugee camp, Gaza Strip, 1967.**
He is weaving typical Mejdel-style dress material of cotton with narrow silk borders. The treadles which operate the heddles are in a small pit. *Photo: Shelagh Weir*

fabrics with stripes were worn in the Nablus and Tulkarm areas, and the blue in the southern plain.

Several silk materials, some imitating Syrian products, were woven in both Mejdel and Gaza: *ghabani*, a white silk with all-over chain stitch embroidery in yellow or white; pure plain silk (*harir asli*) used for women's veils and men's headcloths; *rozah*, a thicker silk, used for veils and dresses, and for men's coats; and *asaweri*, a cotton and silk mixture.

Bethlehem and Beit Jala were the next most important textile centres. Dalman was told that Beit Jala once had three hundred looms (probably an exaggeration) weaving a widely-sold cotton cloth for garments, the cotton being handspun by local women; but this production is said to have ceased around 1860 as a result of competition from European imports.[28]

The main Bethlehem families involved in weaving and the textile trade were, and still are, the Nassers, the Jassers and the Qatans. According to family tradition, the Nassers started as textile traders, importing dress fabrics from a weaving establishment in Egypt with which they were associated. The fabrics they imported, said to have been specially made for the Palestinian market, were a plain linen for everyday dresses worn in the Bethlehem area, called *shrimbawi*[29] (after the place where it was woven), which they dyed with indigo in Bethlehem, and *malak* and *ikhdari* fabrics, like those described above. Later they started weaving these fabrics themselves.

Other products of the Nasser establishment were: a fine silk veil (*tarbi'ah*) woven with silk imported from Homs[30]; pink and blue woollen sashes (still made by them today, partly for tourists); and a flowered, fringed shawl (*shal*, *lefhah*) in pink or maroon wool, cotton or silk, copied from one originally imported from Germany. (Similar, higher-quality shawls were also imported from Spain and Japan.) Later they imported the materials for this shawl, and they and the Jassers added the fringe and large machine-embroidered floral patterns in Bethlehem. A similar article was made by Abu Mishail in Ramallah. The local production of these veils provided paid work for local women, who added the fringes and embroidered the patterns of flowers and leaves.[31]

Two of the main materials used for dresses and veils in the central and southern plain and Hebron hills during the Mandate period were *brim* and *qarawi*, which were woven in Hebron. *Brim*, meaning 'plied', is a cotton or cotton and linen mixture, undyed or dyed blue, with an open weave which facilitated the counting of warp and weft threads for cross-stitch embroidery. *Qarawi* is a finer linen used mainly for veils. A characteristic of *qarawi* and most other dress fabrics for village use is their narrow width of about 40–45cm. This enabled village women to construct their dresses with the minimum of cutting of the side edges (selvedges), which they disliked doing. Dress fabrics were always sold in lengths (*maqta'*) sufficient for a dress: between 10 and 12 *piqs* (roughly 7–8.5 m, a *piq* being about 70cm).

Outside the above centres, Palestinian weavers produced only

Right **Detail from a coat, Druze *dura'ah*, Galilee, late 19th or early 20th century.**
Sleeves of locally-woven cotton; body of silk, satin and brocade probably imported from Syria and Europe; lining of green cotton.
Museum of Mankind: 1968 AS5 2

Below **Men making head-ropes (*'aqal*), Silwan, 1926–35.**
Photo: Grace Crowfoot

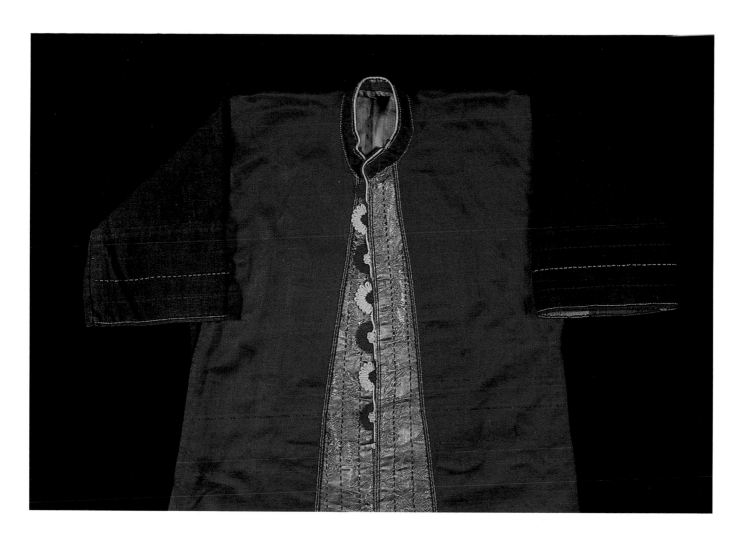

simple cotton and woollen fabrics, mainly from imported yarns. The fabrics made from local yarns, handspun by the drop-and-spin method, were relatively thick and coarse. The thick cotton material for the coats worn by Galilee women in the last century was probably woven in Safad or Nazareth from local cotton, and other centres further south must have woven similar fabrics for men's and women's clothing at one time.

Coats for men and women were woven from local wool, in some places up to the 1930s. A speciality of Nablus was a black and white, or red and white, striped woollen fabric (*busht*) for men's cloaks (*'abayahs*) (and for camel bags for transporting Nablus soap to Jaffa). This material was still being made in 1923, but the cotton weaving which had been carried on before the First World War had died out.[32] Another Nablus speciality which survived into the 1920s was the making of men's head-ropes (*'aqal*) from goat-hair, camel-hair, wool and silk.

Woollen cloth for men's overcoats (*'abayeh*) with broad stripes either in natural colours, particularly brown and cream, or in dark indigo and cream, was woven in many towns and villages, sometimes by single weavers working alone. Weavers in Beth-

Woman plaiting a woollen hairband, Artas south of Bethlehem, 1926–35.
Photo: Grace Crowfoot

Village woman wearing plaited hairbands (*laffayef*), Artas, 1926–35.
Photo: Grace Crowfoot

Facing page **Details of various woollen costume components handwoven by women.** From the left: a bedouin girdle; a plaited hairband, Hebron hills villagers; two belt decorations and a belt, Negev bedouin. *Museum of Mankind: 1966 AS1 23; 1971 AS1 33A; 1975 AS7 10 and 11; 1981 AS23 11*

lehem, Beit Jala and Gaza also wove a coarse red woollen material with narrow stripes used for a sleeveless coat (*bisht*) worn by women in the Bethlehem area, and there were reported to be three or four men still weaving this in Bethlehem in about 1940;[33] the *bisht* went out of fashion soon afterwards.

Bedouin women's belts, and bands for wrapping the hair at the back of village women's headdresses, were plaited from local, handspun wool, mainly by women. Bedouin women also made decorative pattern bands for their belts in twined weave, either in wool or silk. Grace Crowfoot vividly emphasises the local and co-operative production of hairbands (*laffayef*):

The makers of these plaits may be men, women, boys or girls; boys especially seem to take pleasure in the craft. I asked a young woman at Artas who possessed an especially pretty braid, who had made it, and she replied: 'The wool came from my sister's sheep at Surbahar, my mother spun it for me, I dyed it myself with cochineal and my young cousin (a boy) made it for me.'[34]

Up to the Mandate period, woollen hammock-cradles were woven on simple ground looms by village women of the Hebron hills and Ta'amreh bedouin women; these were 'worn' suspended by a band from the forehead, with cradle and baby behind.[35]

During the 1930s and 1940s, when women's 'wardrobes' and trousseaus greatly increased in size and value, the Nassers of Bethlehem developed a sideline producing hand-embroidered dress panels and ready-made garments in the Bethlehem style, which were sold for trousseaus throughout southern Palestine. Similarly, Abu Mishail of Ramallah marketed dresses in the Ramallah style, embroidered by local women, for sale in the Ramallah area; and as business expanded, he opened a branch in Na'lin producing dresses for villages in the hills west of Ramallah. Embroidered panels for women's veils were also produced commercially in Bethlehem, Hebron and Mejdel.

These merchants and others had scores of female outworkers embroidering and sewing for them at home. Some enterprising women also set up their own businesses, often commissioning other women to produce for them. They sold directly to customers who came to their homes or to shopkeepers in the towns, or peddled their wares round the villages themselves. In most villages there were also professional dressmakers and embroideresses who worked on commission for fellow village women who were unable to make and adorn their own clothes. From the 1930s this ready-made trade thrived and expanded, and, most notably in Bethlehem, constituted an important cottage industry unacknowledged in economic surveys of Palestine.

Egyptian textiles

Egyptian cotton and linen yarns for the Palestinian weaving industry, and clothing materials, were imported during the nineteenth century and the Mandate period, though quantities must have fluctuated according to Egyptian production levels, the

Tarabin bedouin girl plaiting a belt component, Negev desert, 1926–35.
Photo: Grace Crowfoot

state of competition with English products, and the volume and success of local Palestinian production.[36]

During the Mandate period *shrimbawi*, mentioned above, a hand-woven linen with an open weave was imported for women's dresses. A similar dress linen, called *rumi* or *ruhbani*, may also have originally come from Egypt, but during the Mandate period came from Turkey and Germany. These fabrics are about 45cm wide, and were sold in dress lengths (*maqta'*) similar to other dress fabrics.[37]

Other Egyptian imports included striped cotton (*dima*) for men's coats (*qumbaz*), and early versions of the *malak* and *ikhdari* fabrics (see above).

Syrian materials

Most of the luxury materials used for making or decorating Palestinian garments were imported from the great Syrian centres of textile production, Homs, Aleppo and Damascus. These included silk (*harir*) yarns and embroidery threads, and cords of silk, silver and gold; and fabrics of silk, mixed silk and cotton, and imitation silk (*harir nabati*) (imported first from Italy and Belgium around 1920).

The floss silk thread used for embroidering Palestinian women's costumes was produced in Homs and Mount Lebanon (sometimes from imported cocoons), and dyed the range of required colours in Homs and Damascus. Before anilin dyes were introduced into Syria prior to the First World War, silk threads were dyed different shades of red, orange and yellow with kermes compounds.[38] From the mid-1930s this beautiful, lustrous thread was gradually ousted from the markets by perlé cotton threads manufactured mainly by the French company, Dolfus, Mieg et Cie (DMC).

The silver and gold thread (*qasab*) for the metallic cord used in Bethlehem couched embroidery, for skirt panels on Bethlehem-style dresses and for various brocade fabrics, was produced in Aleppo and Homs. Later, silver thread was imported from France, then Japan, and lurex has now completely replaced metal thread.

From Aleppo and Damascus came the two most important fabrics used for decorative additions to Palestinian women's costumes: silk taffeta (*heremzi*), and satin (*atlas*) with a silk warp and cotton weft giving a matt finish at the back of the fabric. Satin was also used for entire garments.

Heremzi taffeta (called *kamakh*[39] in the Hebron area) was made in red, green, yellow, orange and, more rarely, purple. This narrow fabric, only 18–22cm wide,[40] was used for decorative patchwork on Galilee women's coats, for complete dresses in the Jerusalem area, and for patchwork and inserts on dresses throughout southern

A Syrian silk shop, pre-1914.
In this stiffly posed but apparently authentic photograph, the man on the left is winding silk onto a bobbin from a reeling apparatus, and the one on the right is weighing silk threads (which were sold by weight). *Photo: Underwood and Underwood, Library of Congress*

Taffeta (*heremzi*) patchwork on a Galilee village woman's coat, and rolls of taffeta as they were sold
W 18–22 cm. Museum of Mankind: 1966 AS1 66; Kawar collection

Facing page **Syrian fabrics of silk or silk and cotton mixed.**
From the top: *ghabani*, white silk with yellow chain stitch embroidery; *asaweri*, ribbed (rep) warp-faced silk with cotton weft; two fabrics, *'atafi*, similar to the *asaweri* but with wider warp stripes (similar ribbed silk and cotton fabrics are *qasabi*, with narrow yellow and black stripes, and *'othmani*, with green, red, black, white and yellow stripes); two *atlas* satins with silk warps and cotton wefts, the first, ikat-patterned satin sometimes called 'birds' tongues' (*lisan al-asfur*).

Palestine. The demand for *heremzi* decreased sharply after 1948, and had ceased by 1955.

Red satin *atlas* (also called *kamakh* in Palestine) with white or yellow stripes was used for patching dresses and headdresses, and for sashes. Another, ikat-patterned, satin (called 'the tongues of birds', *lisan al-asfur*), coloured red with black and/or green, was also used for coats and patchwork. A plain red satin found on older dresses preceded the striped and patterned varieties.

Red *atlas* was also widely used for men's coats, and women's coats in the Nablus region, and a wider range of striped satins (*suratli*) with narrow blue, green and yellow stripes was used for men's waistcoats, jackets and coats. Another fabric (confusingly called *kamakh*, though different from that mentioned above) had red, blue, green or yellow satin stripes alternating with white cotton stripes, and was used for men's coats, women's sashes, and women's pants in the Nablus area. Cheaper striped cottons (*dima*), also woven in Syria (and Egypt), were used for men's everyday coats.

Various mixed silk and cotton materials were important for Palestinian men's and women's costumes. One type (*kermezot*[41]), woven in Aleppo and Damascus, became fashionable in the 1930s for women's dresses in the Jaffa area. This comes in red or purple, has silk warps and thick cotton wefts giving a slightly ribbed texture, is warp-faced on both surfaces, and often has a watered (moire) finish. *Kermezot* was mainly produced as a lining for Syrian men's coats and jackets, and for the vestments of Orthodox priests; perhaps a Palestinian merchant from Jaffa or Lydda, on a trading visit to Syria, spotted its potential appeal as a material for village dresses at a period of change and innovation.

Other ribbed silk and cotton fabrics from the same towns, striped in various colours, were used for men's coats and women's dresses

in the Jerusalem area, and had various names according to their colours and the width of their stripes.

An unusual, coarse silk fabric (*qaz*), used for Galilee women's coats, was woven from yarn handspun from damaged cocoons by the villagers of Mount Lebanon.

More substantial garments and fabrics were also imported from Syria. In Homs, men's overcoats (*'abayeh*) were woven from camel-hair, and embroidered with silver thread round the neck. These had a wide Middle Eastern market including Palestine, where they were worn by the better-off. Aleppo produced broadcloth (*jukh*) jackets with couched embroidery in black silk cord, chiefly for the Kurdish areas of Turkey, Iran and Iraq, and these jackets were also imported into Palestine and worn mainly by male and female bedouin in the Galilee area. After machine looms (*nol franji*) were introduced into Syria from France and England in the late 1920s and gradually replaced the old handlooms (*nol 'arabi*), Aleppo weavers began producing velvet (*mukhmal*), some of which was probably traded to Palestine.

Also from Syria came an imitation striped 'kashmir' material in thick cotton with intricate multi-coloured patterns, which was widely used for men's and women's sashes;[42] and tablet-woven bands used for belts (*kamr*).

Below **Satin (*atlas*) patchwork on the side of a dress, Anabta west of Nablus.**
The dress material is the white cotton 'heaven and hell' (*jinneh u nar*) woven in Palestine.
Museum of Mankind: 1968 AS12 17

Below right **Detail from a coat (*qaziyeh*), early 20th century.**
The material is *qaz* raw silk.
Collection: Violet Barbour

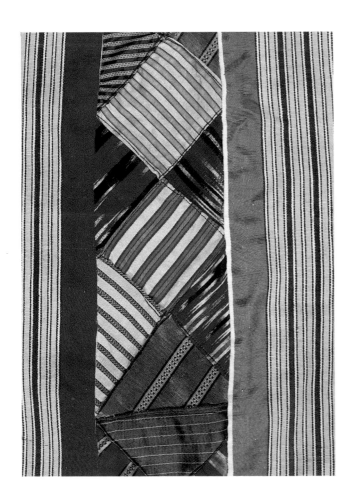

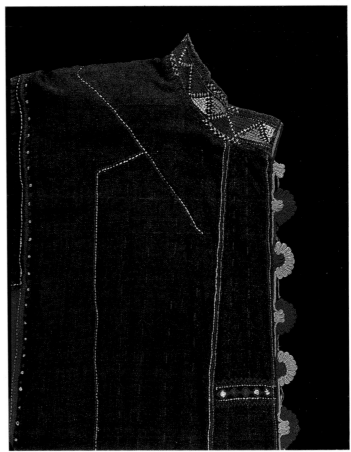

Detail from the back of a dress, Deir Terif or a neighbouring village, Jaffa area, 1930s.
Made from *kermezot* silk and cotton mixture; embroidered with silver cord (*qasab*) filled with satin stitch in floss silk. *Museum of Mankind: 1969 AS8 10*

A variety of fine silk fabrics, some similar to Mejdel and Gaza products, were imported for men's coats, men's and women's head wear and women's sashes.

Three white or cream silks, used for men's coats, turbans and head cloths and women's dresses and veils, were made in Homs and Aleppo: *rozah*, a soft, fine silk bleached white; *malas*, a looser-weave fabric with stripes (the term is also used for black sateen and any soft fabric); and *ghabani* with all-over embroidery in yellow chain stitch (done in Aleppo). A kind of reverse *ghabani* had yellow fabric and white embroidery. Other turban and head cloth fabrics imported from Syria were of fine cotton or silk in various colours, often with stripes and checks.

From Homs and Damascus came a silk crepe ('wrinkled', *kornaysh*) which, dyed black, was used for ceremonial veils (*shambar*) throughout southern Palestine. Homs weavers also produced a large silk veil five metres long with yellow and black stripes, called a *safadiyeh* because it was made specially for the townswomen of Safad in Galilee.

Several silk materials for sashes and headbands were made in Aleppo: a red and yellow silk fabric with green and silver (*qasab*)

Woman shopping in Ramallah market, 1987.
She has just bought some DMC threads. *Photo: Shelagh Weir*

brocade, used for sashes (*zunnar maqruneh*) in the Jaffa area, and headbands ('*asbeh ruwaysiyeh*) in the Nablus area and Galilee; a striped green, yellow and black silk worn as a ceremonial headband (*zamliyeh*) in southern Palestine; and the white, red and green striped silk for the 'Tripoli belt' (*zunnar tarabulsi*), still made today though from inferior materials, and so called according to Aleppo merchants because the greatest demand was initially from the Tripoli area. Imitation *tarabulsi* silk was also made in Homs.

Most silk materials, including *heremzi* taffetas and *atlas* satins, came in two basic categories, 'true' or 'imitation' (*sadiq* or *kadhab*), or 'pure' or 'artificial' (*asli* or *nabati*), and were priced accordingly. The *maqruneh* fabric was, additionally, differentiated by its brocade 'combs' (*musht*) – not by their total number, but by the number of their *teeth*, which could be ten, twelve, fifteen, twenty or thirty.

Squares (*hattah*) of black or maroon silk, or imitation silk, with silver brocade patterns and silver-decorated tassels, worn by Galilee women as veils and headbands, were woven in Aleppo, Damascus and Homs. A flowered muslin with crocheted floral edging, used for headbands in Galilee, may have been made in Syria, but is identical to scarves from Turkey which is its probable place of origin.

European textiles

From the 1830s the quantity of British cotton cloth exported to the Levant greatly increased, and some found its way into the Palestinian markets directly or via Syria.[43] Neale noted, in the 1840s: 'Cotton twist, chintzes of bright and catching colours, and a few bales of strong, coarse cloths, are supplied by Liverpool through Beyrout; and London, via the same route, sends … cochineal, indigo … and other articles.'[44] Some of these plain, dyed and printed cottons must have been used for village clothing – for example for jacket linings, men's pants and shirts, and for women's veils and dresses.

Initially their novelty and scarcity gave them prestige value. Tristram records how (in 1863–4), in a Christian house on Mount Carmel in Galilee, coloured pictures of saints shared wall space 'with labels carefully preserved from Manchester [cotton] bales, and old needle-papers'.[45] The admiration for these new fabrics is also evident in some nineteenth-century village dresses with panels and scraps of colourful European cotton or precious velvet placed in strategic eye-catching positions. The oldest Bethlehem women's jackets (*taqsireh*) – expensive, high-status garments – are usually lined with a bold checked cotton of European, probably British, origin.

Important pre-First World War imports from Britain or Germany were red, green and blue woollen broadcloth (*jukh*) for men's and women's jackets[46] (some may also have come from Aleppo), and a heavy, finely-woven cotton used for bedouin dresses and veils. During the Mandate period there was a great increase in the import of textiles from Europe, especially from the 1930s onwards. This was the period of great expansion in women's 'wardrobes', so the

Refugee women embroidering with canvas, Amman, 1987.
They are embroidering for the *Hai Nazzal* welfare organisation to supplement their incomes. *Photo: Shelagh Weir*

impact on local products must have been offset, to some extent, by increased demand; dresses made from European (and later Asian) materials were sometimes additions to women's enlarging collections, as well as replacing Palestinian-made fabrics.

These new fabrics included black and white machine-made cottons (*baft*[47] and *tubayt*[48]) used for everyday dresses throughout southern Palestine and for jackets in Galilee; and black silk used for festive dresses in central Palestine. The introduction of these finely-woven fabrics was facilitated by the arrival in the 1930s of DMC embroidery threads. These were accompanied in the markets by embroidery canvas which could be laid on the material to guide the stitches, thus obviating the necessity for open-weave fabrics.

Other European textiles popular during the Mandate period were blue, maroon and red velvets (*mukhmal*) imported from Germany and France from about 1935, which were used for women's jackets in the Bethlehem area and dresses in the Jaffa area.[49] Various plain and floral-patterned fine wools and cottons were also imported and used for women's headbands, scarves, sashes and veils. One type of floral material used for sashes in the Bethlehem area came from Austria.

Asian textiles

Japanese textiles, especially cheap cottons, flooded the Syrian markets from 1929, many presumably finding their way to Palestine.[50] Among the earliest imports were flowered shawls (*shal*) of silk, used as head veils in the Ramallah area and competing with those produced in Bethlehem.

Today a number of articles are imported from eastern Asia, including rayon dress materials and other synthetics, for example *trevira* and *banama*, a beige fabric; also white muslin (*shash*) for veils, and flowered squares for sashes, scarves and headbands.

Shopkeepers and merchants

Shopkeepers in many Palestinian towns and large villages imported and stocked the materials villagers needed for everyday clothing, costume gifts, and, most important of all, their wedding trousseaus. Most merchants had shops in the town *suq* (market) which villagers visited on the weekly market day; some also traded from home, partly to serve village women too shy to go to market; others took their bolts of cloth and garments round the villages on specific days. Some shopkeepers stocked a wide range of materials; others specialised in particular items.

The main centres where villagers bought their cloth and clothing were: Acre, Safad and Nazareth in Galilee; Jenin, Nablus, Ramallah, Jerusalem, Bethlehem and Hebron in the hills to the south; Jaffa, Ramleh, Lydda, Yibna, Ashdod, Mejdel, Gaza and Falujeh in the plain; and Gaza and Beersheba, mainly serving the southern bedouin. As times improved and expenditure on clothing increased, some merchants opened small branches in the wealthiest villages. For example, in the 1930s the Jaffa merchant Abu

A shopkeeper selling clothing materials, Amman, 1987.
Note the *atlas* satins. *Photo: Shelagh Weir*

A shop selling embroidery threads, canvases and pattern books, Amman, 1987.
The shopkeepers are Palestinian, and the man on the right is an Egyptian employee. *Photo: Shelagh Weir*

Hasan Zaʿabalawi, already with a branch in Lydda, set up a small shop in Beit Dajan which he opened two days a week.

Merchants dealt with scores of villages in the countryside around their towns. Elias Khalti, a well-known textile merchant in Lydda, claimed his customers came from eighty or ninety villages, and Zabaneh of Ramleh gave a similar number. These figures may be no exaggeration, for, after motor transport was introduced in the 1920s, villagers came from all over the central and southern plain, and from as far as the western hills, to shop in Lydda and Ramleh. With improvements in travel, villagers were no longer restricted to visiting their nearest market, and many southern Palestinians made special long-distance trips to Bethlehem to buy their high-status trousseau products.

Textile retailers did not usually sell embroidery threads or silver cord (*qasab*); these were sold in different shops, or were peddled round the villages by itinerant salesmen. Silks lent themselves to this form of sale, being light, of high value by weight,[51] and often bought in small quantities. This retailing distinction continues today in the shops of Jerusalem and Amman.

Textile merchants had close links with cloth manufacturers and importers within Palestine (some had started as weavers themselves), and sustained trading networks with manufacturers in Syria, Beirut, Egypt, and Europe. Nablus merchants had particularly close trading relations with Syria, and many Palestinian retailers bought their supplies from them. Other shopkeepers gave orders to textile agents who regularly toured Palestine, or they sent messages of their requirements to their suppliers, or they travelled to Syria or Egypt themselves to order their wares.

Merchants had to be familiar with the different village styles in their areas, and the various customs and fashions in trousseaus and other marriage gifts. Sometimes a groom was ignorant of what he should buy for his bride's trousseau, and would rely on the merchant to advise him. Some shopkeepers provided an ancillary dress-making service; Zabaneh's wife employed five women for this work.

Merchants influenced village fashion by importing and stocking new fabrics and clothes, and were always on the lookout for new ideas, especially during the 1930s and 1940s when villagers were eager for change and innovation. However, they had to be careful what they introduced and recommended to their customers; if it was substandard and wore out, they lost their customers' confidence. As Abu Fuad, Zaʿabalawi's son explained:

Peasants had confidence in us. We knew what they bought was for their whole life. So we didn't suggest new things lightly. We had to be sure anything we introduced was good quality and would wear well. The man or woman went to a lot of trouble to save the money, and the woman spent years doing the embroidery, so the material had to be good and durable so her trouble was not wasted.

Buying the trousseau

The buying and giving of cloth and clothing played a major part in

the formalities and celebrations surrounding marriage. When he married, a man was obliged to buy a considerable quantity of clothing materials and costumes as a trousseau presentation (*kisweh*) for his bride, and as gifts for his own and the bride's relatives.

This compulsory purchase of materials and clothing at marriage was a large and difficult expenditure for many farmers, especially since they also had to pay a hefty brideprice to the bride's father. According to Khalti, referring to the 1930s–40s, the trousseau expenditure of the relatively prosperous villagers of the plain averaged as much as P£250, while the poorer hill villagers spent only about £100, depending on their fluctuating olive oil harvests. Merchants therefore became involved in the villagers' financial problems, and are often said to have acted 'like a bank' for them. No doubt this reflects the fact that villagers were often in their debt, but also that the villagers depended on their support. Several times villagers and merchants claimed that a special trust existed between them; for example, the villagers would often give merchants valuables for safe-keeping. Khalti praised the honesty of most village men. He left Lydda in 1948 owed £8000, and over twenty years later some of his customers were still seeking him out to pay their debts. He was confident that 'someday the rest will pay'.

The purchase of the trousseau and other clothing gifts shortly before the wedding involved an expedition to the textile merchant in the nearest town by members of both families.

The wife of the Ramleh merchant, Zabaneh, who began his business around 1920, described her husband's involvement in this event and its attendant celebrations.

Villagers would send advance notice of their visit to buy the wedding clothes and materials to give Zabaneh time to get in food for them. Up to forty or so people would come on the expedition, and in the wedding season (after harvest time) two of these groups could come each week. After arriving at his house – by donkey before the 1920s, by motor bus later – they would set off for the *suq* to choose their materials and clothes at his shop. On their return they would cook a big feast to which the merchant and any friends they encountered along the way were invited. This was a joyful event with much merry-making in anticipation of the impending marriage. There was singing and music, and sometimes a band would be hired from Jaffa.

Farmers often had limited cash, so paid in part with agricultural produce: grain, fruit and vegetables from the villagers of the coastal plain, olive oil from the hill villagers. Zabaneh kept on a large family house in order to store these barter goods, and also to provide the villagers with sleeping accommodation when they could not get home by nightfall.

Elias Khalti of Lydda had a special section of his house set aside for these village expeditions, where they would cook a sheep and rice and, if necessary, spend the night. His customers included many hill villagers who often paid him in olive oil. This he stored in two wells for the two grades of oil; one he sold for food, and the other he made into soap. He was also paid in sesame seeds which he also turned into oil.

Before the *kisweh* party departed, it was customary in the Jaffa area for the merchant to give them a cloth to wrap their goods in as a 'personal' present – a sign that the relationship went beyond the merely commercial.

The groom and his relatives were welcomed back to the village from their important shopping expedition with a special ceremony, called 'the trousseau celebration' (*zaffet al-kisweh*), an exuberant expression of joy at the imminent wedding. Granqvist gives a vivid description of the return of a *kisweh* expedition from Bethlehem to Artas:

One day in the wedding week we heard the women singing with trills (*zagharit*) in broad daylight. 'Ah! it is the bridal outfit which is being brought from Bethlehem', 'Alya said then; she knew everything. I went out and saw a row of women winding down the hill; the foremost of them carried a bundle on her head. The outfit had been wrapped up in a big pink woollen cloth which on the wedding day would form the bride's veil to cover her face, and afterwards be her girdle; the 'veil' was of course also new. After having trilled on the top of the mountain the women began to come down singing and clapping their hands; almost immediately they were answered with trills and songs from the village; some of the bridegroom's female relatives who were at home had gone up on the roof of his house to welcome them thence. It was at the same time the signal for the women of the village to collect at the bridegroom's house and inspect the bridal outfit ... The women sing and dance with the straw trays holding the outfit of the bride and the bridegroom's things on their heads.[52]

A few days later the wedding took place, often attended by the *kisweh* merchant – sometimes for commercial as well as social reasons. On the wedding day the groom received cash gifts from his friends and family at a special ceremony (*nqut*), and this often enabled him to pay any outstanding debts to the merchant.

am singing for Sa'id
or the sake of his mother
What a beautiful *qumbaz*!
With such lovely sleeves!
am singing for Sa'id
or the sake of his sisters

How smart his *qumbaz* is!
Well-fitting to his hands!
Beit Dajan betrothal song

2 Men's Costume

Though plainer and less varied than the richly decorated costumes of women, men's clothing was still a rich medium for visual statements about identity, age and status, and was also subject to changes in fashion as individuals and groups sought to emulate their superiors and display their wealth.

The language of men's costume is best described by examining in turn the different categories of garment, their significance and the changes they underwent.

The shirt

A plain long shirt or tunic (*thob*) was the basic garment of both villagers and bedouin, and was seen as fulfilling one of man's two fundamental needs, to be clothed and fed. As a local saying put it: 'A cotton shirt (*thob*) and a full stomach are God's blessing.'[1] But rare is the human garment which merely protects from the elements and is devoid of social and symbolic significance, and even the humble shirt lent itself to a degree of meaningful variation.

Before this century *thobs* were made from white or indigo blue[2] cotton or fine natural wool, and obeyed the male modesty code by covering the body at least to the knees. There may have been some regional variation in styles, for an ankle-length *thob* with blue and white stripes was noted in Jenin in the early 1860s,[3] and a blue *thob* in Nablus in the 1930s when white had become common elsewhere, but these may have been townsmen's and not villagers' garments.

To keep the long sleeves of the *thob* out of the way when working, they were tied back with a cord (*shmar*) which sometimes had ornamental tassels.[4] In contrast to the narrow sleeves of the village *thob*, bedouin men wore a *thob* with pointed, triangular sleeves (*irdan*). Among those of limited means, the extra fabric needed for triangular sleeves was a display of wealth, as was a blue *thob*, for undyed fabrics were cheaper.

For freedom of movement when working, the *thob* was normally hitched up through a leather belt to form a pouch (where small possessions were kept), so to wear a long, unbelted shirt which trailed on the ground was a display of conspicuous leisure and of wealthy carelessness about conserving valuable clothes. Klein records how, in the late nineteenth century, men of well-to-do Muslim families, 'such as in the village of Deir Ghassan', were characterised as 'going unbelted, trailing their shirts on the ground', for which there was a specific term – *taraffal*. (The same significance undoubtedly attached to the ankle-length overcoats and elongated sleeves of townsmen at the same period.)

During the Mandate period the *thob* was replaced by a long white shirt (*qamis*) cut in the European style.

Overcoats

For warmth in winter the hill villagers and bedouin wore sheepskin jackets (*farwah*) with the wool turned inwards, broadcloth coats (*jibbeh*) with or without sheepskin linings, or baggy sleeveless cloaks (*'aba* or *'abayeh*) of coarse handwoven wool which were draped over the shoulders like a cape. In the nineteenth century

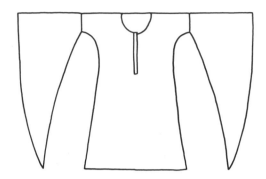

Bedouin shirt (*thob*)
Museum of Mankind: 1966 AS1 182

Bedouin wearing a coat (*jibbeh*) of broadcloth (*jukh*) lined with sheepskin, Bethlehem area, British Mandate period.
Note the elongated sleeve, symbol of wealth and leisure. *Photo: S. J. Schweig*

Previous page **Boy reading the Koran, Artas, 1925–31.**
He is dressed up in a *qumbaz* for a Muslim feast. *Photo: Hilma Granqvist*

'abayehs were made from indigo-blue and white striped wool as well as the natural brown and white which became more familiar later.

Klein points out what a useful all-purpose garment the 'abayeh was. Apart from protecting the wearer against rain and cold, it served as a blanket at night, a sack for carrying goods to market, a prayer rug, a feeding sack for animals, and even a small tent when working in the fields.[5] There were also more luxurious versions of the 'abayeh, called *shaleh*, made from finer woollen materials in plain black, blue, brown or cream and sometimes embroidered round the neck with gold or silver thread, which were worn by notables and the well-to-do.

Around Nablus a coat similar to the 'abayeh, but with short sleeves, was worn; this was also called 'abayeh, or *bisht* or *busht*[6] after the particularly thick handwoven wool from which it was made; this had red and white or brown and white stripes. The Druze of Galilee wore a *bisht* of finer brown or red handwoven wool, sometimes with an intricate brocade pattern on the back; this also had short sleeves, but was much tighter-fitting.

Above **Ta'amreh shepherd boy wearing an 'abayeh, Artas, 1925–31.** *Photo: Hilma Granqvist*

Right **Man wearing a sheepskin jacket (*farwah*), British Mandate period.** Beneath he has a *qumbaz* coat and shirt (*thob*) with horizontal stripes above the hem. He is spinning wool. *Photo: American Colony, Jerusalem*

Far right **Man wearing a locally-woven woollen *bisht* or *busht*, Nablus, 1930s.** Beneath the *bisht* he has a striped *qumbaz*. *Photo: Jan Macdonald*

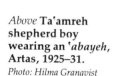

Cloak ('aba or 'abayeh), 19th or early 20th century.
Locally handwoven wool in natural colours.
H 121cm W 133cm Museum of Mankind: 1966 AS1 201

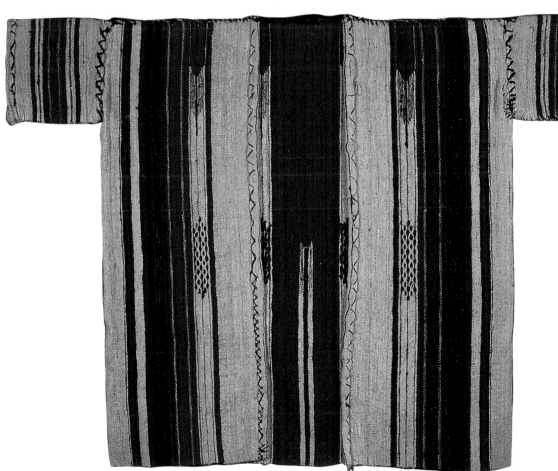

Woollen coat (*bisht* or *busht*), woven in Nablus until the 1920s or 1930s.
H 120cm W 160cm Museum of Mankind: 1966 AS1 200

The long-sleeved coat

In the nineteenth century the *thob* and *'abayeh* were the main garments of both villagers and bedouin, but from the end of the century village men increasingly wore over their *thobs* a calf- or ankle-length coat usually called *qumbaz*, or *hidim*, *kiber* or *dimayeh*. This had long, narrow sleeves, and was made from variously-coloured plain and striped cottons and Syrian silks.

In the nineteenth century the *qumbaz* was mainly a city garment, worn by the Turks (from whom the style derived) and the Arabs of the towns, while in the villages it was a luxury garment worn only by the relatively wealthy minority of village notables in imitation of the urban and ruling classes. As townsmen began to adopt European trousers and jackets at the end of the century, the *qumbaz* moved down the social scale and became a principal village garment.[7]

The widespread adoption of the *qumbaz* in the villages was related, as are all fashion changes, to social aspirations and the increased prosperity which fed them, for its silk versions were expensive, luxury garments. There is no evidence of any regional variation in types of *qumbaz*, but certain colours and fabrics had considerable ritual significance.

Cotton coats were worn for working and everyday purposes, while the more costly and prestigious silk coats were reserved for special family and religious occasions. The finest coats of all, of white *rozah* or *ghabani* silk, were worn by grooms for their weddings.

Silk coats played an important part in the gift exchanges and rituals associated with circumcision and marriage. For example, in many villages the groom had to present the bride's maternal and paternal uncles with coats or their money equivalent prior to his wedding (gifts described in Artas, south of Bethlehem, as 'bribes' for allowing their niece to be taken from her home at marriage). The importance of their sanction of the marriage was symbolised in the wedding ritual when 'her father's brother holds her by the one arm and her mother's brother by the other and thus she comes out of her father's house'.[8]

The gift to the bride's paternal uncle (*'amm*) was recognition that he had relinquished his son's priority right to marry her. In Palestinian village society, marriage between the sons and daughters of brothers was the stated ideal (though not the most common type of marriage actually contracted), and a girl's paternal uncles had to waive their claim before she could be betrothed to anyone other than their sons. Sometimes the Artas groom gave coats to the bride's brother and grandfather as well, but these gifts were not obligatory.

In Beit Dajan the groom presented his bride's maternal uncle with a coat of the finest white *roza* or *ghabani* silk called, in this context, 'the uncle's coat' (*hidim al-khal*). This was in explicit acknowledgement of the specially close relationship (common in patrilineal societies) between a woman's brother and her children. Not only was the relationship ideally a warm and affectionate one, but children were believed to inherit personal characteristics from

A Druze sheikh, probably in Galilee, 1930s. He is wearing a finely woven woollen *bisht*, baggy pants (*sirwal*), a broad sash (*hizam*) and a tall white turban (*'imamah*) *Photo: Jan Macdonald*

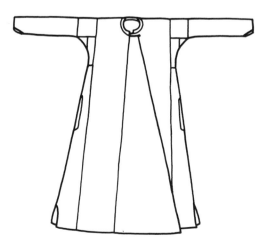

A *qumbaz*.

51

Village men and a boy, Bethlehem area, early 20th century.
They are wearing striped coats (*qumbaz*) and woollen cloaks (*'abayehs*). The boy is wearing the red felt *tarbush* without the turban (*laffeh*) worn only by adults. *Photo: Palestine Exploration Fund*

their mother's brother; it was therefore important to choose a wife with brothers of good character to ensure fine offspring.[9]

Coats were presented as gifts on these and other crucial life occasions in many Palestinian villages,[10] to affirm the existence or transformation of valued relationships, and help sustain the network of gift exchanges which bound individuals and families. The coats the groom presented to his bride's uncles set in train a lifetime of reciprocal gifts from the uncles to their niece, starting with a gift of money at a special ceremony (*nqut*) on her wedding day, and continuing with presents on feast days and whenever she gave birth.

In the specific context of the wedding, a coat of the *qumbaz/hidim* type expressed the protective element in male-female relationships, for a coat belonging to the groom was often draped over a bride's head and body as she rode in procession on horseback or camel from her old to her new home. This covering, and concealing, of the bride symbolised the transference of primary responsibility for her protection and wellbeing from her father to her husband. In Artas, the groom presented this coat to the girl's father at the time the marriage contract was made, and it returned on the wedding day on the back of his bride. In Beit Dajan the coat was made from white *rozah* or *ghabani* silk, and, as will be described in Chapter 6, was associated with transition between statuses.

In many villages, the colour of the male coat draped over the bride signified to which of two political alliances or factions, Qays or Yaman, she belonged – the Qaysi colour being red, the Yamani colour white. These alliances, which encompassed all of Palestine except the Jaffa region, were politically important in the nineteenth century when state control was weak; entire villages or regions adhered to one or the other alliance, or villages were split internally between the two. Although Qays and Yaman have lost their political import, they have survived as an aspect of social identity, and villagers still usually know to which former alliance they and neighbouring villages 'belong'. For example, the villages of the Hebron area are often referred to as 'the Qaysiyat' by themselves and others.

If the bride was marrying into a village of the opposite faction, she wore the colour of her own village for the first part of the procession, and, at the insistence of her husband's people, changed into the colour of his village at a specified place on the way. For example when brides from El-Khadr or Artas, which were Qaysi, married into Bethlehem which was Yamani, they changed at Soloman's Pools. In 'Aboud, which was split between the two factions, there was a special stone where the coat was changed when a bride was marrying from one faction into the other. There, and in other villages, the change was facilitated by a reversible coat, red lined with white and vice versa, which could simply be turned inside out at the designated spot.

Often fights broke out over the colour change – ritual conflict which, like the wearing of 'colours' by the bride, simultaneously asserted the identity and cohesion of the village or village section, and its wider political allegiance. Some women, lauded as heroines, refused to change their faction colour, and proudly entered their new village in the colour of their own, staving off attempts to force them to change with the sword which brides usually carried in their wedding procession.[11]

Jackets and waistcoats

A variety of jackets or waistcoats, copied first from the Turkish ruling élite, then from European visitors and the British, were copied initially by urban Palestinians, then later filtered down to the wealthier villagers and bedouin. The Turkish-style garments included a broadcloth jacket (*damer* or *salta*) with braid or cord trim, satin waistcoats (*sidriyeh*) with braid trim and bobble fastenings, and long-sleeved satin jackets (*mintiyan*) with similar fastenings, worn over the *sidriyeh*.[12]

In the late nineteenth century, European fashions began to catch on in the towns,[13] especially among the better-off Christians of Ramallah and Bethlehem, who had European and American connections and experiences through migration and who were emulated by other villagers. Ulmer comments that it had become fashionable (by 1918) to wear at least one piece of European

Young man of Artas, 1925–31.
He is wearing a European jacket and shoes and a tall, urban style *tarbush* on his head. This youth was an apprentice carpenter in nearby Bethlehem, and adopted urban clothes to go to work (Seger, 1981:62) *Photo: Hilma Granqvist*

Waistcoats (sidriyeh).
Left: white cotton *ghabani* material; right: red and yellow striped cotton (*dima*) with crescent-shaped pocket. *H 50 and 44cm Museum of Mankind: 1966 AS1 185, 183*

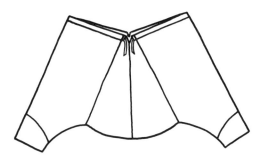

Baggy pants (sirwal)
L from waist to ankle: 80cm.

clothing, be it a collar, shoes or a coat; at a wedding in Ramallah in 1913, the bridegroom wore European shoes, coat and collar, and his host wore a European waistcoat and frock coat.

The European jacket became very popular at all levels of Palestinian society during the Mandate period, largely replacing the older cloaks and overcoats. In the towns it was worn with European-style trousers, but in the villages it was worn over shirts (*thobs*) and coats (*qumbaz*). So village men were often clothed in three historical layers: a 'traditional' shirt, a Turkish-style coat, and a European-style jacket.

Pants

Around the same time as the *qumbaz* started to be worn, village men also began wearing baggy pants (*sirwal* or *libas*), probably in imitation of Turkish officials and to display wealth by their voluminous material. The pants were normally in white, black or blue cotton, and were tight-fitting on the lower leg and very wide at the waist, where they were gathered by a draw-string (*dikkeh*) in folds.[14]

Baggy pants were worn more by villagers than bedouin, who usually went bare-legged, and were not common even among villagers until the late 1920s.[15] Before then they were a luxury which could only be afforded by the better-off.[16] A need for more modest dress may also have been felt because of increased contact with

Men winnowing grain near Sebastiyeh, 1926–35.
Both are wearing the striped *qumbaz*. The man on the left has hitched his up while he works, revealing his baggy black underpants (*sirwal*).
Photo: Grace Crowfoot

A boatman from Jaffa, British Mandate period.
He is wearing baggy pants (*sirwal* or *libas*).
Photo: S. J. Schweig

other villagers and foreigners; this was the reason for the widespread adoption of long pants by women at the same period.

In contrast to the easy popularity of jackets, European trousers were considered strange and foreign, and were also associated with conscription. In the late nineteenth century Turkish military uniform became increasingly European, so 'to put on the pants' came to mean the dreaded call-up for military service.[17] However, this connotation faded with time, and during the Mandate period trousers became common among all groups and classes of Palestinian society, and in the 1980s only a minority of older village men still wear the *qumbaz*, and a minority of bedouin the *thob* and *'abayeh*.

Belts and sashes

For everyday wear villagers and bedouin wore a leather belt (*sherihah* or *kshat*)[18] to which a variety of equipment could be attached, as illustrated in the following description of a villager's belt by Baldensperger:

Encircling his waist was a broad leather girdle, and to this were attached a number of iron hooks, to which were suspended a powder horn of solid wood, a long chain with a knife dangling at the end, a leather bag to hold lead and bullets for firearms, a tobacco pouch with a pipe, and a smaller pouch containing flint and steel and tinder ...[19]

Occasionally a narrow curved dagger (*shibriyeh*) was worn behind the belt. Bedouin often wore leather bandoliers with crossed straps over the chest and slots for bullet cartridges.

Another style of village belt (*kamr*), was tablet-woven in Syria,

Tablet-woven belts (*kamr*).
The top belt, from the Hebron district, has been decorated with taffeta and embroidery for wearing on festive occasions. *L 203 and 213cm Above: Dar al-Tifl collection 37.112; below: Museum of Mankind: 1966 AS1 226*

Above **Bedouin in the Negev desert, 1936.**
They are wearing tablet-woven belts (*kamr*).
The man on the left also has a dagger
(*shibriyeh*). The man in the centre is Egyptian.
All three were working on excavations at Tell
al-Duweir when the photograph was taken.
Photo: Olga Tufnell

Above right **Boys dressed up for a feast, Artas,
1925–31.**
Note their broad sashes and smart coats.
Photo: Hilma Granqvist

usually in red or brown wool edged with yellow stripes, with
leather trimmings and buckle fastenings. In the Hebron area a
ceremonial version of this belt was gaily embroidered.

The better-off, those who wanted to exhibit their high status, and
men dressing up for special occasions, wore a variety of sashes
(*hizam*, *zunnar* or *ishdad*) made from wool, silk or cotton, some with
multi-coloured woven patterns.[20] This was a prestigious garment
because of its status associations with the ruling Turkish élite, from
whom it was copied, because of the fine, expensive materials from
which it was made (the best from Kashmir wool), and because of its
wealth-displaying width and bulk.

Footwear

Before the introduction of European footwear, village men went
barefooted or wore locally-made shoes (*wata* or *madas*) of brown
leather. Bedouin also went barefooted, or wore sandals with a
thong between the first and second toes.[21] Horsemen wore red or
yellow leather boots (*yezmeh*) with iron strengthening on the soles.
These were all made by specialist shoemakers in the cities.[22] The
shoe trade boomed at harvest time because farmers needed protection for walking over the stubble in their fields,[23] and perhaps
because the poorest could then afford footwear.

While head coverings had a positive, noble aura, the covering of
the other bodily extremity, the feet, had negative connotations.
Shoes were considered unclean, and were always removed at the
threshold before entering a house or mosque, while head wear was
kept on. Macdonald points out how topsy-turvy it appeared to
Palestinians that European men removed their hats and kept on
their shoes when entering a house.[24] In certain ritual situations,

Men's footwear.
Left: common style of hide shoe (*wata* or *madas*) worn throughout Palestine, including sometimes by women, up to the late Mandate period
Right: boot (*yezmeh*) of the type worn by horsemen, especially bedouin. It has an iron reinforcement on the heel. *Museum of Mankind: 1977 AS10 2; 1966 AS1 308*

Shoemaker selling his wares in Bethlehem market, 1930s. *Photo: Jan Macdonald*

shoes were also believed to be instruments of harm, especially if their soles were exposed.

Head wear

Until the 1930s, men's head wear[25] was a clear marker of the major divisions of Palestinian society: men were most immediately recognisable as townsmen, villagers or bedouin by what they wore on their heads. Head wear also proclaimed religious affiliation, political position and wealth, and possibly also regional origins.

VILLAGERS The head wear of villagers was the most complicated, and had the greatest range of significance. It comprised several layers. The first was a white cotton skull cap (*taqiyeh*, or *'araqiyeh* meaning 'sweat-cap'). Over this was placed a white or grey felt cap (*libbadeh* or *kubb'ah*), and over that in turn a red felt hat (*tarbush maghribi*, implying north African influence) with a floppy black or navy blue silk or cotton tassel (*dubbahah* or *sharbush*) attached to the crown. In contrast to the *tarbush istambuli* worn by Ottoman officials, Turkish soldiers and urban Palestinians, which was tall, stiff and shaped like an upturned flowerpot, the village *tarbush* was small, soft and rounded at the crown. The purpose of

Above **Bedouin wearing sandals, British Mandate period.**
The man on the left is also wearing an elaborate leather belt, and the one on the right an *'abayeh* coat. *Photo: S. J. Schweig*

Right **Bethlehem market, late 1925–31.**
Most men and boys are wearing the tall urban-style *tarbush istambuli* as a sign of their identification with the town and the ruling élite, rather than the villagers.
Photo: Hilma Granqvist

A hierarchy of miniature *tarbushes* and turbans (*laffeh*), as worn by adult male villagers until the 1930s.
Miniature headdresses were made for sale to tourists and pilgrims.
Top left: green turban and multi-coloured *tarbush*, worn by Muslim religious specialists.
Top centre: Smooth, plain white turban on red *tarbush*, worn by Muslim scholars.
Top right: turban of *ghabani* fabric on red *tarbush*, worn by village elders and notables.
Centre left: orange/yellow turban on red *tarbush*, worn by Muslim and Christian villagers in the Bethlehem region and elsewhere.
Centre right: green turban on red *tarbush*, worn by villagers who belonged to sufi religious orders.
Bottom: orange/yellow turban on felt cap (*libbadeh*), worn by low-class urban workers such as porters. *D approx. 5cm*
Museum of Mankind: 1987 AS7 6

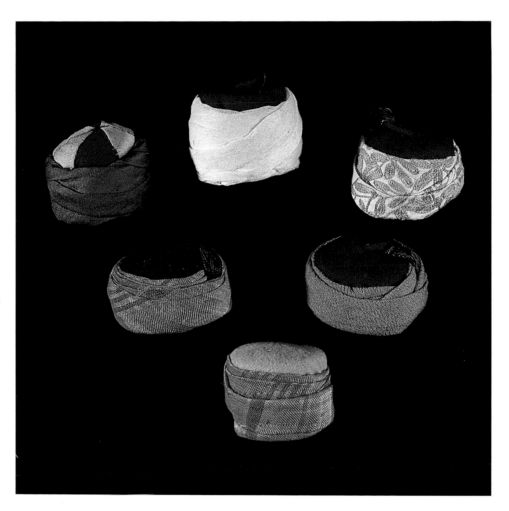

59

Above **A village leader in Artas, 1925–31.**
He is wearing a bulky turban of *ghabani* silk, as befits his age and rank. *Photo: Hilma Granqvist*

Left **Various striped silk fabrics used for turbans (*laffeh*).**
Approx. 100cm square Museum of Mankind: 1966 AS1 257, 258, 266, 261

the *libbadeh*, which was the same shape as the *tarbush* and fitted neatly inside it, was to bulk it out.

The turban (*laffeh*) was made from Syrian fabrics of cotton or silk, usually striped or checked in a variety of colours, and with a sparse, tasselled fringe on two edges. First a plain white cloth was wrapped round the *tarbush* to protect the *laffeh* from sweat, and probably also to make it look thicker (a fat turban being prestigious), then the *laffeh* was wrapped round on top of this so as to leave the crown of the *tarbush* exposed and enclose the end of the tassel.

Often small articles were stored in the folds of the turban, or between the layers of caps. The complexity of all this head gear and storage space is humorously conveyed by Baldensperger (writing in 1913):

Khaleel Ibrahim had come to tell his chief that the hour for departure had arrived. Bringing his prayer to an abrupt termination, Muhammad Moosa rose to his feet and, as he arranged his immense green turban (a sign of his claim to prophetic descent), gave his orders. A complicated piece of work – this arrangement of the Sherif's turban, his caps and their contents; and one that took much longer than the giving of a few brief instructions regarding the loading of the camels. Besides the white cap, or Takiyeh, he wore the red Tarbush, and between these the grey felt Lubbaad. Between the Lubbaad and the Tarbush, Muhammad Moosa kept his cigarette papers, his tax-papers and other documents, and tucked away between the three caps and the turban were little bottles of tar or scent and the wooden comb with which, whilst saying his prayers, he daily combed his beard.[26]

The head was the locus of a man's honour and reputation, and it was proper and dignified that it should be covered, and shameful (*'ayb*) to leave it uncovered (as it also was for women). By association, the head wear itself took on connotations of honour. Men swore oaths on their turbans, and the removal of a man's turban in anger was a slur and provocation, and could necessitate material compensation.[27]

Head wear was not taken off when entering a house, nor a mosque, for it was required to be worn for prayers. Normally it was only removed when going to bed, or in special circumstances – the most notable being at Mecca where pilgrims go bare-headed. Ulmer mentions that youths also removed their head wear for a dance they performed to greet the first spring rain.

The adoption of the *tarbush* and *laffeh* signified manhood, and boys wore only a cap (*taqiyeh*). In some villages, quite elaborate boys' caps were worn early this century. Ulmer describes a cap worn by boys in the Bethlehem region and Ramleh which was made from velvet or broadcloth, and sometimes decorated with zig-zag applique (*tishrifeh*) and embroidered, and he noted another in 'Aboud, north west of Ramallah, with no less than five tassels.

As though in anticipation of their manhood, a highly decorated *tarbush* was worn by small boys for their circumcisions. The circumcision ceremony was the main occasion in a man's life for the celebration and display of his social value, and was in this respect the male equivalent of the wedding for the bride; indeed villagers

A father and his sons in Ramallah, 1905.
The ornamental *tarbushes* mean the boys are probably Muslims dressed up for their
circumcision ceremony. *Photo: Keystone, Library of Congress*

Boy riding on horseback in his circumcision procession, Artas, 1925–31.
Photo: Hilma Granqvist

often comment 'circumcisions were just like weddings', even though most boys were circumcised under the age of six. On his circumcision day a boy was ornamented in similar ways to a bride, and led in procession on horseback or camel through the village, just as a bride was taken in procession from her father's to her husband's home on the first day of the wedding ceremonies.

As with brides, the social value of the boy was expressed by adorning him with precious coins and jewellery. He was also (as she was) decorated with ostrich feathers, to divert the evil eye, and with green leaves for prosperity. In Beit Dajan in the 1920s, the boy to be circumcised usually wore a red *tarbush* ornamented with sequins, and a woman's headdress ornament (*shakkeh*) comprising a row of gold coins attached to a band; later in the Mandate he wore a cap (*qaluseh*) embroidered with silver cord (*qasab*), and a blue or red velvet chest panel (*qabbeh*) sewn with gold coins. A special circumcision *tarbush* worn in Lifta near Jerusalem before 1918 had blue beads attached to it against the evil eye, and on the crown a metal plaque (*qurs*) with *repoussée* patterns, and pendant chains with coins.[28]

The turban was everywhere associated with sexual and social maturity. At weddings in Beit Dajan in the 1920s, grooms wore the *tarbush* alone without the turban (*laffeh*), and added the turban after. In other villages a man wore the turban when he was ready for marriage. In 'Aboud, the turbans of unmarried men had a rakish fringe to one side with a mirror attached to attract the girls. A man's headdress continued to represent him even after death, for Muslim graves had *tarbush*-shaped stones at their heads round which turbans were wrapped.

Turbans indicated social position and religious identity by their

Above **Muslim funeral, Jerusalem, British Mandate period.**
Note the white turban on the body. *Photo: Matson Collection, Library of Congress*

Facing page **Circumcision waistcoat, possibly Hebron hills, British Mandate period or earlier.**
Red *atlas* satin, with one side covered with coins to express the high social value of the boy. *H 30cm Collection: Widad Kawar*

size, shape and colour. Wide bulky turbans, like wide bulky sashes, proclaimed a man's social importance. Conder remarks on the 'huge white turban – emblem of superior holiness and incorruptibility' worn by a Muslim judge (*qadi*) in Nablus in the 1870s,[29] and village notables also displayed their power and status with especially large and cumbersome turbans. Klein describes how a Christian sheikh in Nazareth, who discarded his old headdress, took great care to ensure the new one was as large and heavy as the old, and adjusted its size by adding felt hats and wrapping veils round and round. He said 'a change would have given him headaches'. (Women say the same about removing their heavy coin-encrusted headdresses.) He also notes that these heavy turbans were being replaced at the time he wrote (1881) by Turkish headdresses, by which he presumably meant the tall stiff *tarbush istambuli*.[30]

Learned, religious men wore smoothly wrapped flat white turbans, in contrast to normal turbans which were twisted and bulky. Men who claimed descent from the Prophet Muhammad wore green, as did *hajjis* to show they had made the pilgrimage to Mecca, and men who wanted to emphasise their Muslim identity. Green had been worn in Palestine by purported descendants of the Prophet for hundreds of years,[31] but early this century they lost their monopoly on this significant colour. Around 1918 the green turban was being adopted by so many *hajjis*, and men who wanted to display their affiliation to Islam, that the descendants of the Prophet changed to white turbans to maintain their distinctiveness.[32] The adherents of different sufi orders of Islam each had their own turban colours as well.[33]

Apart from green, which has an intrinsic symbolic value as a holy Islamic colour, turban colours connoting religious affiliation took their significance from their contrast with others. Tristram noticed their contrastive significance in the Nablus region when he visited members of the Samaritan sect there in 1863–4:

All [the Samaritans] wore the red turban, the peculiar badge of the sect, while white is appropriate to the Moslems, green being the exclusive colour of the shireefs or descendants of the prophet, and black or purple left to the Jews or Christians.[34]

This explains why men of Beit Dajan, which was Muslim, say they could wear 'any colour but black'.

In Aboud, a half Christian, half Muslim village, members of the two religions were clearly distinguished by their turban colours: Muslims wore white turbans, often of *ghabani* silk, while Christians wore a red turban called a *mahrameh*.

Apart from those who had a religious statement to make, most village men in the prime of life wore turbans in bright, warm colours. In the 1870s yellow and brown were the commonest turban colours in southern Palestine,[35] while orange was popular during the Mandate. Vibrant colour was associated with youth, as it was in women's costume, and when men reached their fifties it was considered appropriate to exchange their coloured turbans for

turbans which were predominantly white.

There is evidence that turban colours might sometimes have indicated regional or village origins. Around 1914, a turban of white linen with a coloured border was worn in the area north of Jerusalem, and of yellow and red silk around Hebron.[36] And Beit Dajan informants distinguished between a turban (*samasmiyeh*) worn in the Gaza area, which was patterned red and yellow and wound directly round the skull cap without a *tarbush*, and the *ghabani* turban worn on the *tarbush* common in the Jaffa area. This may, however, have been more a reflection of wealth than regional identity, though the two amounted to the same thing.

Turban colour could also indicate political affiliation. At the beginning of this century, a white turban not only signified a Muslim, especially one who was an Ottoman official, but was also worn by members of the Yaman political faction, while those of the opposing Qays faction wore red.[37]

Individuals and groups could change their turban colour to maintain a separate identity, or to establish identity with another group. So, historically, there were probably shifts in the patterns of contrasting turban colours as a change in one group caused a chain reaction of changes through other groups who wished to maintain their distinctiveness.

BEDOUIN Until the 1920s the bedouin were distinguished from villagers and townspeople by their square head cloth (*hattah* or *keffiyeh*), worn folded diagonally, and bound to the head with head-ropes (*'aqal*) of black goat hair or brown wool or camel hair. Sometimes a white cotton skull cap (*taqiyeh*) was worn beneath the cloth. The *hattah* came in cotton, silk and fine wool, and in various colours and patterns. In the nineteenth century, head-ropes were relatively thick, and later became thinner; and high status bedouin wore ropes of wool or camel hair bound at intervals with gold thread (called *'aqal mqassab*). There were, and are, a variety of ways the *hattah* could be worn according to whether the paramount concern was practical considerations, like shielding the eyes and nose from dust, or else the wish to appear à la mode in the way the points were arranged, for fashions in the way the cloth was draped changed, and still do.

In view of the association of turban with 'village' (*fellah*) identity, and head cloth and head-ropes with bedouin identity, it is interesting to note that in the nineteenth century the men of the Ta'amreh tribe, who lived in tents, and conducted a semi-pastoral, semi-agricultural existence in the hills east of Bethlehem, were, according to Conder (1880) 'remarkable for wearing the turban, which none of the other tribes use'. Costume was such a powerful symbol of social identity that Condor concluded that because the Ta'amreh 'also wear shoes, instead of sandals ... they are indeed not true Bedawin, but of the same stock with the peasantry'.[38]

The Ta'amreh are often described as 'semi-settled bedouin' or 'not true bedouin' in the literature, and the reason they were not easily slotted into the social category of either '*fellah*' or '*bedouin*'

Young sheikh, Beersheba area, British Mandate period.
He is wearing ornamental head ropes (*'agal mqassab*), a white *hattah* draped over a checked *keffiyeh*, and a dagger (*shibriyeh*) with niello decoration.

Ta'amreh bedouin wearing turbans, pre-1920.
They are doing a celebration dance (*fantasia*). *Photo: Palestine Exploration Fund*

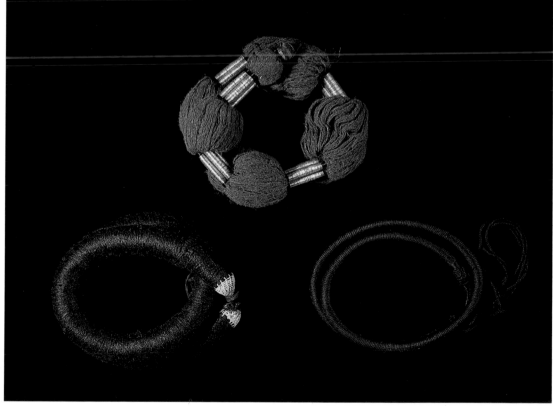

Bedouin head-ropes ('aqal).
Goat hair and wool, the latter bound with gold cord. In the nineteenth century, head-ropes were fatter than those worn more recently.
Museum of Mankind: 1966 AS1 296, 301 and 1987 AS7 7

was probably due to their clothing as much as their mode of subsistence – for many 'bedouin' cultivated grain as well as herding animals, but did not *appear* anomalous because they wore 'proper' bedouin head gear. The Taʿamreh turbans probably meant that the tribe *wanted* to dissociate themselves from 'true' or 'pure' bedouin identity at that period and identify with villagers – probably because of the fear with which villagers regarded bedouin in the nineteenth century when they were often raided by them. This would have been of concern because of the close economic and social relations the Taʿamreh had with the villagers of the Bethlehem area. They marketed their grain in Bethlehem, wove rugs, cradles and bags for the villagers, and sometimes intermarried with them.[39]

In the late 1930s a significant change took place in village men's headdresses. The distinctive bedouin-style head wear, the head cloth (*keffiyeh*) and headropes (*ʿaqal*), was adopted by many villagers and townsmen as an expression of Palestinian nationalism, and the *tarbush* and turban (*laffeh*) went out of fashion except among old men. Photographs show that the head cloth at this period was white, but later black and white and red and white checked patterns became popular.

After the war of 1967 and the Israeli occupation of the West Bank and Gaza, the black and white *keffiyeh* adopted by Yasser Arafat, Chairman of the Palestine Liberation Organisation, became a potent symbol of Palestinian national identity. Young men, in particular, wore it as a statement of their aspirations and allegiance, its distinctive black and white pattern became a popular motif in Palestinian cartoons, posters and paintings, and its meaning has passed into the international language of costume.

Right **Villagers in Halhul north of Hebron, 1940.**
They are waiting for an open-air film show. The younger men are wearing bedouin-style head cloths and head-ropes, while the older men retain the *tarbush* and *laffeh*. *Photo: Matson Collection, Library of Congress*

Below **Two men in Dhahariyeh, south of Hebron, 1940.**
The younger man has adopted the *keffiyeh* to express his nationalistic sentiments, whereas the older man retains the *laffeh* and *tarbush*. He is also wearing a fur-lined jacket (*jibbeh*). *Photo: Matson Collection, Library of Congress*

Ta'amreh bedouin wearing dark *keffiyehs* and head ropes, British Mandate period.
Photo: S. J. Schweig

Above **A variety of head cloths in Ramallah market, 1987.** *Photo: Shelagh Weir*

Above right **A bedouin cotton head cloth (*keffiyeh*), with indigo-dyed pattern, British Mandate period; and a woman's scarf made from a man's head cloth, 1980s.**
Black and white checked *keffiyehs* became a symbol of Palestinian nationalism in the 1960s, and scarves made from *keffiyeh* material, and ornamented with the colours of the Palestinian flag, are popular among refugee women in Jordan in the 1980s.
Museum of Mankind: 1966 AS1 290 and 1988 AS6 22

Right **'Prisoner's day', painting by Palestinian artist Sliman Mansour.**
The black and white checked *keffiyeh* has become a popular motif in Palestinian art.

Left **A man and his wife picking figs in their orchard, Artas, 1925–31.**
Photo: Hilma Granqvist

Right **Girl embroidering, probably British Mandate period.**
Photo: Library of Congress

3
Women's Costume
Body garments

We embroidered the side panels for such a long time!
remember Halimeh when we were pals?
We embroidered the chest panels for such a long time!
remember Halimeh when we were girls?

Henna night song, Beit Dajan

Women's costumes, especially their festive garments, are far more diverse and richly ornamented than men's; there is great regional and local variation in garments, and coats (in Galilee) and dresses (in southern Palestine) are lavishly embellished with colourful taffeta, satin and velvet patchwork, and embroidery in lustrous silks and gleaming silver or gold cord. This elaborate, intricate work was an entirely female enterprise.[1] Most women decorated their own costumes, and a minority sewed and embroidered professionally for others.

The great variety of women's costumes and their complicated decorative elements constitute a correspondingly complex language about identity and status. Many features, some major, some very small, indicated women's marital and sexual status, displayed the social and economic status of family and village, and announced village or regional origins.

The fact that women created their own costumes is a significant aspect of female clothing, not merely because of the hours of skilled work required for their elaborate ornamentation, but because women were thereby creating their own exclusive language, influenced, but barely comprehended, by men; within certain constraints, they were choosing what statements their clothes should make, defining their own identity and deciding how to portray it.

This chapter and the next describe the main regional variations in the garments worn on the body and the head respectively, indicating their significance. The final two chapters attempt a deeper, more detailed understanding of Palestinian women's costume language by focusing on the costumes of Beit Dajan.

The trousseau and the wedding

The central event for understanding women's costume is the wedding, partly because a girl's wedding trousseau contained her first collection of ceremonial costumes, and partly because the symbolism of many costumes becomes clearer in the context of the wedding rituals.

In central and southern Palestine the trousseau was called the *jihaz*, literally 'equipment', and was indeed essential equipment, symbolic and practical, for a girl's new womanly status. It contained jewellery, lavishly decorated dresses (*thob al-tal'ah*, 'going out dresses'), veils and girdles, for wearing at ceremonial, festive occasions such as weddings, circumcision ceremonies and pilgrimages, and for important social visits and expeditions to town. Most dresses illustrated in this book are such festive dresses. The trousseau also included plainer dresses (*thob al-khidmah*, 'service dresses', or *thob basitah*, 'simple dresses') and plain veils and girdles for everyday, working purposes in the home and fields.

The trousseau was divided into two distinct categories: items presented by the groom, called the *kisweh*;[2] and items paid for by the bride's father and usually made by the bride or her mother during the months or years preceding marriage. The latter were not distinguished by name; they just made up the *jihaz*.

The *kisweh* contained only luxurious ceremonial garments or the materials for making them – dresses, jackets, girdles or veils, depending on local fashion and economic circumstances. Most *kisweh* items were bought in the market (as opposed to home-made), and their purchase was highly ceremonialised (as described in Chapter 1).

The bride's contribution to the trousseau included both everyday and festive items, the most important of the latter being heavily embroidered dresses in the style of her village. The number and quality of these garments depended on her father's means (for he paid for the materials), as well as how much time the bride had free from agricultural and household chores for embroidering.

The most lavishly ornamented of the dresses prepared by the bride was worn for the first time during her wedding celebrations. These celebrations appear to have had the same basic ritual structure everywhere, with minor local variations. The rituals extended over several days, and began and ended with ceremonial processions in which the bride was main participant. In the first procession ('going out from her father's house', *tal'at min dar abuha*), which took place on the wedding day (*yom al-'urs*), she rode on horse or camel-back, shrouded in coats and veils, from her father's home to the groom's. This will be referred to as 'the wedding day procession'.

In the second, entirely female, procession the bride walked to the village well, spring or stream to fill her water jar, surrounded by the women of her village; this proclaimed and celebrated her transformation into a married woman, and could only take place after the consummation of the marriage and a variable period of seclusion of up to a week. For this joyful procession (*tal'at al-bir*, 'going out to the well', 'spring' or 'stream' as the case may be), which will be referred to as 'the going out ceremony', she wore the most splendid of the dresses she had prepared for her trousseau. Some

Wedding procession, Artas, 1925–31.
The bride, shrouded in coats and veils, is transported by camel to the house of the groom, with cushions, rugs and quilts piled around her on the camel. In some villages, the trousseau costumes were carried in bags on the camel; in others they were carried separately in a wooden chest.
Photo: Hilma Granqvist

of the most heavily embroidered dresses illustrated in this book were worn for the first time on this important ritual occasion.

In addition to costumes, the bride's (and her father's) contribution to the trousseau usually included furnishings for her new marital home: a mattress (*firash*), a quilt (*ilhaf*), gaily patched and embroidered cushion covers (*mkhaddeh*), and a chest (*sanduq*) for her trousseau. (Women in the Hebron hills wove camel bags specially for transporting the trousseau to their new home.) Many girls also made decorative antimony (*kohl*) holders (*mukholeh*) to hang on the wall, and in the Sinjil area, which specialised in basketwork, they made colourful boxes (*quteh*) to store embroidery threads, combs and other trinkets.

As well as these items, the bride's father provided her with a set of jewellery, and coins for attaching to her married woman's headdress. These were usually paid for with the brideprice received from the groom.

Regional styles and changing fashion

A woman's garments indicated by their colour and style whether she was a townswoman, villager or bedouin, and varied in more detailed ways according to the region, village or tribe to which she belonged. Differences increased with social and geographical distance, and were more subtle between groups in close proximity and with regular contact. Villagers mixed and intermarried mainly within a radius of four or five neighbouring villages, and generally name the same villages when asked which had costumes and embroidery most like their own.[3] Thus Palestine was made up of scores of overlapping village clusters with similar fashions. It can also be divided into larger stylistic regions with regard to specific features of costume.

In addition to the enormous geographical diversity of costume, several distinct styles of festive dress and other garments co-existed in each village and each woman's collection at any one time, with richer individuals and villages possessing the greatest variety of garments and the most lavishly ornamented. As economic conditions improved, costume collections also became larger, and garments more richly decorated; in the nineteenth century, women possessed, on average, a smaller number of dresses and veils, with less embroidery, than during the more affluent British Mandate period. In addition to this overall growth in quantity and quality, the fashions of each region were in a constant state of flux in response to new materials, local economic and social change, improved communications, and the ever-present drive to emulate the fashions of individuals, groups or villages who were socially and economically superior.

In order to keep up with fashion, a woman therefore endeavoured to replace or alter her trousseau clothes, her foundation collection, several times in her lifetime as they became unfashionable or wore out. The vivid, ostentatious costumes of her prime years were also exchanged for more restrained clothes as she grew old.

Women inside their house, Ramallah, 1906.
In the background can be seen folded bedding stored in a niche, the edge of a basketry tray, and wall paintings. The woman on the left is wearing a white dress with coloured stripes and a chest panel of striped satin (*atlas*), a type worn in the Nablus area. She is also wearing an embroidered veil and a ceremonial girdle (*kashmir* or *ishdad*), both decorated with fringed bands (*dikkeh*). Both women are wearing Bethlehem-style jackets (*taqsireh*) and the local headdress (*saffeh*).
Photo: Standard Scenic Company, Library of Congress

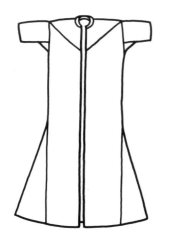

Galilee coat (*dura'ah*). *H 132cm*

Coat (*qumbaz*, *hidim*), Lower Galilee, late
19th/early 20th century *H 140cm*
Note the long side openings.

The remainder of this chapter describes the garments worn on the body, indicating the main regional variations in style, materials and embellishment. Unless stated to be bedouin, the garments described were worn by villagers.

Coats

Galilee and the Nablus area

STYLES AND MATERIALS The main garment of the Galilee villagers and the women of Nazareth[4] until early this century was a short-sleeved front-opening coat (*dura'ah* when relatively plain, *jillayeh* when heavily ornamented). Coats were usually made from locally-woven cotton, mostly indigo blue in colour, sometimes a rusty red or light brown, and sometimes a combination of the two. More luxurious examples were made from pink or red satins, often lined with fine cotton. Another type (*qaziyeh*) was made from unlined black or purple *qaz* silk.

During the second half of the nineteenth century, this short-sleeved coat was replaced in many villages by another style of coat (*qumbaz*), with long, tight-fitting sleeves, a scooped neckline, and long side openings; the three flaps were usually hitched up through a girdle. The *qumbaz* is Turkish in style, and was adopted first, in emulation of the ruling class, by the townswomen in Acre and Nazareth,[5] then copied by the villagers of the southern Galilee hills (Lower Galilee).

Similar coats (*qumbaz*, *hidim*) were also worn in the Nablus region until the 1960s, mainly for festive occasions. Their cut was similar to that of men's coats, with overlapping fronts and short side slits (or none at all), and they were sometimes worn over the head with the sleeves flapping loose.

These coats are mainly made from brightly coloured, striped and patterned Syrian satins (*atlas*); and, in the Tulkarm area, from white (*ghabani* and *rozah*) silks as well.

DECORATIVE PATCHWORK The older, short-sleeved coats of thick blue cotton are often beautifully decorated with patches of red, yellow and green taffeta (*heremzi*), or striped or ikat-patterned satins (*atlas*), applied inside or outside the front opening of the coat and sleeves, and sometimes across the back. The patches are rectangular, or cut and slashed in irregular shapes, their outlines clearly marked with silk thread on the reverse of the coat. Often the coat and its patchwork are so neatly sewn that the coat was clearly intended to be reversible. This type of exuberant patchwork decoration is usually combined with rich silk embroidery. Other plainer coats, without embroidery, are decorated more simply with silk and brocade facings to their front openings, the latter usually edged in coloured cord.

EMBROIDERY The back and sides of blue Galilee coats (*jillayeh* when heavily ornamented) are often richly embroidered in mainly red silks, in predominantly geometric designs: squares, diamonds,

Left **Coat (*dura'ah*), probably Druze, Galilee, late 19th or early 20th century.**
Cotton sleeves and facings; reddish-purple raw silk (*qaz*) body with green satin panels; blue cotton lining.
H 123cm Museum of Mankind: 1971 AS1 17

Right **Back of a coat (*dura'ah*), Majd al-Kurum, Galilee, circa 1920.**
Cotton material; cotton embroidery; blue and green silk brocade facings to front opening.
H 127cm Museum of Mankind: 1968 AS4 36

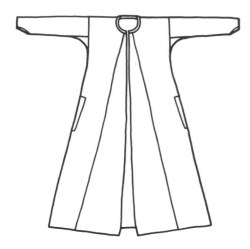

Front and back of a coat (*qumbaz*, *hidim*), Nablus area.
When worn, the front edges are overlapped.
H 136cm

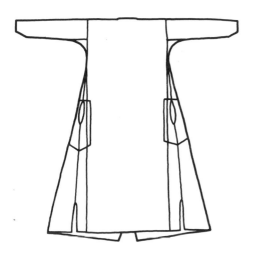

Right **Detail from the back of the coat on the facing page.**

Facing page **Coat (*jillayeh*), Galilee, probably 19th century.**
Cotton with satin and taffeta appliqué patches and silk embroidery. *H 122cm Museum of Mankind: 1966 AS1 65*

triangles and chevrons. A variety of stitches – running stitch, cross stitch, satin stitch, hem stitch, stem stitch and drawn thread work – are used in Galilee embroidery, often on the same garment.

It is clearly one such splendid *jillayeh* which impressed Tristram when he first encountered it in the village of Al-Bussah north of Acre in 1863–4:

Their dress was unlike any costume we had yet seen; consisting of rather tight blue cotton trousers tied at the ankle, slippers without stockings, a chemise of cotton, blue or white, rather open in front, and over this a long dress, like a cassock, open in front, with a girdle and short sleeves. This robe was plain patched or embroidered in most fantastic and grotesque shapes, the triumph of El Bussah milliners being evidently to bring together in contrast as many colours as possible.[6]

Examples of these beautiful coats are known from Kefr Kenna, Safsaf, Buqei'a,[7] and Beit Jann, and they were probably worn throughout Galilee in the nineteenth century. However, they went out of fashion too long ago for the regional styles and significance of their embroidery to be known.

Above **Coat (*qumbaz*), Lower Galilee, late 19th or early 20th century.**
Atlas satin, with long side openings and scalloped edges. *Dar al-Tifl Museum: 37.240*

Above right **Women in the Nablus area, 1930s.**
Note the coats (*qumbaz*) worn both on their bodies, and draped over their heads and shoulders. *Photo: Jan Macdonald*

Right **Girl in Sebastiyeh near Nablus, 1968.**
She is demonstrating the way coats were worn over the head. She is also wearing ikat-patterned pants (*sirwal*) and a *zunnar tarabulsi* sash.
Photo: Shelagh Weir

Facing page **Coat (*jillayeh*), Galilee, probably 19th century.**
Cotton with taffeta (*heremzi*) patchwork. This coat is clearly made to be reversible. *Museum of Mankind: 1966 AS1 66*

Left **Coat (*jillayeh*), Galilee, probably 19th century.**
Cotton with taffeta patchwork and silk embroidery. *Museum of Mankind: 1967 AS2 21*

Right **Back of a coat (*jillayeh*), Majd al-Kurum, Galilee, circa 1920.**
Cotton with silk embroidery.
Museum of Mankind: 1968 AS4 37

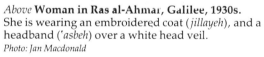

Above **Woman in Ras al-Ahmar, Galilee, 1930s.**
She is wearing an embroidered coat (*jillayeh*), and a
headband (*'asbeh*) over a white head veil.
Photo: Jan Macdonald

Above right **Detail from the back of a coat (*jillayeh*),
Kefr Kenna, Galilee, probably 19th century.** *Dar al-Tifl
Collection: 38.68*

Below right **Detail from the back of a coat (*jillayeh*),
Galilee, probably 19th century.**
Cotton with silk embroidery. *Museum of Mankind: 1966
AS1 69*

Dresses

Galilee bedouin

The dresses (*thob* or *shirsh*[8]) worn by the nomadic and semi-nomadic groups of Galilee were, and remain, quite different in style, material and embroidery to the garments of the Galilee villagers. They have long tight sleeves and a long neck opening, and in the nineteenth century were made from locally-dyed light blue cotton.[9] By the 1920s, dresses were made from imported black cotton (*malas*[10] in Galilee), which probably superseded locally-dyed blue cottons in the late nineteenth century; a vestige of the latter fabric was sometimes retained in light blue bands inserted above the hem and in the sleeves of otherwise black dresses.

Although black cotton was still being used by older Galilee

Detail from the skirt of a dress, Arab al-Hayb bedouin, Tuba, 1960s.
Cotton sateen material with cotton embroidery. Each pattern, created by leaving spaces between the stitches, is named.
Museum of Mankind: 1968 AS4 48

Above **Embroidering a dress panel, Tuba, 1968.**
Photo: Shelagh Weir

Above right **Woman of the Arab al-Hayb bedouin in Tuba, Galilee, 1968.**
The Galilee bedouin are now mostly settled in villages. *Photo: Shelagh Weir*

Below **Galilee bedouin dress (*thob* or *shirsh*), 1960s.**

bedouin women in the early 1980s,[11] a shinier black satin became more fashionable among younger women in the 1960s, and black velvet in the 1980s.

Dresses either have simple decorative cotton stitching along the seams, in lines above the hem, around the neck opening and on the sleeves; or they are more richly decorated with four or five horizontal bands of cotton embroidery above the hem. Several embroidery stitches are used (all named), but not the cross-stitch so widely used in southern Palestine.[12] The distinctive skirt embroidery is executed in a zig-zag stitch with gaps to create geometric black patterns where the dress material shows through. In the 1930s embroidery was entirely white (suggesting a different colour language from village dresses), and by the 1960s was multi-coloured.

The style and embroidery of Galilee bedouin dresses is similar to village dresses in southern Syria and north Jordan (for example around Remtha and Suf). The Galilee bedouin have historic connections with these areas, having once pastured their flocks to the east of Lake Tiberias.[13]

The Arab al-Aramsheh group claim never to have embroidered their dresses, while the Arab al-Hayb were still doing embroidery in the 1980s, though hand embroidery had become rare by the early 1980s, and passable imitations were increasingly made by machine.[14]

Coat-dress with short sleeves (Ramallah area type).

Dress with pointed sleeves (most of southern Palestine).

Dress with long tight sleeves (south west Palestine).

Southern Palestinian villagers

STYLES AND MATERIALS Women did not wear coats south of the Nablus region (except on their wedding day), but in some areas a kind of hybrid garment, best described as a coat-dress, was worn, similar in cut to the Galilee *dura'ah* or *jillayeh*. This was worn in the Ramallah, Jaffa and Ashdod areas up to the 1920s, but may once have been more widespread. It has short sleeves, and an opening in the front of the skirt extending from below the waist to the hem, where it is sometimes permanently fastened.[15] Richly embroidered coat-dresses are called *jillayeh*, but more modestly embroidered coat-dresses may have been referred to by another term.[16]

The most common style of southern Palestinian dress (*thob*, or *jillayeh* when highly decorated) has a full skirt and extravagant, pointed sleeves (*irdan*) which displayed leisure as well as means, for the points hampered work, and had to be tied behind the neck. In the villages along the coast south west of Ramleh, dresses had tight sleeves (*kum*), and a narrower cut.

Necklines and collars distinguished the dresses of certain areas. Most dresses have round necks and chest slits, but south-west coast dresses sometimes have V-necks, and some Jaffa area dresses (from Kufr 'Ana, Saqiyeh and Salameh) sported closed, scooped necklines in the 1930s – possibly to reveal the material of new print underdresses. Some villages, such as Halhul, Dhahariyeh and Dawaimeh in the Hebron hills, were 'noted for their high collars', regarded as a reflection of their conservativeness.

Since 1948, dresses have become less baggy and are customarily made with tight sleeves. A recent fashion, emanating from refugee camp welfare projects, and popular among girls and young women in the West Bank and Jordan in the 1980s, is an ankle-length, narrow-skirted dress (*shawal*) with bust darts in the western fashion, and short slits, tied with coquettish bows, in the sides of the skirt.

Central and southern Palestine can be divided into three regions according to whether their main garments (coat-dresses and dresses) were white (*abiyad*), mid to dark blue (called 'black', *asmar*), or whether they could be either white or 'black'.

In the Nablus and Tulkarm areas, dresses were always white, usually cotton (*tubsi, jinneh-u-nar*) with coloured cotton stripes, or silk stripes for festive and wedding dresses. Dresses of white *rozah* silk were also worn for special occasions.

In the coastal plain south of Ramleh and in the Hebron hills, dresses were only 'black', the festive, heavily-embroidered versions made partly or wholly from cotton fabrics with variously coloured silk stripes (*jinneh-u-nar, jiljileh, abu mitayn* and *biltajeh*). The only place in this southern region where there is evidence of white dresses having been worn is Falujeh.[17]

In the Ramallah and Jaffa areas, and around Jerusalem (but not as far south as Bethlehem), both white *and* 'black' dresses were worn. These were made from various cottons and linens (*durzi, bayt al-sham, qarawi, brim, rumi, ruhbani, shrumbawi*), the linens tending to

Right **Coat-dress (*jillayeh*), Ramallah area, late 19th or early 20th century.**
Indigo-blue handwoven linen with embroidery in cross-stitch and double-sided cross-stitch in orangey-red silks, with details in yellow, green, white, pink and mauve (the latter two colours are anilin-dyed). This dress has been taken in above the waist. *Museum of Mankind: 1967 AS2 15*

Below **Woman wearing a coat-dress, Ramallah, 1930s.**
This style of dress was out of fashion among young women by this period, but had presumably been part of the owner's trousseau around 1900. *Photo: Jan Macdonald*

be used more in the wealthier villages, and for festive dresses. The co-existence of undyed and dyed dresses, and the darker hue of the 'black' dresses, reflects the superior circumstances of these regions; they could afford a greater variety of dresses, and to pay for several dyeings.[18]

As one would expect, dress colour, as the most obvious feature, was a major means by which women identified the regional origins of others. For example, a woman from Masmiyyeh south west of Ramleh, where only 'black' dresses were worn, remarked that 'the mountain villagers (*al-jabaliyeh*) wore white dresses with coloured stripes!'. And a woman from the Hebron area, where dresses are also only 'black', said with some wonderment 'the people in the north wore *white* dresses!'.

In addition to the above fabrics, festive dresses were often made from more luxurious materials. In much of southern Palestine the *kisweh* contained up to three dress lengths of *malak*, *ikhdari* and

Left **Dress, Lifta near Jerusalem, 1906.**
Natural linen; three taffeta sleeve inserts;
Bethlehem-style couching in metal and silk
cord on the sleeves and chest-panel; silk
cross-stitch embroidery on the chest-panel
and skirt. This is the only known example of a
richly-embroidered white dress from so far
south in the hill region of Palestine. This dress
was one of those prepared by the bride for her
wedding trousseau in 1906. The bride's
contribution to the trousseau would also have
included 'black' dresses. Lifta dresses were
named after one of their vertical 'branches' of
embroidery, for example: 'the pigeon branch
dress' (*erq al-batt*), 'the duck branch dress'
(*erq al-wazz*), 'the cock branch dress' (*erq
al-duq*), and 'the vine leaf dress' (*erq al-
daliyeh*). Birds and leaves remain the most
popular motifs on Palestinian dresses up to
the present day. *Collection: Ivy and Sari Nasir*

Right **Back skirt panel (*'alam*) of a dress (*thob
malak*), Bethlehem, late 19th or early 20th
century.**
Note how yellow stripes have been used to
accentuate the costly silver wire. *Museum of
Mankind: 1967 AS2 11*

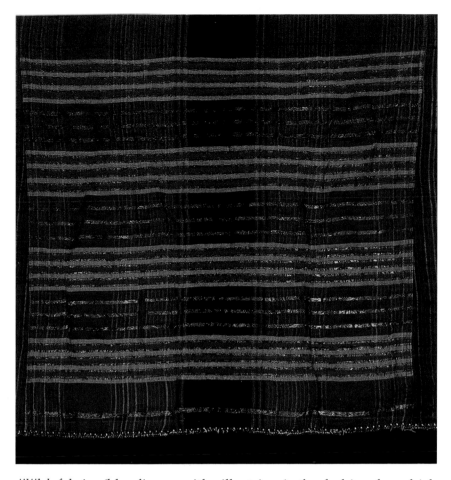

jiljileh fabrics (blue linens with silk stripes), the fashion for which
probably originated in Bethlehem – the village which most
influenced southern Palestinian fashions. When made up into
dresses, the silk stripes of these materials correspond in position to
the vertical bands of cross-stitch on embroidered dresses. The
panel of woven silver wire at one end also falls in the same position
at the back of the dress as the embroidered panels (*shinyar*) on
dresses made from plain materials. This shimmering, eye-catching
metallic panel, appropriately called a 'banner' ('*alam*), added further to the value of these luxurious materials, and proclaimed
wealth.[19]

The relative prosperity of the villages surrounding Jerusalem –
Lifta, Deir Yasin, 'Ain Karim, Al-Malhah, Beit Safafah, Abu Dis,
Silwan and Al-'Aizeriyeh – was reflected in especially luxurious
trousseau dresses, some made from the same silks as the finest
men's coats (*qumbaz*): white and black *rozah* silk; white *ghabani* silk
with yellow chain stitch; and variously-coloured striped, ribbed
silks. Another trousseau dress, worn mainly in Lifta, the wealthiest
of these villages, was made entirely from alternating panels of red
and green taffeta (*heremzi*), and called 'father of stitches' (*abu qutbeh*)
after the fine stitch used to join the panels. A similar dress was
worn in the Hebron hills, in imitation of Lifta. As one dressmaker
said, 'I would ask women, do you want like Lifta?'.

Facing page, top left **Dress, Rafidiah next to Nablus, 1930s or earlier.**
'Heaven and hell' (*jinneh-u-nar*) material; chest panel of red cotton edged with zig-zag appliqué in green taffeta; side skirt inserts of red cotton and green taffeta; simple embroidery in yellow and green cotton. This is a trousseau and wedding dress. *Museum of Mankind: 1984 AS10 7*

Facing page, top right **Woman from 'Anabta east of Tulkarm, 1968.**
She has dressed up in the outfit she wore for her wedding: a *jinneh u nar* dress, a *zunnar tarabulsi* sash, and a coat (*hidim*) over her head. *Photo: Shelagh Weir*

Facing page, bottom **Women going to (or returning from) market, Nablus region, British Mandate period.**
Their dresses are the everyday versions of the *jinneh u nar* dress, without side skirt inserts and decorative chest panels. Note the pants, worn beneath dresses in this region earlier than others, and the characteristically wide sash of the area. *Matson Collection, Library of Congress*

Right **Dress, Yatta, southern Hebron hills, 1930s or earlier.**
Indigo-blue handwoven linen; silk taffeta (*heremzi*) appliqué patchwork on the front skirt, cuffs and hem; broadcloth patches above the chest panel; yoke of European cotton print. The dress has panels of solid silk embroidery, mainly in red, on the chest, sleeves and back skirt panel. The fabric of these is of a lighter blue than the main body of the dress, and they have clearly been removed from another, presumably older, dress. The vertical 'branches' of small motifs on the skirt are typical of the Hebron hills. The relative sparseness of the embroidery reflects the poor circumstances of the hill villagers around Hebron. *Dar al-Tifl Collection: 37.96*

In the 1930s, some of the wealthiest villages began to use European velvets (*mukhmal*) for trousseau dresses. Black velvet, for example, became fashionable in 'Ain Karim (replacing the earlier black *rozah* silk). In Beit Jala and Beit al-Husan near Bethlehem, an imitation *malak* fabric in velvet competed with the Bethlehem product, whilst red and blue velvets became popular around Jaffa, as did red and purple *kermezot* silk.

From the 1950s, imported machine-made fabrics – cotton sateen (*tubayt*[20]), satins and synthetics, in black, white, blue and red, and shades not previously worn, such as beige, yellow and brown, became increasingly popular for village dresses (including those of refugees).

PATCHWORK AND INSERTS Festive dresses, notably *jillayehs*, are often ornamented with appliqué patches, inserts and trimmings in taffeta (*heremzi*), satin (*atlas*) and velvet. These luxury embellishments were normally applied by professional embroideresses for a fee.

Red, green and orange (or yellow) taffeta was used in several

Made from *abu mitayn* material (woven in Mejdel until 1948, and by Mejdel weavers in The Gaza Strip in the late 1960s for the dresses of refugees from the coastal villages living in Gaza). *Museum of Mankind: 1968 AS12 8*

Facing page, top right **Women in Ramallah, late 19th or early 20th century.**
In Ramallah and certain other wealthy villages, women could afford both white and 'black' dresses. The women appear to have dressed up specially for this posed picture.

ways: panels were inserted in sleeves and in skirt sides, patchwork was applied to chest panels and skirt fronts, and taffeta was used to edge and patch hems and cuffs.

The 'fashion idea' of taffeta sleeve, skirt and chest panels probably originated in Bethlehem. Bethlehem-style festive dresses from the nineteenth century, made from *ikhdari* and *malak* fabrics, have a single sleeve panel of yellow silk or taffeta, and of red in the skirt sides. Later Bethlehem dresses, made from the same materials, have three taffeta panels in each position; on the sleeves the centre panel is usually red with orange (or yellow) on each side, while on the skirt sides the centre panel is usually green with red on each side; orange or yellow panels do not normally appear on the skirt sides. The same colour arrangement was generally followed in other villages.

Taffeta skirt and sleeve panels were an index of wealth. For example, the villagers of Silwan, next to Jerusalem, are said to have had 'only one side panel in their skirts', while the wealthiest village of the Jerusalem area, Lifta, 'always had three'. The height of extravagance was reached around Falujeh, where festive dresses

Right **Dress (*thob ikhdari*), Bethlehem area, probably late 19th century.**
Indigo-blue linen with silk stripes; silk sleeve and skirt inserts; taffeta chest square with striped satin panel above; yoke of European cotton print. *Museum of Mankind: 1966 AS1 58*

Facing page, bottom **Woman outside her house, Ashdod (Isdud), British Mandate period.**
Both mother and child are wearing the narrow-cut Mejdel-weave dresses typical of the southern coastal area. The painted house decoration is reminiscent of the large chevron patterns embroidered on festive dresses from this area. *Photo: Matson Collection, Library of Congress*

Facing page, top left **Dress (thob abu qutbeh), Jerusalem area, probably 1920s or earlier.**
Narrow taffeta panels; Bethlehem-style couching on the chest, sleeve and side skirt panels; velvet strip above the chest-panel; cotton yoke (probably not original). Lifta is best known for this luxurious dress, although other Jerusalem area villages wore it too. A similar dress made from strips of taffeta was also part of the trousseau in some Hebron area villages. *Collection: Widad Kawar*

Facing page, top right **Watercolour of a woman, probably from Lifta or another of the Jerusalem area villages, 1849.**
She is wearing the taffeta *abu qutbeh* dress, and the broad, low *shatweh* headdress worn in the Bethlehem and Jerusalem areas in the 19th century. The painting is entitled 'A girl of Bethlehem', signed MB and dated 16th April 1849. MB is an unidentified, probably British, watercolourist. *Searight Collection, Victoria and Albert Museum*

Facing page, bottom left **Dress, Jerusalem area, probably 1920s or earlier.**
Striped Syrian silk (*qasabiyeh*) with three green and red taffeta skirt inserts, embroidered in cross-stitch; Bethlehem-style couching on the chest-panel and sleeves; yoke of probably European velvet. One of the set of trousseau dresses presented by the groom in the villages bordering Jerusalem.
Museum of Mankind: 1969 AS8 9

Facing page, bottom right **Woman in Silwan near Jerusalem, 1926–35.**
Her dress is made from the striped ribbed silk used for trousseau dresses in the Jerusalem area, and has a single taffeta insert panel in the skirt. Her winged sleeves are tied at the back. Suspended from her head is a hammock cradle for carrying her baby. *Photo: Grace Crowfoot*

Right **Chest panel (qabbeh) from a dress, Bethlehem area, probably late 19th century.**
Early silk and linen *malak* fabric, before the addition of red flowers; taffeta (*heremzi*) appliqué chest panel, edged with *tishrimeh*; silk cross-stitch embroidery and edging stitches, surmounted by strips of red broadcloth and probably European brocade (which smacks of church vestments); yoke of European cotton print. All four decorative fabrics had status connotations as scarce, luxurious imports. *Museum of Mankind: 1966 AS1 59*

sometimes had as many as five insert panels, in alternating red and green taffeta, on each side of the skirt. Sleeve and skirt panels were in contrasting colours, partly to make it obvious, at a glance, how many there were.

Bethlehem chest panels can be so heavily embroidered that the background taffeta can hardly be discerned, but some early, lightly-embroidered panels reveal their 'grammar': the central square is usually made from red taffeta, often surrounded by borders of alternating green and red taffeta, and the borders and the whole panel are edged with zig-zag appliqué (*tishrimeh* or *tishrifeh*) in contrasting colours.

Tishrimeh is an important decorative technique in southern Palestine, widely used to edge and frame different areas of the dress and headdress. The zig-zag edge is achieved by making small cuts in the material at intervals, and folding it under to make points.

In the 1920s and 1930s, plain or embroidered taffeta sleeve, skirt

Left **Coat-dress (*jillayeh*), central Palestine between the Jaffa and Ramallah area, early 20th century.** Indigo-blue linen; skirt patchwork in yellow and green taffeta and red satin; yoke of cotton and probably European brocade; silk embroidery.
Collection: Val Vester

Right **Dress, Hebron hills, circa 1920s.**
Cotton and silk-striped *jiljileh* skirt, *abu mitayn* sleeves and bodice; taffeta patchwork on skirt front, and taffeta sleeve and (five) skirt inserts; *atlas* satin yoke; embroidery in silk cross-stitch. Dresses in this style were part of the trousseaus in the villages north west of Hebron, including Nuba, Kharas, Tarqomiyah, Idna, Beit 'Ula and Surif. *Museum of Mankind: 1971 AS1 1*

Dress front, Tulkarm area, probably pre-1920. Cotton with cotton stripes (another version of *jinneh-u-nar*); satin chest panel with cotton trim of zig-zag appliqué. *Museum of Mankind: 1966 AS1 62*

Front skirt of a dress, Falujeh area, circa 1920s. Three vertical panels of taffeta patchwork applied to cotton material with silk stripes (*abu mitayn*); three taffeta insert panels at each side; panels and hem edged with zig-zag appliqué (*tishrimeh*) in red and white striped *atlas* satin. *Museum of Mankind: 1970 AS15 3*

and chest panels, mostly made in Bethlehem and Beit Jala, were popular additions to trousseau dresses made from silk striped fabrics or plain cotton or linen, throughout central and southern Palestine. Panels were bought in the markets as sets, and attached to dresses in the village.

Taffeta patchwork (*baqaj*) was also popular for decorating the skirt fronts of festive dresses and coat-dresses in the Hebron hills to the south of Bethlehem, around Jaffa, and in the southern coastal plain.

The front skirt openings of Jaffa area *jillayehs* are usually bordered with alternate red, yellow and green taffeta appliqué patches with diagonal slashes, often edged with *tishrimeh*. (Ramallah *jillayehs*, by contrast, are never decorated with taffeta.)

Festive dresses from the Hebron hills and the coastal plain south of Ramleh have large panels (*farij* or *hajriyeh*) of taffeta on the fronts of their skirts. These come in a variety of designs, each village or area having its distinctive forms, but there is a common underlying structure: a central panel, often with a pointed top, flanked by two narrower panels. Many skirt front panels are entirely red, while others alternate triangular or diamond-shaped patches of red, green and orange taffeta (some sleeves are decorated with similar patchwork). Panels can be plain, slashed diagonally, or embroidered.

The hems of many festive dresses are also decorated with red or orange (but not green) taffeta panels or zig-zag appliqué edging.

Satin (*atlas*), mainly red striped with yellow, or (on older dresses) plain red or red striped white, was widely used for ornamental yoke panels. Satin yokes were applied to dresses from the Hebron hills, the Jaffa area, and the coastal region south of Ramleh – the same areas where skirt fronts are decorated with taffeta – but not in the Ramallah or Nablus areas. Red satin was, however, used in the Nablus area as a more luxurious alternative to the cheaper and more usual red cotton for chest panels on wedding dresses; and other satins were sometimes used for decorative patchwork on the skirts and sleeves of trousseau dresses from the same area.

Red and yellow striped satin was also used more widely, the Nablus area included, for zig-zag appliqué edging for hems and cuffs; the front skirt openings of some Ramallah area coat-dresses are sometimes edged in the same way,[21] and patches of satin are occasionally combined with taffeta on skirt fronts.

Before velvet and other European fabrics became available and affordable in the 1930s, they were expensive and prestigious luxuries, used sparingly in prominent positions on the chest and yoke. The oldest surviving festive dresses from Bethlehem, which date back to the late nineteenth century, have small patches of Syrian satin, and European velvet, brocade and cotton prints – obviously cherished for their scarcity and novelty as well as their beauty – sewn above the chest square and on the yoke of the dress.

In the 1930s velvet became especially popular in the Jaffa area, replacing táffeta and satin for sleeve inserts and yoke panels.

Above **Back skirt panel of a dress, Masmiyyeh area east of Ashdod, 1920s–30s.**
Cotton material with satin panels, approx. 10cm wide, at each side.
Museum of Mankind: 1969 AS8 5

Right **Detail of embroidery on the side of a dress, 'Aboud, 1930s–40s.**

CROSS-STITCH EMBROIDERY The only area of southern Palestine where dresses are not richly decorated with silk embroidery is that around Tulkarm and Nablus. There the only decorative features on dresses are the silk stripes of the white dress fabrics, taffeta and satin inserts and patches, and rudimentary cotton embroidery on the chest panel, sleeves and skirt.

Women from the area attribute this remarkable cultural exception to their disdain for embroidery as a waste of time and money, and (more convincingly) to their heavy involvement in agriculture; they say 'embroidery signifies a lack of work'. A woman from Zababdeh near Jenin explained: 'We didn't admire embroidery. And women had many responsibilities in the fields. Agriculture was our only source of income; we had no crafts or tourists like other areas.' A woman from Deir Istia, west of Nablus, who married into Dawaimeh near Hebron, related how the women of her natal village made fun of her when she visited them in a richly-embroidered dress in the Dawaimeh style. 'They said, what a waste of money!' She denied that the lack of embroidery in the villages of the Nablus region was because they could not afford it; as she rightly pointed out, they were better off than the villages of the Hebron area who embroidered lavishly.

Lack of leisure cannot, however, be the only explanation for the absence of embroidery in this area, since the work could have been commissioned, for example from nearby Ramallah. Either disposable income was insufficient for embroidery, or the need for that form of visual communication and display was, for some reason, weak or lacking.

Festive dresses in the rest of southern Palestine are richly embroidered, using two main techniques: cross-stitch with floss silk thread; and couching with silk or metallic cord. Cross-stitch, described first, was used by all women throughout the region, with the exception of the Nablus area, while couching, described second, was a professional speciality of the Bethlehem area (though it was copied elsewhere).

EMBROIDERY PRODUCTION A girl normally began embroidery (*tatriz*) as soon as she could wield a needle. Around the age of six or seven she was given a few piastres' worth of silk thread, and was taught cross-stitch and the simpler motifs of her village by older girls or women. When she had learnt to sew neatly, perhaps by the age of ten, and had built up her repertoire of village patterns, she began embroidering the panels for her trousseau garments, her mother's measurements being used to gauge her eventual size.

Dress panels were embroidered piecemeal, and sewn together to make the garment only when the embroidery was completed – sometimes only after the wedding was arranged. Dresses were then sent to professional dressmakers for decorative patchwork and inserts to be added. This was paid for by the groom as part of the *kisweh*.

Beit Dajan women say 'learning to embroider was our school – for us embroidering was like going to school was for our daughters", an

Left **Basketry box (*quteh*), Sinjil area near Ramallah.**
Decorated with floss silk; used for keeping embroidery
threads and other trinkets. *H 40cm*
Museum of Mankind: 1968 AS12 74

Below **Women embroidering, probably Ramallah, 1920s or
earlier.**
They are embroidering both white and blue dress panels.
Photo: Matson Collection, Library of Congress

Young girl embroidering, probably Ramallah, 1900.
While the two women in the foreground pose stiffly at their wheat quern, the girl in the background embroiders a chest panel. Note how the pointed sleeves of their dresses are tied behind their backs while they work. *Photo: Library of Congress*

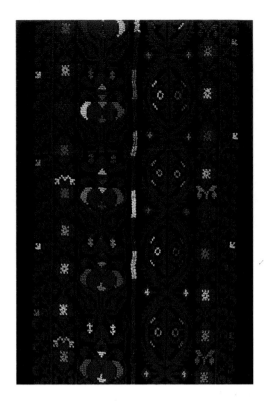

Detail of embroidery from the side of a linen dress, Ramallah, probably 1930s.
Museum of Mankind: 1966 AS1 32

apt analogy, for just as school was to educate their daughters for the society of their time, so embroidery, with its mass of detailed knowledge, educated the girls of an earlier era for their female social world. Like all languages and artistic endeavours, it also united those who shared it in a sense of community, both as women, and as women of a specific village. Significantly, girls who married into another village were pressured to adopt their style of costume and embroidery; to fit in properly they had to conform to their standards and speak their language.

Women have a strong sense of village identity and pride which is expressed in specific designs and motifs, and in an aesthetic idiom. The women of each village say they embroidered one way rather than another because 'that was our custom (*sibrna*)', or 'because it looks better that way'. To be good it had to conform to local conventions, which were generally the 'best', although the embroidery of other villages was objectively assessed, and was admired and copied if it equalled or bettered the standards of one's own.

The embroidery aesthetic was also linked to fashion and generation. What was beautiful and correct for each woman interviewed tended to be what was in fashion in her village at 'her time', as they call it – meaning the period when she married, and as a young woman kept up with village fashions and wore the gayest festive dresses.

Women take the importance and seriousness of embroidery for granted, and it was and is the focus of absorbing interest and profuse comment. When Beit Dajan women were invited to identify a group of dresses from their village, it was striking how carefully they examined and discussed each one, weighing its merits and faults in similar terms and as earnestly as an art critic evaluating an Old Master.

Ideally girls and women did their own embroidery, but in practice many bought embroidered panels or complete dresses. Sometimes weddings were arranged at short notice, leaving insufficient time to make the trousseau dresses wanted; it was essential a girl have, at the minimum, the dress worn for the 'going out' ceremony. Similarly, some girls wanted a larger, more impressive array of dresses than either they or their mothers could make. After marriage, household and child-care responsibilities, and work in the fields or orchards, prevented many women from embroidering. Others lacked the skill; as one woman said, 'embroidery was like a language – some women just couldn't learn it'.

So there was a demand for ready-made embroidery which was supplied by professional embroideresses. Such women were free from the work which consumed the time and energies of others; they were typically unmarried or childless, were the daughters or wives of the landless, or were from wealthy families who hired agricultural labour. Embroidery and dressmaking were the only professions open to most village women, and could provide significant income, especially during the 1930s and 1940s when trousseaus grew and embroidery became more lavish.

Women in mourning, Artas, 1925–31.
They are engaged in a ceremony for the deceased at the graveyard. The woman on the right has exchanged her white veil for black to signify mourning (see Seger, 1981:169).
Photo: Hilma Granqvist

A few women embroidered for money in most villages, and their numbers undoubtedly increased in the 1930s when embroidery became more commercialised; but some villages, most notably Bethlehem, specialised in commercial embroidery and dress-making. Bethlehem was the major centre for the production of trousseau garments and embroidered panels for southern Palestine; Ramallah was likewise an embroidery centre for its surrounding villages; and Beit Dajan supplied the villages around Jaffa. These embroidery centres were more prosperous, well-connected and 'urban' (*madani*) than other villages. The women worked less in the fields, had more time and money to ornament their own costumes, and became leaders of fashion; other villages emulated them because of their high status and exceptionally fine embroidery.

THE SIGNIFICANCE OF EMBROIDERY Lavish embroidery and patchwork in vibrant colours was fundamentally associated with marital status and prime womanhood; it was shameful ('*ayb*) to wear heavily-embroidered dresses before marriage, and inappropriate after the menopause when dresses with sparser, more muted embroidery were adopted. The dominant red of southern Palestinian embroidery is therefore implicitly associated with menstrual blood and the blood of defloration – an association made explicit among the southern bedouin.

Bright rich embroidery also indicated normality and happiness. It was worn as a sign of rejoicing at celebrations, and was covered, turned inside out or dyed blue when in mourning. Bereaved women also donned one of their best dresses and rent the chest panel to express grief, often wearing it torn for the forty-day mourning period. 'No one was to blame them for not having exhibited their deep and sincere feelings for their deceased relative

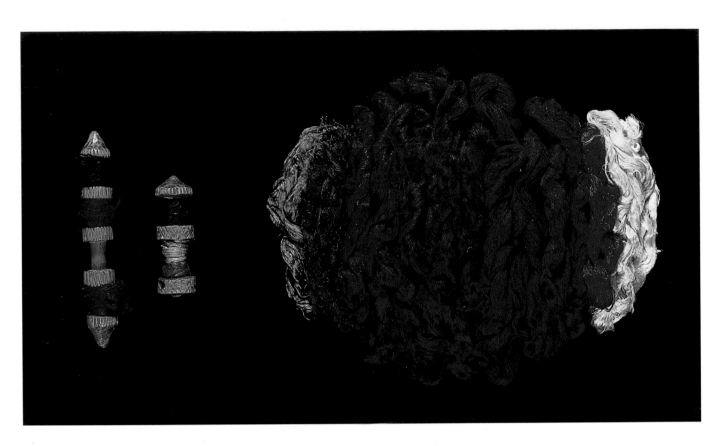

– they had not spared their fine garments!'[22] In Artas the dress was preferably one which had been bought, not received as a gift; when presenting a dress, the donor would say, 'God bless thee, and the dress! May it not be torn or worn for mourning!'[23]

Lavish embroidery was above all a celebration and demonstration of wealth; embroidery threads and fabrics were expensive luxuries for village farmers, and women's time and labour were also precious.

STITCHES Until the 1930s and 1940s, when perlé cotton threads became gradually more popular, all village embroidery was done in floss silk. This was twisted into threads of the required thickness by the embroideress, and wound round a wooden spool (*milwah*) for working. The main technique used for embellishing dresses and other garments in southern Palestine is cross-stitch, called 'the village stitch' (*qutbeh fallahi*); usually two warp and weft threads of an open weave cotton or linen fabric were covered by the cross, although women embroidering for money would encompass three to rush the work.[24] Light cross-stitch was also done on taffeta panels.

Another common stitch was satin stitch (*tifsireh*) framed with couched thread, called *shibrik* in many areas. This imitated Bethlehem cord couching (described below).

A variety of other stitches were used for edging, hemming, joining seams and attaching appliqué patches, each of which is named. The most important of these are:

sabaleh ('ears of corn')
herringbone stitch; used as a joining stitch for seams, for framing appliqué panels and for reinforcing and decorating hems.[25]

habkeh ('binding')
oversewing stitch for edges; used round neck and sleeve openings, and doubled as a joining stitch for seams.

menajel ('sickles')
a joining stitch for seams, especially sleeves because it is not as strong as *sabaleh*; also called *'arayjeh* ('zig-zag' stitch).

tinbiteh ('planting')
running stitch; used on seams and hems.

'owaynet al-sus ('chick's eye')
zig-zag edging stitch used to attach appliqué patches

Even stitches, the smallest units of costume and embroidery, could be significant – especially within villages and village clusters. For example, a Lifta woman distinguished her village, which did the *habkeh* stitch round the neck, from neighbouring Silwan, which bound it with fabric; and a Beit Dajan woman claimed that her 'quarter' (*harah*) of the village was superior because they hemmed their dresses with *tinbiteh* stitch, whereas another quarter used *sabaleh* 'which wasn't so good because it collected dust'.

Stitches were also subject to changes in fashion, leading to differences between generations. In the 1970s, a Beit Dajan dress

Facing page, above **Floss silk embroidery threads, and wooden spools (*milwah*) for holding threads while embroidering.**
Silks: Collection Serene Shahid; spools: Collection Widad Kawar

Facing page, below **Detail from the front skirt panel of a dress, southern plain, circa 1920s.** Taffeta panels; centre panel embroidered in cross-stitch, side panels in *shibrik*; panels joined by *menajel* stitch, and attached with *'owaynet al-sus* stitch.
Museum of Mankind: 1971 AS10 1

Detail from the yoke of a dress, Masmiyyeh area, east of Ashdod, 1920s–30s.
The sleeve seam at top right is joined by double *habkeh* stitch, the *tishrimeh* zig-zag appliqué is attached with *'owaynet al-sus* stitch, and divided by lines of *jadleh* stitch. *Museum of Mankind: 1969 AS8 5*

was commissioned in Amman for a foreign dignitary, and as time was short several women co-operated to embroider the different panels. When it came to doing the cuffs (*sfifeh*), an argument developed about the stitching. Some thought they should be decorated with *habkeh* stitch, others herringbone (*sabaleh*), and others a couched design called *mlawlaw*. Eventually the disagreement was resolved when they realised they were *all* correct, but for different periods. Each woman had wanted the stitch which had been correct at her 'time' (when she married).[26]

The way stitches were executed was also significant. Certain villages, such as Dawaimeh west of Hebron and Na'ani south of Ramleh, were noted for their small, neat stitching. Such careful work was admired partly because it took longer, partly because tiny, neat stitches were considered more beautiful. Because it required a greater investment of time and money, solid embroidery which concealed the fabric was also valued more highly than lighter embroidery with spaces between the motifs.

COLOUR Embroidery silks were bought in various shades of red, and a variety of subsidiary colours. It is not clear how soon, after they were invented in the 1880s, chemical ('anilin') dyed silks were used in Palestinian embroidery; they were not widely available until after 1920, but some colours such as bright pink and green may have been imported earlier.

Different shades of red, and a variety of shades and proportions of subsidiary colours, were favoured in different regions, and were self-conscious expressions of local identity. Colour preferences changed through time, so within a village, embroidery colour could also be a marker of generation.

In Ramallah, for example, the main embroidery colour on coat-dresses and dresses from the late nineteenth century is a shade of orange-red, with details in green, yellow, mauve, white and magenta pink, while on later dresses the dominant colour is a deep pink, often (only on white dresses) combined with black. The deep pink of Ramallah may have been influenced by the Bethlehem and Jerusalem areas, where a similar shade was fashionable early this century.

In the Jaffa area, the southern plain and the Hebron hills, brighter scarlet and crimson shades were favoured at the early period, with variable amounts of subsidiary pinks and other shades depending on area. In Beit Dajan, a deep maroon-red became the dominant embroidery colour in the 1930s, combined with touches of green, mauve and orange. In the southern plain and Hebron hills, a beautiful medley of brown, crimson, purple and pink is often created in the same panel of solid embroidery. Sometimes different shades have clearly been deliberately selected for the individual triangles which make up the pattern; at other times the colour changes seem more haphazard, and probably derive from inconsistency in the shades available in the markets – for many women could only afford to purchase their silks bit by bit as they needed them. The absence or presence of uniformity of shade in one dress

Details of dress sleeves from (left) the Mejdel area and (right) the Beit 'Ummar area, south of Bethlehem.
The seam stitch on the Mejdel area sleeve (on *abu mitayn* material) is characteristic of tight-sleeved dresses from the southern coastal region; the cuff is edged with *tinbiteh* running stitch. The sleeve on the right (made from *ikhdari* material with flowers) has both *habkeh* and *menajel* seam stitching, and a cuff of *qasab* couching with a wavy line of *jadleh* stitches in the centre, framed by *sabaleh* herringbone stitch and *tishrifeh* zig-zag appliqué. *Museum of Mankind: 1968 AS12 8; 1970 AS 14 1*

can therefore be evidence of its owner's spending power.

Though the boundaries of distinctive colours, and the colours themselves, have shifted over time, embroidery colour still has meaning, not only among those still living in their villages, but also, more surprisingly, among refugees in Jordan. Women's senses are therefore finely tuned to the most subtle differences between shades, and when buying their perlé cotton threads they demand a specific shade of red (often by its DMC number). Anything even slightly lighter or darker will not do. The specialist shopkeepers who sell the threads are familiar with these regional differences, and a woman has only to say she is from Ramallah or the Hebron area, for example, for the correct shade and number of perlé cotton thread to be produced.

From the 1950s the colour language of Palestinian embroidery changed. On many dresses the dominant red was replaced by yellow, orange, green or blue, alone or combined, and shaded threads (*muwannas*) are popular in the 1980s. These changes were facilitated by the ready availability of a wide range of colours in perlé cotton but, in view of the symbolic associations of embroidery colour with regional and sexual identity, may have deeper significance.

Facing page, above **Back panel of a dress, Bir Zeit north of Ramallah, 1930s.**
Dark red became the dominant embroidery colour of the Ramallah area at this later period, and new brilliant anilin-dyed shades became popular for the subsidiary colours. Note the 'tall palms' pattern characteristic of back skirt panels in this area. *Museum of Mankind: 1984 AS10 10*

Left **Details of three dress hems.**
From top to bottom: hem trimmed with satin and zig-zag taffeta appliqué (*tishrimeh*) with cross-stitch embroidery, Beit Jibrin area, southern plain; hem with diagonally slashed taffeta border, southern plain; hem with herringbone stitch alone, Beit 'Ummar area west of Bethlehem. The hems of most southern Palestinian dresses from the Mandate period and earlier are strengthened with reddish-brown *dendeki* cotton, and embroidered in herringbone stitch (*sabaleh*). *Museum of Mankind: 1970 AS15 1; 1968 AS4 9; 1970 AS14 1*

Facing page, below **Detail from the front of a linen coat-dress (*jillayeh*), Ramallah, late 19th or early 20th century.**
The 'palm' pattern in double-sided cross-stitch entirely covers the background. The dominant orangey-red shade is characteristic of the area at this period. Some of the subsidiary colours are early anilin-dyed silks. *Museum of Mankind: 1967 AS2 15*

PATTERNS The earliest Palestinian embroidery combines predominantly geometric and abstract patterns – triangles, chevrons, eight-pointed stars, squares and lozenges – with a few representational motifs such as flowers and trees. Later, at different periods in different regions, these patterns were supplemented, and eventually largely supplanted, by more complex, mainly representational motifs introduced first by European missionaries and educationalists (as early as the late nineteenth century in the Ramallah and Jerusalem areas),[27] and from the 1930s by magazines and copy-books sold with embroidery threads. Among the earliest European motifs were dainty wreaths, urns, human figures and several species of bird; birds are still popular motifs, but have become plumper, and usually appear in pairs.

Every embroidery pattern, like every stitch, is named. Some have the same name throughout southern Palestine, others vary regionally. The names of some enduring patterns have also changed through time, even within the same village. Patterns are named after things in the familiar world – natural, cultural and social – though do not necessarily resemble them. For example, the visual inspiration for 'palms' (*nakhleh*), 'cypress trees' (*saru*), 'head of corn' (*'aranis*) and various 'birds' is fairly clear, but is less so for 'moons' (*qamr*), which are either rectangles or eight-pointed stars, and 'apples' (*tufah*) which are usually triangular. A few patterns have political-historical connotations, for example 'the tents of the Pasha' (*khiyam al-basha*), and 'the officer's pips' (*nishan al-dhabit*); and, more recently, 'the Bar Lev line', and 'Sadat and Begin'.[28] The passion for naming even extends to parts of patterns; for example the little squares attached to some 'cypress trees' (which take a variety of forms) are called 'seeds' (*bizr*).

Above **'Cypress trees'** (*saru*).
This motif is one of the most popular in southern Palestinian costume, and takes a variety of forms in different areas.

Facing page, top right **Woman and her daughters, Ramallah, 1987.**
Her dress is embroidered with the yellow shaded (*muwannas*) threads popular in the 1980s. She is also wearing a narrow embroidered belt, another new fashion. The little girl is wearing a miniature dress in the *shawal* style, with the Ramallah-style back skirt panel transposed to the front. *Photo: Shelagh Weir*

Right **Dress, probably 1960s or 1970s, Jerusalem area.**
Black *tubayt* cotton; embroidery in perlé cotton shaded threads (*muwannas*). The patterns are entirely from imported copy-books, and include the widely popular paired birds. This style of dress is often called 'the six-branched dress' because of the six vertical bands of embroidery on the skirt.
Museum of Mankind: 1988 AS6 14

Refugee woman machine-embroidering, Amman, 1978.
From the 1950s, machine-embroidered dresses became a popular, cheaper alternative to hand-embroidered dresses. Some imitate hand-embroidery remarkably well, and the traditional embroidery structure is usually preserved. *Photo: Shelagh Weir*

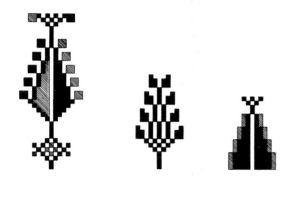

The fact of patterns being named is of generally greater significance than the names themselves; it enabled patterns to be referred to, discussed and commissioned and, like the myriad other details of costume, to form part of a rich, exclusively female discourse and body of knowledge.

The early geometric patterns, some of which have survived until today, are often considered by outsiders to be the 'traditional', 'authentic' Palestinian patterns, in contrast to later 'inauthentic foreign intrusions'. This view is usually coupled with an understandable aesthetic preference for the forms and colours of the older embroidery. However, if authenticity is defined as a totally indigenous artistic form, the earlier patterns are probably no more 'authentic' than the later ones. Village women were not inspired by their natural surroundings when they created their earliest patterns, despite their often naturalistic names, but by other decorated artifacts they saw around them – costumes, uniforms, vestments, church furnishings, architectural motifs, tiles, carpets and so on. The origins of these were often, at the time, as foreign as missionaries and magazines.

A better criterion of authenticity is meaning. Whatever the origin of an innovation, be it pattern, colour, thread or fabric, or any other element of costume, it can be considered authentic if it is absorbed into Palestinian culture, having acquired social or symbolic significance for the Palestinians who make and wear it. It is then integrated into the indigenous (but constantly changing) language of costume. Such innovations are not a sign of 'decline'; on the contrary, the capacity to enrich itself from outside sources is an index of the vitality of a costume language, as of any other.

Facing page, above **Back skirt panel (*shinyar*) from a dress, Lifta near Jerusalem, 1906.**
Motifs imported by Europeans in the late 19th century are combined with older motifs, including indented squares and eight-pointed stars. *Collection: Ivy and Sari Nasir*

Facing page, below **Members of the Arab Women's Union of Ramallah, British Mandate period.**
European patterns influenced Ramallah embroidery from the late 19th century, when the Quakers opened schools there (the first in 1870) and encouraged embroidery to provide women with income. *Photo: Matson Collection, Library of Congress*

Above right **Embroidery sampler, Ramallah, circa 1930s.**
This was collected by Grace Crowfoot, who published it with the names of the individual patterns (Crowfoot, 1935).
Museum of Mankind: 1981 AS23 24

Below right **Embroidery sampler, Beit Jala near Bethlehem, 1967.**
Embroidery in perlé cotton thread on imported machine-made cotton fabric. Embroidery canvas would have been used. The patterns are from European copy-books which were imported from the 1930s, and became widely popular replacements for the older geometric patterns.
Museum of Mankind: 1968 AS12 2

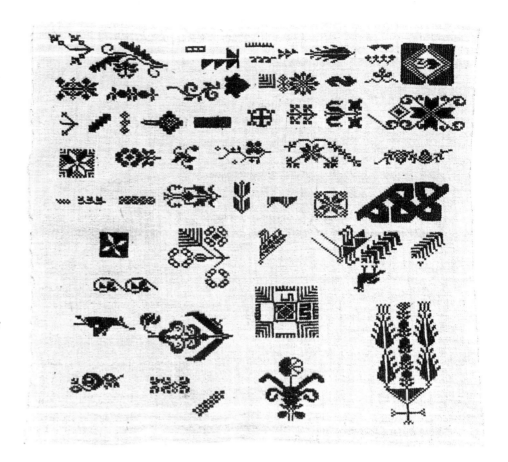

115

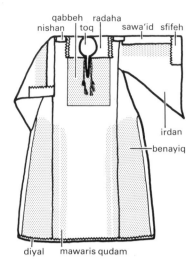

qabbeh radaha
nishan toq   sawa'id sfifeh

irdan

benayiq

diyal mawaris qudam

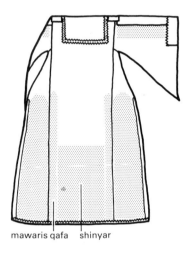

mawaris qafa shinyar

Diagram of a dress from Beit Dajan near Jaffa.
Most of the names for the parts of the dress, including embroidered panels, are the same as those used elsewhere in southern Palestine, though there is some regional variation in nomenclature.

STRUCTURE A fundamental, though tacit, 'grammatical' rule concerned the proper arrangement of the embroidery on the dress. It was always symmetrical, and ordered in the following main sections: the chest panel (*qabbeh*), a panel at the lower back of the skirt (*shinyar*), the front and back seams (*mawaris*, literally 'furrows'), and the skirt sides (*benayiq*). When a section is empty of embroidery, it is sometimes outlined with stitches; the structure or 'grammar' of dress embroidery is still implicitly present.

This structure initially developed from the functional sewing-together of the fabric pieces, the vertical bands on the skirt (and horizontal bands on some sleeves) growing from decorative seam stitching, and the chest panel embroidery emerging from the building outwards of the stitches binding the neck opening.

Within the framework of the basic embroidery structure common to all southern Palestinian dresses, embroidery varied regionally in the shape of the different sections, in the ways the patterns were arranged within them, in certain exclusive patterns, and in the shades of the silks. There was also variation within villages, for usually several types of dress, differentiated and classified according to their embroidery, co-existed at any one time.

No fixed boundaries can be drawn between stylistic areas, for the embroidery styles of one merged into the next; regional styles were also constantly in flux as villages influenced and copied one another, or changed their fashions to maintain their distinctiveness, or for other reasons. As with colour changes, this led to generational differences within villages. For example, women from the southern plain emphasised that back skirt panels of solid embroidery were the fashions of their mothers' generation (around 1920), while panels with horizontal rows of motifs were their own.

Overall, the trend in dress embroidery from the nineteenth century until 1948 was from relative simplicity to greater richness and complexity, especially during the 1930s and 1940s when the relative prosperity of the villagers was reflected in increasingly lavish embroidery. This period also coincided with the widespread adoption of a rich profusion of European motifs, quite different from the older geometric patterns.

Chest panels (*qabbeh*) are usually rectangular, with a similar basic internal structure: narrow panels of solid, chequered embroidery border the neck opening, beneath which a large chevron (*qos*, 'arch') divides the panel into four sections. In the simplest and earliest panels these sections are empty, or contain individual motifs surrounded by background fabric. In later panels, and those on festive, more heavily embroidered coat-dresses or dresses, the chequered neck borders and chevron pattern have been extended so that the entire panel is solid with embroidery. This type of panel is sometimes called 'the amber chest panel' (*qabbet anbar*). The chest panels of different regions are generally quite similar, varying mainly in the patterns used to fill the empty sections.

The chest panels of early dresses from the villages along the southern coast differ from those of other regions in being embroidered directly onto the main fabric of the dress, rather than

Above **Chest panel of a linen dress, Ramallah area, probably late 19th century.**
This panel clearly shows the basic structure of rectangular neck frame and chevron. On earlier chest panels the spaces between these elements contained geometric patterns, but as early as the late 19th century in Ramallah, these were replaced by floral, curvilinear patterns imported by Europeans. There is no other embroidery on this dress. *Museum of Mankind: 1966 AS1 34*

Below **Chest panel of a dress, Al-Naʿani south of Ramleh, 1930s or 1940s.**
The chest panel has become solid with embroidery, and European patterns have been incorporated into the basic structure, which can still be discerned. This dress exemplifies the fine stitching for which Naʿani is famous. Ties with imitation pearls (*bnud lulu*) are characteristic of the Jaffa area and the area just south of Ramleh. In the 1930s, Bethlehem-style couching became a popular addition to the yoke panels of dresses from the area just south of Ramleh and in the Jaffa area. *Museum of Mankind: 1970 AS15 2*

Front and back of a child's dress, Ramallah area, 19th century.
White linen; embroidery in red with details in mauve, purple, yellow and green. This shows the basic embroidery structure common to all southern Palestinian dresses. *Museum of Mankind: 1966 AS1 40*

onto a separate panel, and in being V-shaped, not square; usually a large chevron is combined with 'cypress trees' (*saru*), one of the most popular Palestinian embroidery patterns. In the 1930s this region was influenced by fashions elsewhere, and at the same time as new copy-book patterns were adopted, chest panels began to be square.

Skirt embroidery shows greater regional variety. On the simplest coat-dresses and dresses from the Ramallah area, dating back to the last century, there are narrow vertical panels (*mawaris*) made up of four or six vertical 'branches' (*'erq*) of geometric motifs along the front and back seams of the skirt; later, but before the Mandate period, these 'branches' became wider, and contained only floral, curvilinear patterns of European origin. Dresses worn by villagers in the West Bank and in the refugee camps of Jordan have retained this structure up to the present day, and are referred to as 'six-branched dresses' (*thob sitteh 'uruq*) or 'the Jerusalem area dress' (*thob al-Quts*). This fashion developed after the partition of 1948, and consequent severe disruption to village life and culture. As one Aboud woman put it, 'after 1948 we all began wearing the six-branched dress'.

In other areas there is greater emphasis on ornamenting the sides of the skirt between the front and back seams. In the Bethlehem area and the villages of the Hebron hills to the south, the skirt sides of dresses from the Mandate period are often filled with narrow, parallel rows of 'branches' containing small, delicate motifs.

In the western Hebron hills, and the southern plain, the sides of dresses are more heavily embroidered. In some dresses, skirt patterns were arranged in vertical parallel 'branches', more closely packed, and with thicker stitches, than in the hills further east; in others, they are filled with large, solid opposed chevrons (*quwas*, 'arches'), the spaces between filled with 'cypress trees' and geometric patterns (including *wisadeh*, 'cushions'). Some informants claimed the later patterns are older, and that the 'branches' were copied from the hill villagers; others suggested the chevron patterns came from the Falujeh area and villages to the north and west.

The skirt sides of early Mandate dresses from the south-west coast between Gaza and Yibna, are also decorated with large chevrons (*qelayed*, 'necklaces'), but the spaces around them are not filled in with embroidery. The chevrons are often combined with 'cypress trees' like the chest panels from the same area, and can be alone, or opposed to form diamonds or diagonal crosses. At the back of the dress, the panels at each side are often divided by up to six horizontal bands of simple embroidery.

In the villages of the Jaffa area, for example Beit Dajan, Safriyeh, Kheriyeh and Yazur, dresses from the 1920s or earlier have vertical panels of paired triangles making solid diamond-shaped patterns, called 'pockets' (*jiyab*) or 'amulets' (*hijab*), which are combined with upside-down 'cypress-trees'. Similar patterns are found on the skirts of dresses from villages south of Ramleh, for example Na'ani and Masmiyyeh, except that the diamonds are composed of small empty chevrons (not filled in as they are further north), and are

Right **Dress, Kaukaba and Huleiqat area, south west Palestine, circa 1920s.**
Cotton fabric with silk embroidery. In this area, chest panels of this period are V-shaped, not square. *Museum of Mankind: 1968 AS12 11*

Left **Dress, between Ramallah and El-Bireh, circa 1900.**
White linen, red embroidery with details in black and pink. This dress was published in Crowfoot, 1935. *Museum of Mankind: 1981 AS23 3*

Above **Detail from the skirt of a cotton dress, south west coast, early British Mandate period.**
The villages of this area were unable to afford solid embroidery and taffeta appliqué, such as on the dress illustrated opposite. *Museum of Mankind: 1981 AS18 1*

Facing page **Front skirt of a dress, southern plain, 1920s or earlier.**
Linen material with taffeta appliqué and silk cross-stitch. *Collection: Widad Kawar*

combined with stars (not trees). In the 1930s, these patterns were replaced by closely packed vertical 'branches', a fashion also attributed to the hill villages.

Back skirt panels also vary regionally. In the Ramallah area they tend to be small, are usually subdivided by up to three vertical lines of small motifs, and always contain a repeat zig-zag pattern made from rows and lines of chevrons. This pattern, called 'the tall palm' (*nakhleh 'ali*) in the 1930s, also covers the entire skirt of the ceremonial version of the Ramallah coat-dress (*jillayeh*). The 'tall palm' pattern was particularly associated with Ramallah, and was widely copied: one Ramallah woman boasted 'We taught the whole world how to do the ''palm'' (*nakhleh*)'. However, some villages apparently tried to maintain stylistic independence. Another Ramallah woman claimed that in neighbouring El-Bireh, most women disdained to use the pattern, and those who did were mocked by their fellow villagers, who asked 'Have you caught a disease from Ramallah?'. This pattern is still used on back skirt panels, but is no longer exclusive to the Ramallah area; like the 'six-branches', it has become a widespread fashion and has lost its exclusively regional associations.

Around Bethlehem and in the Hebron hills, back skirt panels are often embroidered with vertical rows of small motifs, as on the skirt sides, an arrangement not found elsewhere. In the Hebron area and throughout the plain, the patterns on back skirt panels are arranged in horizontal rows, or the panels are solid with embroidery, often worked in rows of triangles and chevrons. In the relatively poor Hebron area, these heavily-embroidered panels have often been recycled from older dresses; the embroidery was too valuable to discard when a dress wore out or its owner died. Only in the Hebron hills and southern plain are the sleeves of older dresses heavily embroidered with cross-stitch, also often recycled. Elsewhere only a little light embroidery is used on sleeves, mostly along the seams.

There are many local variations on these basic formats, and in the patterns used. For example 'cypress trees' are particularly popular motifs in the southern plain, where back skirt panels are often double the height of those in the hills.

All this diversity of structure and pattern was of significance to the village women, who could and can identify the regional or village origins of a woman from her dress, more or less exactly, depending on how far her village was from their own, or how famous its embroidery was. For example, when shown dresses from their own region, they could usually identify the village or group of two or three villages from which it came; and when identifying dresses from another region, they would be more likely to say (if they were from the plain) 'that was made by the hill people (*jabaliyeh*)', or (if they were from the hills) 'the girls of the plain (*banat al-sahel*) made it', or (if from the Jerusalem area), 'that was made by the *qaysiyat*', meaning the villagers of the Hebron hills who all belong to the Qays faction.

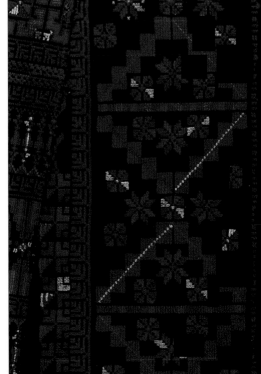

Below **Detail from the skirt of a dress, Masmiyyeh or Al-Na'ani area south of Ramleh, circa 1920s.**
The small opposed chevrons are typical of this area at this period, and contrast with the filled-in patterns ('pockets', *jiyab*) in Beit Dajan and other Jaffa area villages to the north. *Museum of Mankind: 1970 AS15 5*

Right **Dress, southern plain, circa 1920s.**
Cotton fabric, *abu mitayn* fabric on sleeves; taffeta and satin skirt, sleeve and yoke panels. The rows of narrow vertical 'branches' on the skirt sides are probably a later fashion than the opposed chevrons.
Museum of Mankind: 1971 AS10 1

Above **Back of the skirt of a dress, south west coast, late 19th or early 20th century.**
The embroidery is, unusually, entirely in red. *Museum of Mankind: 1970 AS12 1*

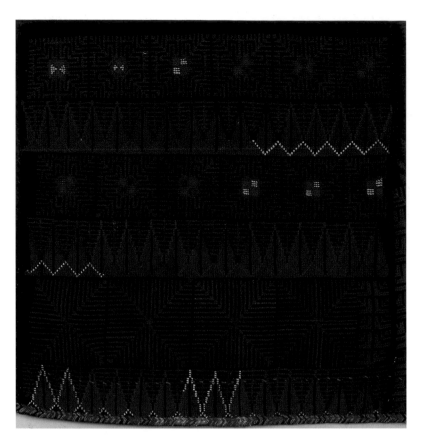

Left **Detail from the back skirt panel of a cotton dress, Hebron hills or south eastern plain, early British Mandate period.**
Museum of Mankind: 1968 AS4 6

Below **Back skirt panel from a linen dress, Ramallah, circa 1900.**
The zig-zag pattern forming four almost solid blocks of embroidery is the 'tall palm' pattern, a distinctive feature of Ramallah dresses up to the end of the Mandate, though it has since become widely popular in the West Bank and among refugees in Jordan. *Museum of Mankind: 1981 AS23 3*

Back of a linen dress, central Palestine between the Jaffa and Ramallah areas, late 19th or early 20th century.
Collection: Val Vester

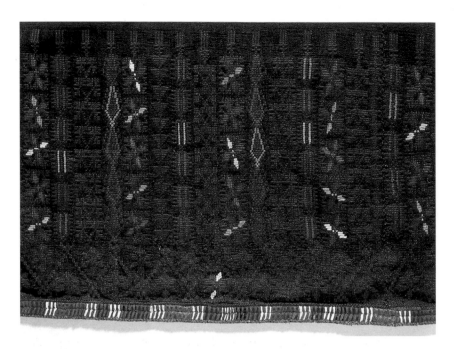

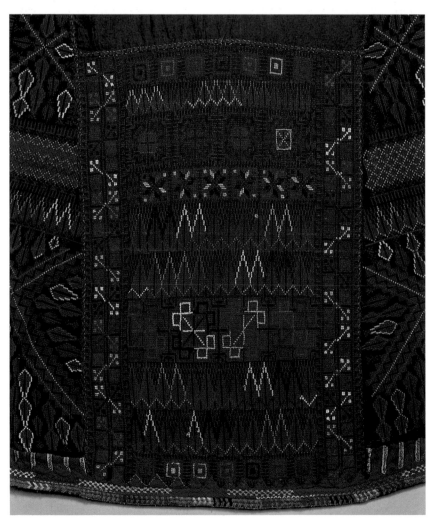

Left **Detail from the back skirt panel of a dress, Beit 'Ummar area, north Hebron hills, 1930s–40s.**
The dark pink embroidery is characteristic of Bethlehem and the villages around at this period, and it is common for the motifs to be arranged in vertical rows, as here, on the back skirt panels of dresses from this area. *Museum of Mankind: 1970 AS14 1*

Bottom left **Back skirt panel from a dress, Tell al-Saffi area north of Falujeh, circa 1920s.**
Horizontal rows of 'cypress trees', indented squares and other geometric motifs are common on dresses from this and the Jaffa area at this period. *Museum of Mankind: 1970 AS15 1*

Below **Back skirt panel from a dress, 'Aqir, south of Ramleh, 1930s.**
Patterns from European copy-books have replaced the older geometric patterns, but the horizontal structure has been retained. *Museum of Mankind: 1968 AS12 13*

BETHLEHEM COUCHING A distinctive style of embroidery developed in Bethlehem and the neighbouring villages of Beit Jala and Beit Sahur, strikingly different from the dominant cross-stitch embroidery of southern Palestinian dresses. The main technique of Bethlehem embroidery is couching with silver, gold and silk cord; this is twisted into elaborate floral and curvilinear patterns, attached to the fabric with tiny stitches, and framed and filled with herringbone and satin-stitches in vividly coloured silks. The general term for this technique is 'Bethlehem work' (*shughl talhami*); if it is in silk cord, *tahriri* (or *rasheq* when copied crudely in other villages); and in silver or gold cord, *qasab*. Chest panels, sleeve panels, cuffs and side skirt panels were decorated with this embroidery and attached to festive, trousseau dresses made from *malak* and *ikhdari* materials. Small amounts of couching were also added to the chest panels and sleeves of everyday dresses embroidered in cross-stitch.

Chest panels were the most important couched areas, the simplest and earliest examples having an open free-flowing pattern on a central panel of red taffeta or broadcloth, with green, red and yellow borders and zig-zag appliqué (*tishrimeh*) edging. The similarity with the relatively plain taffeta chest panels described above suggests that couching was initially applied to such panels as an alternative to the chevrons of cross-stitch with which some were embroidered. Later, chest panels became more complicated; they were couched with a greater profusion of patterns, and on the most costly chest squares the couching, mainly in gold cord, is so dense and intricate that it completely obscures the background material. However, chest squares were always made in a range of qualities and prices to suit the market, and simpler, open patterns made from cheaper materials continued to be produced for the less well-off.[29]

The couching on sleeve and skirt panels is much lighter than on chest panels, though cuffs are often as densely couched. Bethlehem women claim they did not couch their skirt panels, preferring them to be modestly embroidered with the 'apple branch' pattern ('*erq al-tufah*) in cross-stitch. Possibly this restraint developed as a reaction to the growth in popularity of Bethlehem-style couching outside the Bethlehem area; as the dresses of the *nouveaux riches* villagers competed in lavishness, the 'old rich' of Bethlehem retreated into stately understatement to maintain their superiority.

The development of 'Bethlehem' embroidery, as it is usually called, relates to the social and religious position of Bethlehem and its neighbouring villages. Bethlehem, Beit Jala and Beit Sahur are mainly Christian villages, and local women were constantly exposed to ornate church vestments and furnishings richly embellished with gold and silver brocade and embroidery. Being close to Jerusalem, they were also familiar with the braid and couching which ornamented the uniforms of both the Ottoman and the British officials and military personnel. All this decoration was attractive to the female eye because of its intrinsic value, its ostentation, and its status associations with the male-dominated

The Greek Orthodox patriarch, Jerusalem early 20th century. *Photo: Library of Congress*

Tinted photograph of Bethlehem, probably early 20th century.
Palestine Exploration Fund

world of religious and political power. Male ceremonial apparel, both religious and secular, was therefore a major source of inspiration for 'Bethlehem' couching.

The other main factor in the emergence of this costly style of embroidery was the relative wealth of Bethlehem and its neighbouring villages. Bethlehem was (and remains) a market centre for surrounding villages and bedouin groups and, as an important Christian site, has always attracted a constant stream of pilgrims. This generated much local work and income, for women also, for example making mother-of-pearl souvenirs.[30] From the mid-nineteenth century the large Christian population also attracted European schools which raised educational levels above those of the surrounding Muslim villages. A professional class of well-to-do businessmen and officials developed in Bethlehem whose members interacted with and worked for the Ottoman and British administrations. Another consequence of their religion, education, linguistic skills and cash resources, was that many Bethlehem and Beit Jala men were able to seek work abroad, mainly in the Americas, their remittances further enriching their families back home.

The women of these villages therefore became accustomed to working for money, were free of agricultural work, and were relatively urbanised and sophisticated.

Embroidery sampler, Bethlehem, 1930s.
This shows the main couching patterns of the period. The sampler was collected by Grace Crowfoot, who provides a detailed description of the patterns and techniques (Crowfoot, 1936). *Museum of Mankind: 1981 AS23 5*

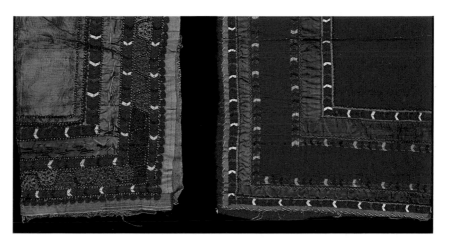

Corners of two unfinished chest panels, Bethlehem, 1920s.
These pieces show the order in which the embroidery for a couched cord chest panel is executed. First the frames of herringbone (*sabaleh*) stitch are sewn round the edges of the differently coloured taffeta patches, then the couched cord is added, and finally the satin-stitch filling. Even though the taffeta backing is usually concealed by the embroidery, the centre panel is usually red, with green borders, as in the earlier panels.
Collection: Widad Kawar

Chest panel, Bethlehem area work, probably late 19th century.
The centre panel is of red broadcloth, and is framed by cotton zig-zag appliqué. The open, free-flowing pattern of flowers and tendrils in couched silk cord filled with satin stitch probably preceded the denser, more intricate couched chest panels which became more common later. *Museum of Mankind: 1966 AS1 60*

Below **Chest panel from a dress (*thob ikhdari*), Bethlehem area, late 19th century.**
The couching is in gold cord, and yellow and green silk cord. The flowing open floral patterns reveal the green and red taffeta background and, combined with the silk satin stitch filling, give a beautiful lustrous effect. Note the small piece of purple velvet, a scarce luxury at the period the panel was made. *Museum of Mankind: 1966 AS1 14*

Right **'Royal' dress (*thob malak* or *malakeh*), Bethlehem area, late 19th or early 20th century.**
Museum of Mankind: 1967 AS2 11

Right **Chest panel from the dress above.**
This is an exceptionally finely and densely embroidered panel, with a high proportion of gilt cord. The bird motif is said to have been introduced by Miriam Ibrahim Jadallah, a noted Bethlehem embroideress.

Left **Side skirt panel from the *malak* dress on the previous page.**
The narrow, vertical cross-stitch pattern at the centre of each panel is called 'the apple branch' ('*erq al-tufah*). The dominant couched pattern, shaped like a wreath, was later transformed into a circular pattern called a 'watch' (*sa'ah*) in the Bethlehem–Jerusalem area, and 'domes' (*qubab*) in the Jaffa area.

Right **Side skirt panel from a dress, probably 'Ain Karim near Jerusalem, 1930s or 1940s.**
The wreaths of the earlier dresses have been transformed into the 'watches' (*sa'ah*) which are found on all Bethlehem–Jerusalem area side skirt panels after about 1920. *Museum of Mankind: 1971 AS1 6*

Bethlehem woman, probably British Mandate period.
Note the side skirt panels with a single vertical 'apple branch' pattern. Bethlehem women claim they preferred this restrained type of embroidery on the skirt to the couched panels they embroidered for sale to other villages. The chest panel is richly embroidered, and the headdress (*shatweh*) is completely concealed by the white veil, as was the custom. *Photo: Library of Congress*

BETHLEHEM INFLUENCE Economic and social superiority, and costly, sumptuous couching, made Bethlehem the 'Paris' of Palestinian village fashions. Throughout southern Palestine villagers strove to wear or imitate Bethlehem embroidery and costumes, and with improved conditions during the Mandate period, the demand for garments, trimmings and embroideries in the Bethlehem style grew, and scores of Bethlehem and Beit Jala women were involved in professional dressmaking and embroidery.

The demand for Bethlehem fashions came particularly from brides, who required Bethlehem-made items in their *kiswehs*: either dresses (*malak*, *ikhdari*, *jiljileh*), or couched taffeta panels to add to locally-made dresses. In the Jerusalem area couched chest, sleeve and side skirt panels were added to silk and velvet dresses; in Ramallah sleeve panels (but never skirt panels) were added to black linen dresses embroidered in cross-stitch, and gold or silver couching was added (in Bethlehem) to cross-stitched chest panels; in the Hebron hills and southern plain, chest, sleeve and skirt panels were added to dresses made from a variety of materials, and sometimes also heavily embroidered with cross-stitch; and in the Jaffa area couched panels were added to dresses of cotton, linen, velvet and watered silk (*kermesot*), and extra lines of couching were added to the skirts, yokes and back skirt panels of linen dresses.

Bethlehem couching remained a largely commercial enterprise because it was paid for by the groom as part of his *kisweh* presentation; no bride would therefore have dreamt of doing her own. If customers were well-off or in a hurry, the dresses were bought ready-made in Bethlehem, or from merchants elsewhere. Otherwise the fabrics and embroidered panels were bought separately, and sewn up into garments by the customer. When the groom could afford it, he bought a matching set of panels of equivalent high quality, but more often he had to settle for sleeve and side panels of inferior quality to the more important chest panel, and even the latter often falls short of the highest Bethlehem standards.

In addition to the couched panels of variable qualities produced in Bethlehem for their varied clientele, imitations of Bethlehem-style embroidery (*rasheq*) were produced by the women of other villages. This was usually inferior to Bethlehem work, but during the 1930s a high standard of professional couching developed in Beit Dajan.

The influence of Bethlehem couching continues up to the present, especially in machine embroidery used to imitate couching with lurex and other threads. Dresses called *malak* are even produced on red velvet, clearly inspired by the colour schemes and patterns of the old Bethlehem *malak* dresses, though their owners and makers have probably never seen one.

Left **Bethlehem women embroidering in the courtyard of an old house, British Mandate period.**
Photo: Matson Collection, Library of Congress

Facing page, above **Painting of the Michel Dabdoub family of Bethlehem, 1900.**
The strong influence of European culture on well-to-do Bethlehem families at this period is evident from the costumes of the children and the domestic furnishings. *Collection: Julia and Michel Dabdoub*

Left **Bethlehem women working alongside men to make mother-of-pearl rosaries, circa 1880.**
From: Wilson, 1880, Vol. I: 133

Facing page, below **Girls in the Russian seminary in Beit Jala, 1895.**
They are wearing Bethlehem-style dresses with chest panels embroidered with simple couching.

Above **Doll in Bethlehem dress, circa 1926.**
Bethlehem women made dolls for sale as souvenirs and
presents. This was made as a gift for an English girl.
Museum of Mankind: 1970 AS5 1

Above left **Chest panel (*qabbeh*) from an everyday linen
dress, Bethlehem, British Mandate period.**
The basic form of the panel is similar to those in much of
southern Palestine. The dark pink embroidery is
characteristic of Bethlehem and nearby villages, and is also
found on the veil (*shambar*) made for sale in Bethlehem. The
idea of adding borders and lozenges of couching, which
presumably originated in Bethlehem, spread as far north as
Ramallah during the Mandate period, and continues to be
popular in the 1980s. *Museum of Mankind: 1970 AS15 8*

Below left **Chest panel of a linen dress, Ramallah, early 20th
century.**
The fine gold cord couching was probably added in
Bethlehem. *Museum of Mankind: 1984 AS1 1*

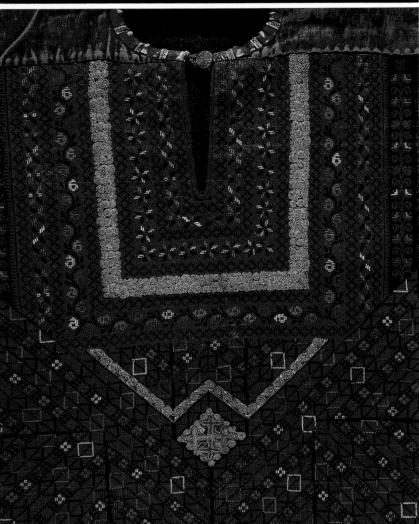

Right **Back of the skirt of a dress, Hebron hills, 1920s or earlier.**
Skirt of *jiljileh* fabric; back skirt panel recycled from an older dress; side skirt panels of taffeta with crude silk cord couching (*rasheq*) imitating Bethlehem work. *Museum of Mankind: 1968 AS4 10*

Below left **Dress, Deir Terif near Jaffa, 1930s or 40s.**
Kermezot material, with taffeta inserts; Bethlehem-style couched embroidery on the yoke, chest panel, sleeves and skirt probably done by local specialists. *Museum of Mankind: 1969 AS8 10*

Below right **Side skirt panels of the dress on the left.**
Couching in silk and gold cord probably done by local women. The patterns, particularly the 'watch' pattern called 'domes' (*qubab*) in this region, are clearly inspired by Bethlehem work.

Left **Modern *malak* dress, Jordan, 1980s.**
Velvet with machine embroidery in lurex threads. *Museum of Mankind: 1988 AS6 12*

Below **Women of the In'ash al-Usrah (Family Welfare) organisation, 1987.**
The woman on the right is wearing a lurex-embroidered dress. This organisation, based in El-Bireh near Ramallah, commissions embroidered cushions, dresses and other items from hundreds of women in West Bank villages, which are sold to help provide them with an income. The organisation also runs biscuit and dressmaking factories, has a small museum, and publishes books on folklore. The president, Sameeha Khalil, is third from the right. *Photo: Shelagh Weir*

Bedouin dress, Negev desert, 1930s or earlier.
H 138cm W 130cm

Below **Back skirt panel from a dress, Jaffa area.**
Black cotton material with orange cord couching (*rasheq*). The 'watch' ('*domes*') motif used only on the sleeves and skirt sides of Bethlehem dresses is here transferred to a new site. *Museum of Mankind: 1969 AS8 4*

Southern Bedouin and Jericho area villagers

The dresses (*thob*) worn by the bedouin of the Negev desert were similar in shape to early village dresses, though more voluminous. From the 1960s their long, pointed 'winged' sleeves were also replaced by narrow sleeves, both short and long. The main dress material in the nineteenth century was light blue machine-made cotton, later replaced by black cotton (*tubayt*), as among the Galilee bedouin.

Up to the 1930s, dresses were relatively plain with little or no embroidery. However, as perlé cotton threads became available, dresses began to sport cross-stitch embroidery, with similar geometric patterns to the village embroidery which they emulated. The arrangement of the embroidery also follows the structure of village dresses, with panels on the chest, back of the skirt, sleeves and sides – plus an additional line or panel of embroidery on the front of the skirt, something never found on village dresses. The lines of satin-stitch around the hems (*diyal*) of bedouin dresses are also distinctively different from village dresses.

The dominant colour of southern bedouin embroidery is red, and is explicitly associated with sexual maturity and marital status. Unmarried girls wore dresses embroidered in blue; only after marriage or becoming pregnant were they permitted to adorn their dresses with red embroidery.[31]

After copy-books arrived in the 1930s, the new floral and curvilinear motifs also appeared on bedouin dresses, and a greater variety and mixture of embroidery colours came into use. Machine embroidery was also popular among the bedouin in the 1950s and 1960s, and many tents boasted a Singer sewing machine.

An enormous dress (*thob*) was worn by villagers in the Jericho area, and by semi-settled bedouin groups, such as the Taʿamreh and ʿObaydeh in the hills and valleys east of Jerusalem and Bethlehem. This huge garment is over twice the size of the human body, the excess material being pulled through a belt so that it fell in a fold (*ʿob*), forming three layers. The long point of one sleeve was thrown over the head as a veil, and the other was often left trailing. This dress had its functional aspect, since air trapped in the folds was cooling, and the Jordan valley, which is below sea level, is exceedingly hot. However the giant dimensions of the dress were as much to do with ostentation as comfort; it was more prestigious to have a fold which fell low, close to the hem, demonstrating that more material had been used. A narrower but equally long version of this dress was still being worn in Jericho in the 1960s. Later a shortened, normal-length version (*madraqah*) became more popular.

Early dresses were embroidered on the front with simple patterns in vertical rows or zig-zag patterns in white, or white and green, cotton. Later dresses had vertical 'branches' of predominantly red cross-stitch motifs.

Left **Detail of the back skirt panel from the dress below.**

Below left **Bedouin dress, Khan Yunis area, western Negev desert, pre-1937.**
Heavy black cotton material; cotton cross-stitch embroidery on the sleeves, skirt sides and back skirt panel. The embroidery is all in the geometric patterns pre-dating copy-book designs which arrived in the 1930s. The large diagonal cross patterns on the skirt sides are also found on bedouin festive veils. The hem, with rows of blue cotton satin-stitch, is typical of bedouin dresses, and not found on village dresses. This hem, unusually, has two layers, the lower being made from indigo-blue cotton obviously salvaged from an earlier dress.
Dar al-Tifl Collection: 37.185

Details of two bedouin dress hems, Negev desert, 1930s or 1940s.
The lines of satin stitching are distinctive features of bedouin dress hems. Predominantly blue embroidery indicates a girl's unmarried status, while mainly red embroidery indicates sexual maturity and marital status. *Museum of Mankind: 1972 AS4 1; 1970 AS15 4*

Chest panel from a dress, Negev bedouin, 1960s or earlier.
Black cotton material; cotton cross-stitch embroidery. The all-over diamond pattern, also found on the back skirt panel, is typical of bedouin dresses from the 1930s onwards. The buttons, which appear to be men's blazer or military buttons, are marked 'Waterbury Button Co' on the reverse. *Collection: Widad Kawar*

Woman of the Abu Jwayd bedouin of the Negev desert in Gaza, 1968.
Facial tattoos were for beauty and to promote well-being; they have now gone out of fashion among the young. *Photo: Shelagh Weir*

Left **Bedouin dress, Negev desert, 1940s or later.**
Black cotton material with cotton cross-stitch embroidery. Older geometric patterns are used on the front of the skirt, while copy-book patterns dating from the 1930s onwards are used on the sides, back, sleeves and chest square. The tight sleeves were a development of the 1950s and 1960s. Unmarried girls wore dresses embroidered in blue; only married women could wear red embroidery. *Collection: Widad Kawar*

Facing page, above **Back skirt panel from a dress, bedouin, Negev desert.**
Cotton cross-stitch embroidery. The patterns are all derived from copy-books, and one obviously had particular appeal. *Collection: Widad Kawar*

Facing page, below **Embroidery on the back skirt panel of a dress, bedouin, Negev desert, 1960s or later.**
Cotton machine embroidery, using similar patterns and colour schemes to hand embroidery. The patterns are all derived from copy-books; the 'branches' ('*erq*) of birds are very popular motifs on village dresses, from which they were probably copied.
Museum of Mankind: 1988 AS6 15

Woman, probably of the Ta'amreh bedouin, outside Bethlehem, British Mandate period.
The fold of her *thob 'ob* can clearly be seen. She is using one of her voluminous sleeves as a head veil, and the other to carry her possessions. *Photo: Matson Collection, Library of Congress*

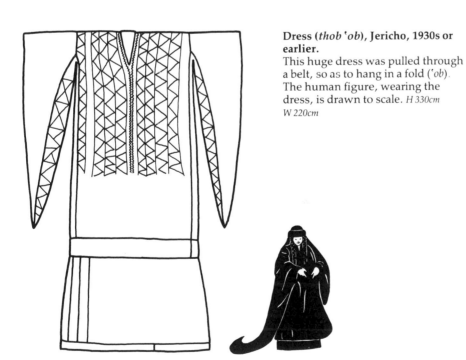

Dress (*thob 'ob*), Jericho, 1930s or earlier.
This huge dress was pulled through a belt, so as to hang in a fold (*'ob*). The human figure, wearing the dress, is drawn to scale. *H 330cm W 220cm*

Woman, Jericho, 1967.
Vertical lines of cross-stitch embroidery had become fashionable by this period. Note the fold of her 'double-dress'.
Photo: Shelagh Weir

Jericho women, British Mandate period.
The fold is unfortunately out of the picture, but the simple white embroidery is clearly visible. The woman in the centre is wearing a triangular amulet, and the woman on the right an amber necklace. Many Jericho people, like these women, are descended from African pilgrims.

Shirt or underdress (*qamis* or *thob*), Galilee, 19th or early 20th century.
Worn beneath the coat and over underpants so as to reach to the calf. *H 120cm*

Undergarments: shirts, underdresses and pants

The garments worn beneath coats, coat-dresses and dresses were not underwear in the western sense; rather they were clothing considered proper in the house, but insufficient for appearing in public.

Galilee

The short-sleeved coat (*dura'ah* or *jillayeh*), and the long-sleeved *qumbaz*, were worn over long-sleeved shirts (*qamis* or *thob*) of locally-woven fine white or blue cotton, or natural silk. From the late nineteenth century European-style dresses (*fustan*), with long sleeves and a waisted cut, and made from a variety of imported cotton prints, gradually replaced the traditional *qamis*.

Beneath the *qamis* ankle-length pants were worn. Early pants (*elbas* or *sirwal*) are made from thick hand-woven cotton, usually indigo blue and sometimes white, their lower legs often richly embroidered. Shirts and dresses, worn over the pants, were short enough to reveal the embroidery. Some pants have baggy legs which were gathered at the ankle; others are tight-fitting on the calf. In the 1930s, examples of the baggy-legged variety were collected in Kefr Kenna, and of the variety with narrower legs in Safsaf and Buqei'a,[32] but both types were widely worn and could have co-existed in the same villages.

Corresponding to the spread of the Turkish-style *qumbaz* was the fashion for baggy-legged pants (*sirwal* or *shintiyan*) made from cotton or fine silks and satins in brightly-coloured patterns; these, like the *qumbaz*, were inspired by Turkish fashions, and were adopted first in Nazareth, then copied by the villagers.

Similar pants of (unembroidered) blue cotton and coloured and

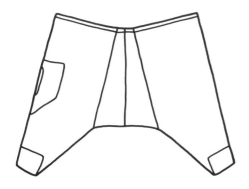

Pants (*sirwal* or *elbas*), Nablus area, 1930s.
White or blue cotton pants with a similar cut were also worn in Galilee.

Below **Embroidery on the leg of a pair of pants (*elbas* or *sirwal*), Safsaf, Galilee, 1930s or earlier.**
Indigo-blue handwoven cotton; silk embroidery. *Dar al-Tifl Collection: 37.222*

patterned satins were worn under white dresses in the Nablus area.

From the beginning of this century, and especially after the First World War, pants with baggy legs were replaced in the Galilee and Nablus areas by pants (*elbas*) with tight calves and often frilled cuffs. These were worn with the European style dress (*fustan*). Both garments have remained in fashion until today.

Southern Palestine

White cotton underdresses were worn beneath coat-dresses and dresses. Some of these were lightly embroidered; for example in Beit Dajan, underdresses worn beneath the *jillayeh* had six vertical rows of *sabaleh* stitching, and zig-zag appliqué (*tishrimeh*) round their hems and the cuffs of their sleeves; the latter were pointed (*irdan*), and pulled through the short sleeves of the coat-dress.

During the Mandate period, white underdresses went out of fashion, and were replaced by print *fustans* like those worn further north. Ankle-length underpants were also adopted for the first time, because greater modesty in dress was felt to be required with the increased exposure of women to strangers and foreigners.

Bedouin women also adopted the *fustan* as an undergarment, often made from especially gaily coloured and patterned prints. The fashion for short-sleeved overdresses may be explained by the wish to show off the long sleeves of these underdresses.

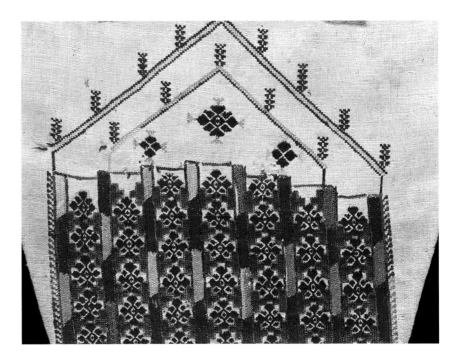

Detail of the silk embroidery on the leg of cotton pants (*elbas* or *sirwal*), Buqei'a or Safsaf, Galilee, 1930s or earlier. *Dar al-Tifl Collection: 37.271*

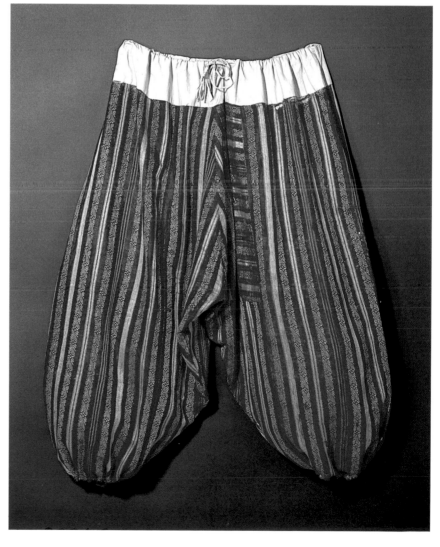

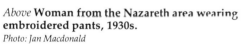
Above **Woman from the Nazareth area wearing embroidered pants, 1930s.**
Photo: Jan Macdonald

Above right **Woman of the Al-'Azazmeh bedouin in the Negev desert weaving a bag or rug, 1970s.**
Note the brightly coloured sleeves of her cotton print underdress, and the piece of colourful cotton with which she has patched her overdress. *Photo: Klaus-Otto Hundt*

Below right **Pants (*sirwal* or *shintiyan*) of imported cotton, Nazareth or Nablus area, late 19th or early 20th century.** *Museum of Mankind: 1966 AS1 70*

Girdles and belts

Coats, coat-dresses and dresses were, with few exceptions, worn with a girdle or belt over them. Even this relatively simple article of attire indicated status and regional identity by the material from which it was made and the way it was worn. Girdles have been remarkably resilient symbols of regional identity, and several styles dating back at least fifty years are still worn, both by women in their villages and by refugees.

Villagers

A girdle worn only in Galilee and the Nablus area was the *zunnar tarabulsi*, made from three long pieces of checked red, white, black and green silk, joined lengthways with a distinctive thick red silk stitch. This was wound twice round the waist and knotted at the back. Imitation silk versions of this girdle are still being made in Syria in the 1980s, and are still worn by women from the Nablus area.

Other girdles are made from squares of material folded diagonally, and tied once or twice round the waist. A type of girdle once worn all over Palestine, of thick cotton with floating warp threads, has an all-over pattern in white, black, dark blue and other colours. This is similar to the broad sashes worn by Palestinian men of high status in the nineteenth and early twentieth centuries, and to girdles worn in Turkey where the material was probably woven. Like several garments and decorative features, it therefore travelled down the social hierarchy from the foreign ruling class, to townsmen, then village men, and finally to village women.

The most popular luxury girdle in most of southern Palestine, which is still worn today, is made from red and yellow striped *atlas* satin, and called *zunnar kashmir* or *ishdad* in different areas. A ceremonial version had a band (*dikkeh* or *sfifeh*) with a long, heavy red silk fringe and tassels attached to the ends. This eye-catching decoration was considered sexually provocative, as illustrated in the saying: 'If you want to know the way, follow the tassels on the belt'. In Ramallah, girdles made from red *atlas* were worn mainly by younger women, while older women, and women in mourning, wore 'black girdles' (*zunnar asmar*) of black and red striped satin.

Another luxury girdle, called *zunnar maqruneh*, of green, red and yellow silk with silver brocade 'combs' (*musht*), was worn in the Jaffa area, and remains an important expression of regional identity among refugees. 'They only have to see our girdles to know we are from Beit Dajan', as one old lady put it. This came in several qualities and prices, depending on the number of 'teeth' in the 'combs': ten, twelve, fifteen, twenty or thirty. This girdle was turned inside out for mourning, to conceal the shiny brocade.

Other popular southern Palestinian girdles (*ishdad* or *hizam*) were made in Bethlehem from pink or blue wool; bright, warm pink was for young women, while older women, and women in mourning, wore the more sombre blue girdles. In Artas, the pink girdle was used to wrap the *kisweh* for its ceremonial return to the village, and

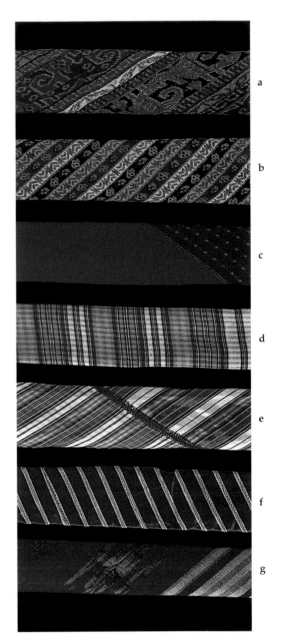

a

b

c

d

e

f

g

Left **A variety of Palestinian girdles.**
a, b. Patterned cotton girdles, common everyday wear throughout Palestine up to the end of the British Mandate.
c. Pink woollen girdle (*ishdad* or *hizam*), made in Bethlehem, and worn all over the southern hills of Palestine up to the present. Pink was worn mainly by girls and women before the menopause (and by Qaysi brides as a face veil), while a blue version was worn by women who were older or in mourning.
d. Checked cotton girdle worn in the Nablus area in the Mandate period.
e. The *zunnar tarabulsi* worn up to the present day in the Nablus area, and previously in Galilee.
f. The *zunnar kashmir* or *ishdad*, worn throughout southern Palestine.
g. The *zunnar maqruneh* worn in the Jaffa area. The same fabric was worn as a headband (*'asbeh*) in Galilee and the Nablus area.
Museum of Mankind: 1966 AS1 127, 120; 1988 AS6 33; 1966 AS1 131; 1968 AS8 1; 1977 AS10 3; 1984 AS10 3

Below left **Ramallah woman, 1979.**
She is wearing the 'black' girdle (*zunnar asmar*) considered more suitable for older women and those in mourning. *Photo: Shelagh Weir*

Below right **Beit Dajan woman in Nablus, 1978.**
She is wearing her girdle (*zunnar maqruneh*) below her waist, as is the custom for the women of her village. *Photo: Shelagh Weir*

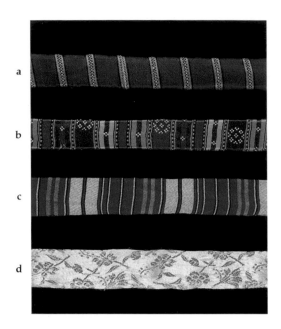

Part of one woman's collection of belts, Ramallah, 1987.
Each style is worn with a different dress. Missing is a dark belt worn for mourning.
a. *kashmir* or *kamakh*, an everyday belt.
b. *'ajami*, worn with *malak* or other brightly coloured dresses.
c. *tarabulsi*, worn with coloured dresses.
d. *shamlah*, worn with black dresses.

Two women in Jerusalem, 1987.
They are both wearing 'six-branched' dresses, and the recently-fashionable narrow belts, made from the same fabrics as the wider sashes which have been worn for most of this century if not longer. *Photo: Shelagh Weir*

was later worn over the bride's face during the wedding-day procession (signifying that she was from the Qaysi faction). These pink and blue girdles are still being made and worn in the 1980s, and have also found a wider market among townspeople and tourists as shawls.

The way girdles were worn was and remains an important indicator of village or regional identity, and women often volunteer this significant information. A Yibna woman, for example, emphasised that their girdles were always tied at the back, while in other areas, such as the Jenin area, they are tied at the front. Beit Dajan women, who tie theirs once at the front, then knot it at the back, always wear them below the waist with the dress pouched over the top. Hill villagers used to poke fun at this style in the following ditty:

we are from the hills and you are from the coast
look how lop-sided your belt is on your waist!

Recently, narrower belts have become fashionable among younger women; in the Ramallah area these are worn above the waist, so as to cut across the large embroidered chest panel – thus emphasising how the panel has expanded to cover the entire front of the dress.

Bedouin

Among the bedouin, women favoured long, narrow handwoven belts instead of the folded squares of the villagers. In the Mandate period, Galilee bedouin wore a tablet-woven woollen belt, called *shwahiyeh*, made in Syria. This was wound twice round the waist, and tied so that its tasselled ends hung down at the side.[33]

The 'double-dress' of the bedouin and Jericho women was bound with a long, narrow belt, also called *shwahiyeh*, or *sfifeh*, which was plaited by the women themselves from hand-spun wool, and had tasselled ends. This was also wound more than once round the waist, and the excess dress material was pulled through it to form a large pouch.

The bedouin of the Negev desert wore an elaborate and highly decorated 'home-made' woollen belt. It had two components, each plaited and woven from home-spun wool: a white and black striped underbelt (*hizam*), and a narrower overbelt with a decorative twined weave panel and/or tassels at one end, threaded with shells and beads, and sewn with cowrie shells or shirt buttons. This was wound round the waist several times over the wider belt, then fastened so that the decorative ends hang down at one side.[34] For festive occasions additional panels (*jada'*) with colourful geometric patterns in twined weave were suspended from the front or back of the belt.

Left **Woman of the Tarabin bedouin, Negev desert, 1926–35.**
She is wearing the type of belt illustrated below, with ornamental tassels. Note the embroidery on the skirt of the dress. *Photo: Grace Crowfoot*

Below left **Bedouin woman's belt or sash, Negev desert, pre-1960s.**
The belt comprises a wide underbelt (*hizam*) made from plaited strips, and a narrower plaited overbelt (*shwahiyeh*) decorated at the end with twined weave panels, tassels, cowrie shells, buttons and shell and glass beads. *L (hizam) 194cm, W 10cm, L (shwahiyeh) 285cm, W 4cm Museum of Mankind: 1975 AS3 9; 1974 AS29 6*

Below right **Belt or sash (*shwahiyeh*), Lake Huleh area, Galilee, 1930s.**
Tablet-woven wool (imported from Syria), terminating in a section of twined-weave and plaited bands and tassels, all added locally. *Dar al-Tifl Collection: 37.289*

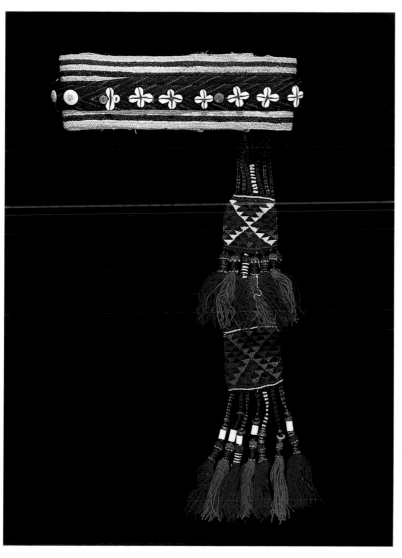

Christian women in Nazareth, 1900.
This stiffly posed picture clearly shows several
garments worn in Nazareth at this period, all
of which were copied by the surrounding
villages: the coat (*qumbaz*) with side slits
through which the white shirt (*qamis*) can be
seen; the baggy pants (*sirwal*); the short jacket
(*mintiyan*), that on the right of broadcloth with
cord couching; a girdle (*zunnar*) of checked
material; and, on the left, a head-scarf (*mandil*)
of flowered gauze bound with a headband
('*asbeh*). *Photo: Library of Congress*

Jackets

In some areas of Palestine, jackets were worn over coats, coat-
dresses and dresses, both for warmth and display.

Galilee

Galilee villagers sometimes wore a long-sleeved, waist-length
jacket (*mintiyan*) of indigo blue handwoven cotton, like *dura'ahs* and
jillayehs, and with similar, though lighter, embroidery; or of broadcloth, sometimes couched with silk cord.

Galilee bedouin women wore a long jacket (*damer*[35]) of blue
broadcloth (*jukh*) or black cotton (*malas*), and both styles were still
worn in the 1960s. The broadcloth version is often couched with red
silk cord, and the cotton version embroidered in red cotton. Longer
coats (*jubbah* or *kiber*) were also worn.

Southern Palestine

Southern Palestinian villagers often wore plain, simple cotton or
quilted jackets (*mudarabiyeh*), but only in Bethlehem were they
decorated with embroidery.

The most splendid Palestinian women's jacket was the beautiful
taqsireh of Bethlehem. This has short sleeves, through which were
pulled the pointed sleeves of the dress beneath. The earliest jackets
are mostly made from red, blue or green woollen broadcloth (*jukh*),
and embroidered with silk cord couching filled with silk satin
stitch.

As prosperity increased during the Mandate period, jackets were
made from richer materials. From the mid-1920s, velvet, usually in
navy blue or purple, gradually replaced broadcloth, and gold cord
was increasingly used for the couching, either alone for the more
expensive version, or combined with silk cord for the cheaper
model.

Bethlehem women got their inspiration for the *taqsireh* from the
uniform jackets of official and military personnel. In Ottoman and
British times, these jackets were often made from broadcloth, and
richly embroidered with metallic couching or thread (by male
tailors in Lebanon and elsewhere). Though the imitation and
adaptation of this prestige male garment for female purposes
happened beyond human memory, one *taqsireh* specialist recalled
sitting behind the standard bearer (*qawas*) in church, memorising
the pattern on the back of his jacket, then rushing home to copy it
on a *taqsireh*. One of the denser couched cord motifs used in
Bethlehem was called 'the guard's branch' ('*erq al-qawas*).[36]

The *taqsireh* was one of the chief articles in the *kisweh* over a wide
area of the southern hills, from Ramallah in the north to the Hebron
hills in the south.

For everyday purposes, women in the Bethlehem and Jerusalem
areas wore a sleeveless woollen coat (*bisht*) instead of the *taqsireh*.
The *bisht* was also preferred by older women for whom the *taqsireh*
was too gaudy. The *bisht* was made from locally-spun wool, and
handwoven on horizontal treadle looms by male weavers in Bethlehem and Beit Jala. It was usually striped in red and black or red and

Above **Jacket (damer or saltah), Lake Huleh area, Galilee, 1930s.**
Broadcloth; silk braid trim and cord couching; broadcloth lining and appliqué decoration; two inside pockets. Possibly made to be reversible. *H 90cm Dar al-Tifl Collection: 37.289*

Below **Jacket (taqsireh), made in Bethlehem or Beit Jala, early 20th century.**
Red woollen broadcloth; embroidered with silk cord couching (*tahriri*) filled with satin stitch. Jackets such as this were made commercially by the women of Bethlehem for many villages in the Jerusalem and Bethlehem areas. *Museum of Mankind: 1966 AS1 3*

153

Left **Panel of embroidery on the back of the jacket on the previous page.**
This jacket might have been made for a Lifta woman, for the women of that village preferred broadcloth jackets even after velvet was introduced in the 1930s, and liked a large couched design on the back – in contrast to Bethlehem women who preferred a more restrained border design.

Right **Detail from the front of a jacket (*taqsireh*), made in Bethlehem or Beit Jala, 19th or early 20th century.**
The velvet probably pre-dates that imported in the 1930s; the simple wreath pattern in gold cord couching is similar to those found on the skirt side panels of Bethlehem *malak* dresses from the late 19th and early 20th century. *Museum of Mankind: 1967 AS2 12*

Jacket (*taqsireh*), made in Bethlehem or Beit Jala, 1930s or 40s.
Velvet embroidered with silk (*tahriri*) and gold (*qasab*) cord couching filled with satin stitch. *Taqsirehs* were usually lined with European cotton print material, as here. *Museum of Mankind: 1969 AS8 18*

brown, and the more ornate versions had bands of floral cord couching around the hem and on the shoulders – the latter possibly mimicking epaulettes on military uniforms.

The various bedouin groups and the Jericho people sometimes wore short-sleeved jackets, some made from the same black cotton as their dresses. Examples from the 1930s are plain with only a little decorative seam and edge stitching, whereas later jackets are heavily embroidered with patterns similar to those used on dresses. Other jackets (*damir*) are made from dark blue broadcloth with decoration in black cord couching.

Shoes

Until the 1920s most village and bedouin women went barefooted; shoes were only worn by those who regarded themselves as urban (*madani*), like the women of Bethlehem. Putting on shoes was therefore synonymous with upward mobility; a woman from the prosperous village of Ain Karim near Jerusalem admitted: 'the people of our village were *nouveaux riches* because the women wore shoes'.

Granqvist relates how proud the Artas people were of a splendid wedding procession which had impressed neighbouring villagers

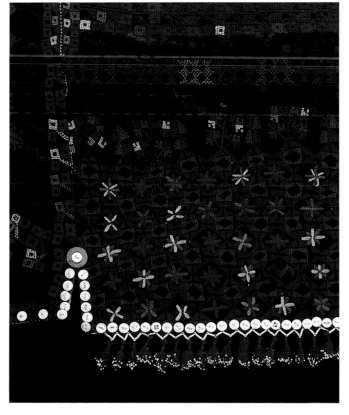

Below left **A consular guard (*qawas* or *cavas*).**
He is wearing an elaborately decorated jacket and waistcoat of
the type copied by Bethlehem and Beit Jala women. Note his
broad sash made from the same material as some women's
sashes. *Photo: Matson Collection, Library of Congress*

Above left **Coat (*bisht*), Bethlehem area, British Mandate
period.**
Handwoven in Bethlehem and Beit Jala from wool locally spun
and dyed; couched epaulettes in silk cord. *Museum of Mankind:
1968 AS12 1*

Above right **Jacket, bedouin, Negev desert, probably 1940s or
1950s.**
Cotton material; coin and button decorations; cotton cross-
stitch embroidery. Note the camel motifs. *Collection: Widad Kawar*

Below right **Detail from the back of the jacket illustrated above
right.**
Embroidery in cross-stitch and chain-stitch; hem edged with
white shirt buttons and tassels with tiny white beads.

Bethlehem women dancing at a wedding, 1930s or 1940s.
Few village women wore shoes before the 1930s, but women from Bethlehem, as semi-urban sophisticates, wore the latest fashions in shoes. *Photo: Matson Collection, Library of Congress*

partly because '... all the Artas women [were] in shoes and stockings! The el-Hadr people stared in amazement'.[37] In Artas, as elsewhere, shoes and stockings were status symbols because of their association with European fashions; when a woman turned up for her sister's wedding in patent shoes but no stockings, one woman drily remarked: 'Only half European.'[38]

In Artas, shoes and stockings were considered improper by conservative traditionalists, so women were divided on the propriety of wearing them to attend a wedding:

... some of them even have stockings and shoes and are very proud of them. But in the eastern part of the village the women confided to us that they would not dare to dress themselves in such a European fashion: 'We have all got shoes and stockings', they asserted. But they also said the old men would 'kill' them if they ventured to put them on; it is condemned as a modern idea which is only evil and brings trouble and sorrow; only the Meshani and Shahin families [in Artas] as yet allow their women such a luxury.

Shoes had specific meanings in the context of the wedding rituals. During the wedding-day procession, a pair of the groom's shoes were placed on the bride's feet for protection against the 'evil eye'; for this reason, and presumably because it was not then customary for women to wear shoes, the wedding day was sometimes referred to as 'the day of the putting-on of shoes'.[39]

The removal of these shoes on the wedding night also had significance. When the bride and groom were left alone to consummate their marriage, a small, private ritual called 'loosening the shoes' (*fakk al-wata*) took place, in which the bride staged a mock resistance to the groom's advances, insisting on gifts of coins before she would allow him to approach and remove her shoes and clothing.[40]

4
Women's Costume
Head Wear and Jewellery

Safiyeh is a golden headdress
stamped by a jeweller
blessed is he who bought her
and compensated the loser!
Safiyeh is a golden headdress
the pride of her father
blessed is he who bought her
he compensated her father!
Safiyeh is beautiful
what more can we say?
Her elegant long neck
is adorned with necklaces!

Beit Dajan wedding song

Townswoman of Hebron, 1930s.
In contrast to village women, many Muslim townswomen wore all-enveloping cloaks (*izar*, *habarah*, *emlayeh*) and face veils when they went out in public. In Hebron, a flowered muslin scarf (*mandil*) was worn over the face.
Photo: Jan Macdonald

Previous page **Bride dressed for her 'going out ceremony', Qubeibeh ibn 'Awad, southern plain, 1932–3.** *Photo: Olga Tufnell*

Village and bedouin women did not veil their faces like townswomen, with the sole exception of their wedding-day – hence the saying 'today the sun is a bride' on a cloudy day.[1] However, the modesty code dictated that in public their heads, like men's, should always be covered.

Head wear usually comprised a headdress – a tight-fitting cap or bonnet – and, draped or tied over it a scarf or veil, sometimes bound with a headband. Headdresses and veils, like other garments, varied regionally, indicated marital status – they were first adopted to show readiness for marriage – and displayed wealth, in the case of headdresses and jewellery, with precious metals and actual coins. Some headdresses and veils, and of course jewellery, were made commercially, which added to their monetary value.

Veils and headbands

Galilee villagers

Galilee villagers wore a variety of fringed and tasselled veils or scarves (*hattah*) of silk or cotton, often black and maroon silk, less often white (the dominant veil colour in the south). Dark-coloured veils were worn mainly by the old, light by the young.

An unusual silk veil called a *zurband* is recorded for Nazareth in the second half of the nineteenth century.[2] Examples (one 3m long) were collected in the 1930s from the villages of Kefr Kenna and Buqei'a,[3] so it was probably quite widely worn. It sometimes doubled as a veil and a sash, half covering the head and hanging ostentatiously down the back like a train, half divided and tied round the waist.

A headband ('*asbeh*), made from a square of material folded and rolled diagonally, was tied round the forehead, over the *hattah* or *zurband*, and knotted at the back of the head; some ceremonial headbands were edged with fringed and tasselled bands (*dikkeh*) which hung down the back. Headbands were made from flowered muslin, black silk with silver brocade, or yellow, red and green silk with silver brocade 'combs' (the same *maqruneh* material used for girdles in the Jaffa area). The latter was also worn in the villages of the Nablus area, where it was called *gharawiyeh* or *ruwaysiyeh*.

Druze women differed from other Galilee villagers in wearing a long, flowing white headveil, like the southerners. They once wore a black '*asbeh*, like other villagers, but some time after the 1930s, their religious leaders forbade them to continue wearing it in order to distinguish them from Muslims and Christians.

Galilee bedouin

Galilee bedouin wore, and still wear, a black crepe veil (*shambar* or *milfa'*) bound with an '*asbeh*, often of brocaded silk like that of the villagers, but broader. The ends of the veil are sewn together to make a large tube which is draped round the head twice so that the excess material fills the neck opening of the dress. This veil was reported as being red in the 1930s.[4]

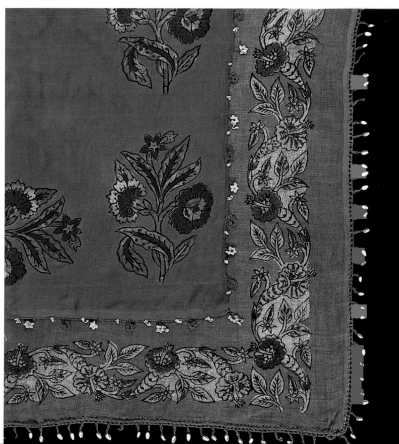

Above **Woman in Nazareth, Galilee, 1930s.**
She is wearing a *zurband* with a separate girdle, a short velvet jacket (*mintiyan*), a coat (*qumbaz*) with long side slits, a white underdress (*thob*), and baggy pants of cotton print (*sirwal* or *libas*). *Photo: Jan Macdonald*

Above right **Detail from a scarf (hattah), Galilee, Mandate period or earlier.**
Silk with yellow metal brocade patterns and tasselled fringe (on two edges) bound with metal thread. Roughly square cloths such as this were worn by villagers both as head covers and (folded and rolled diagonally) as headbands (*'asbeh*). Similar headbands were also worn by the Galilee bedouin. Among both villagers and bedouin the headband signified marital status. *110 × 120cm (excl. fringe) Museum of Mankind: 1971 AS1 11*

Below right **Details of scarves (mandil), Galilee, Mandate period or earlier.**
Cotton muslin with block-printed floral patterns, and edgings of crocheted flowers and tiny shells respectively. These scarves were rolled diagonally and worn as headbands (*'asbeh*) by Galilee villagers. Scarves such as this were copies of Turkish fashions, and may have been imported from Turkey. (Similar scarves were worn as face veils by the townswomen of Hebron in the Mandate period and later). *60 × 70cm and 70 × 70cm Museum of Mankind: 1966 AS1 82, 86*

In the 1930s an unusual head-covering (*malas*) was worn by the hut-dwellers in the Lake Huleh area north of Lake Tiberias, possibly only by unmarried girls. An example from Khalsa[5] is made from a rectangle of red and yellow ikat-patterned Syrian satin which is folded in two, with one open edge sewn together for half its length. This was worn like a bonnet with the face pushed through the open half of the joined edge, and the spare material tucked into the neck of the dress.

Above left **Druze women at Al-Hammeh, Galilee, 1930s.**
Note the headbands (*'asbeh*) which were later banned. *Photo: Jan Macdonald*

Left **Druze women, Galilee, 1967.**
Note the absence of headbands; this, together with the long, flowing white veils, now distinguishes Druze women from Muslims and Christians. *Photo: Shelagh Weir*

Above **Woman of the Arab al-Hayb bedouin, Tuba, Galilee, 1968.**
She is wearing the black crepe *milfa'*, a brocade silk headband (*'asbeh*), and a row of gold coins. *Photo: Shelagh Weir*

Girl in Mallaha, north west of Lake Huleh, Galilee, probably 1940.
She is wearing the satin hood (*malas*), usually worn without a headband, which was probably reserved for girls approaching marriageable age. Over her cotton print dress (*fustan*) she is wearing a tablet-woven belt (*shwahiyeh*) with the tasselled fringe falling to the side. The women of the lake Huleh area specialised in weaving mats, which were used for floor covers and for the roofs and walls of their homes. *Photo: Matson Collection, Library of Congress*

Southern Palestinian villagers

Headbands were not worn by southern Palestinian women, except at weddings. Brides often wore an '*asbeh* on their wedding day and, in the Hebron hills, a headband (*zamliyeh*) of green, yellow and black stripes was worn at weddings by all the female guests.

Southern veils were (and still are) predominantly of white cotton; a long, flowing white veil (*shash*) was and remains a clear signal, even from a distance, of a woman's village, as opposed to bedouin, identity, for the veils of the latter are mainly black. Along the southern coast, everyday veils were sometimes of checked cotton, and more recently of beige and white striped cotton. Festive veils (*tarbi'ah*) of luxurious *rozah* silk, or fine cotton or linen with floral patterns embroidered in wool, were worn in the Bethlehem and Jerusalem areas, and of thicker cotton or linen with thick fringes (*hadab*) of white cotton or colourful silk (*dikkeh*) elsewhere; in the hills from Ramallah southwards, and in the southern plain, the latter are sometimes richly embroidered.

Veils from the hills north of Jerusalem are made from two pieces of fabric joined lengthways, while those from the Jerusalem area, the Hebron hills and the southern plain tend to be made from three pieces.

Ramallah-embroidered veils (*khirqah*) underwent a process of change similar to that of dresses. Early examples have relatively sparse geometric patterns, which are later combined with motifs of European origin. These changes took place within a fixed structure: a narrow band of embroidery along the two long sides of the veil, wider bands along the two short sides (invariably with the characteristic 'tall palm' design), and three or four crosses of embroidery

163

one above the other in each half of the veil. Large individual motifs are arranged within the spaces between these main elements.

In the Jerusalem area festive veils were made from three pieces of material and were almost square in shape (in contrast with the elongated rectangles common elsewhere). These were embroidered all over with small, delicate patterns, the most dominant being diagonal crosses, and were often sprinkled with sequins.

In the south-eastern plain and Hebron hills, festive veils (*ghudfeh*) have a wide panel of embroidery (*rus*) on one or both short sides, narrower bands of embroidery bordering the long sides, and either large diagonal crosses combined with 'cypress trees', or rows of 'branches', in the centre of each panel. Veils with embroidery only at one end were worn doubled, with the embroidery falling to one side. Some embroidered panels, and most fringed *dikkehs* for *ghudfehs*, were made commercially in Bethlehem and Hebron.

In the nineteenth century, an unusual festive veil was worn in Bethlehem. This was made from two pieces of very fine cotton or linen joined lengthways, with delicate silk embroidery bordering all four sides, and a *dikkeh* band and fringe matching the embroidery along the two short sides. The embroidery patterns and technique, and often the colours, are quite different from other Palestinian embroidery, and even other Bethlehem embroidery. Bethlehem women interviewed had no clear memory of this veil or its origins, but its embroidery resembles that of the Greek islands, so it may have been imported by Greek women who came to Bethlehem as pilgrims or brides.

The most important commercially-produced veil in southern Palestine was the *shambar* (also *shinbar* and *shunbar*), made by women in Bethlehem, Beit Jala and Hebron. The *shambar* has four main components: a body of fine black silk or silk crepe; an embroidered cotton panel (*naqleh*) about 50cm high; a fringed *dikkeh*

Left **Woman from Mejdel in Jabaliya refugee camp, Gaza Strip, 1967.**
Beige and white striped veils were still being woven by Mejdel weavers in Gaza at the time of the photograph. The chest panel of her dress is decorated with machine embroidery, all many refugees could afford at the time.
Photo: Shelagh Weir

Right **Ramallah woman wearing an embroidered veil (*khirqah*), late 19th or early 20th century.**
Photo: Library of Congress

band; and tassels (*sharashib*). The *naqleh* was embroidered on a frame, using large stitches in mainly cyclamen-red silk, and was not considered 'proper embroidery'.

Bethlehem women preferred to wear a simpler *shambar*, without a *naqleh*, and ornamented only with a *dikkeh* which had the added refinement that the ends of its fringe were delicately knotted. The fringe was either entirely red, or a mixture of up to eleven colours. They considered this more restrained *shambar* a reflection of their higher social standing as aspiring townspeople. They say 'the *shambar* with the *naqleh* was not for *us*, it was for the *villages*'.

Both the ornate and simple versions of the *shambar* were popular throughout southern Palestine. In many villages they were an essential part of the *kisweh*; in less affluent villages, or at leaner times, only a *dikkeh* was supplied.

The black of the *shambar* was in striking contrast to other village veils, and reflected the special, abnormal, celebratory aspects of the occasions on which it was worn. Women wore it for weddings and feast days, and in many villages it was worn by the bride for her 'going out' ceremony. 'It could *never* be worn on the wedding day', said one woman, 'because it was *black*!'

Another type of festive veil (*shal*) which became popular during the 1930s was made from pink or maroon silk or wool, had a long silk fringe, and was embroidered with large floral patterns. This style of veil, which was first imported, then made locally, replaced the *shambar* as a ceremonial veil, and similar veils are still common everyday wear among older women in Ramallah.

Southern bedouin

The veils (*qun'ah*) of the southern bedouin are also long and flowing, but contrast with village veils in being of the same blue or black material as the dresses. Older veils are plain, but some from the 1930s are decorated with red zig-zag appliqué borders, or embroidered all over with patterns similar to those found on dresses and jackets from the same period. For journeys outside the home, a plain black *'abayah*, similar to a man's mantle, was worn instead of the *qun'ah*.

Jericho (villagers) and Ta'amreh women, who wore the huge 'double dress', threw the material of one sleeve over their heads as a veil, and bound it to their heads with a plain black or coloured, patterned headband (*'asbeh*). Alternatively, Jericho women wore a flowered scarf (*mandil mshajar*) of cotton or wool, folded diagonally, with the ends tied behind their heads.

Above **Detail from the veil on the right.**
Note the sequins sewn to the distinctive 'tall palm' pattern, and the addition of simple European bird motifs to a local feathered pattern.

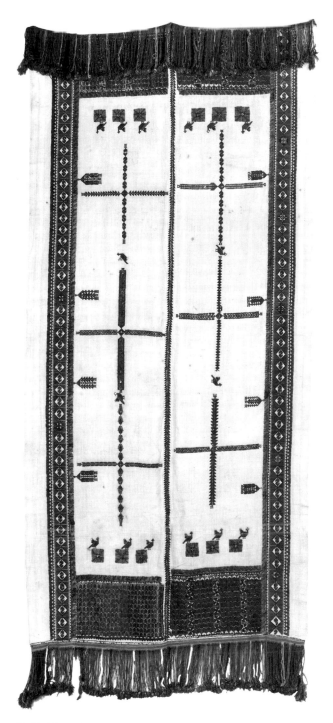

Veil (*khirqah*), Ramallah, early 20th century.
Two pieces of linen, red embroidery with
details in black, purple, green and yellow. A
dikkeh band with a multi-coloured, tasselled
silk fringe is attached at each end. This piece
clearly shows the basic embroidery structure
of Ramallah-area veils. *L approx. 200cm Museum of
Mankind: 1981 AS23 14*

Veil (*khirqah*), Ramallah, early 20th century.
Two pieces of linen, embroidery in red with
details in black. The field of the veil has
become filled with motifs of European origin,
while the basic structure has remained
unchanged. *L approx. 200cm Museum of Mankind:
1981 AS23 13*

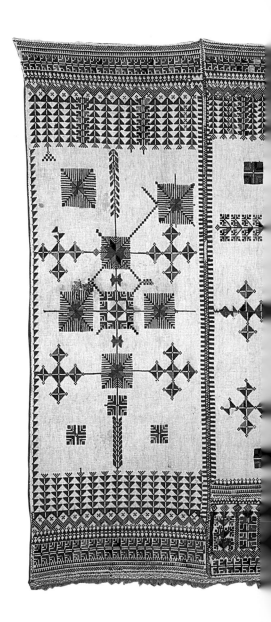

Left **Veil (*ghudfeh*), southern plain or Hebron hills, 1920s–30s.**
Cotton material; cross-stitch embroidery. These veils are sometimes twice this length, and worn doubled with the embroidered panel falling to one side. *L 152cm Museum of Mankind: 1968 AS4 17*

Below **Veil (*ghudfeh*), Jerusalem area, early 20th century.**
Cotton material; silk embroidery in cross-stitch. *W 130cm Museum of Mankind: 1968 AS4 16*

Below left **Detail from a veil panel, Hebron hills, 1920s–30s.**
Linen; embroidered in double-sided stitch. *Museum of Mankind: 1986 AS16 1*

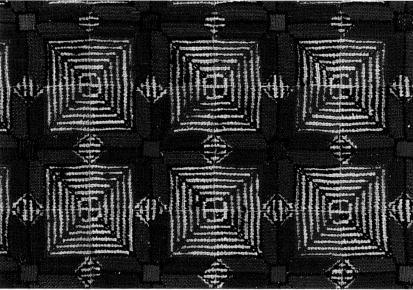

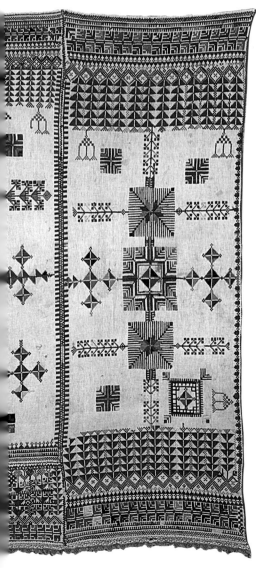

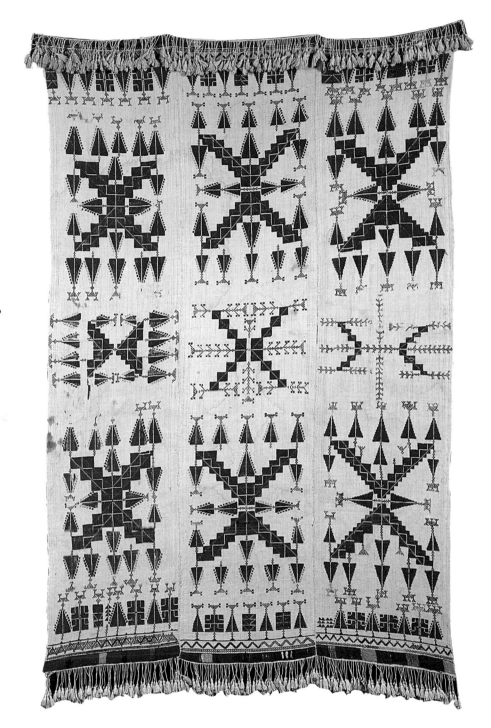

Above **Veil (*ghudfeh*), Falujeh, southern plain, 1920s or earlier.**
Three pieces of linen; linen fringe with cotton tassels; embroidered in cross-stitch
with satin stitch borders. *L 195cm Museum of Mankind: 1979 AS11 1*

Girl from the Bethlehem or Jerusalem area, 19th century.
Tinted studio portrait of a girl wearing a veil with embroidery similar to that illustrated; a headdress (*shatweh*) of the lower, wider type worn in the last century; a red and green taffeta *abu qutbeh* dress with a chest panel bordered with zig-zag appliqué; a jacket (*taqsireh*) with large zig-zag patterns; and a magnificent silver chin-chain (*iznaq*) with many pendant coins. The headdress was normally concealed by the veil, and is revealed for the photograph.

Facing page **Detail from a veil, Bethlehem, 19th century.**
Two 48cm-wide pieces of fine cotton joined lengthways; silk embroidery in stem stitch and broken running stitch forming a narrow border on all four sides of the veil; matching multi-coloured fringe at the two ends. The embroidery is quite different from other southern Palestinian embroidery, and was possibly influenced by that of the Greek islands which it resembles. *L 3m (excl. fringe)
Museum of Mankind: 1966 AS1 16*

Detail from a veil, Bethlehem, 19th century.
Silk embroidery on fine linen. *Collection: Church's Ministry Among the Jews*

Left **Detail from a veil (*ghudfeh*), Hebron hills, British Mandate period.**
Linen material; embroidery in a double-sided stitch and drawn thread work. This type of embroidery, unusual for Palestine, was done by Bethlehem embroideresses for sale to the villages in the Hebron hills. *Museum of Mankind: 1968 AS4 18*

Below **Panel from a veil, Bethlehem, 19th or early 20th century.**
Embroidery in silk and wool on fine linen. The patterns of a vase and flowers, and rosettes, are similar to those found on early Bethlehem chest squares and jackets. A similar panel is sewn to each end of the veil. Veil trimmings of imported European lace were popular in the Bethlehem–Jerusalem area. *L 175cm W 85cm Collection: Church's Ministry among the Jews*

Above **Detail from a veil (*shambar*, *shinbar* or *shunbar*), made in Bethlehem or Beit Jala, 1930s or earlier.**
Silk embroidery done on a frame. *Collection: Widad Kawar*

Above right **Imm Munir Salih and her daughter Hiyam in 'Aboud, west of Ramallah, 1979.**
Imm Munir is wearing a flowered silk shawl (*shal*) and dress dating from the 1940s. *Photo: Shelagh Weir*

Below right **Veil (*shal*), Ramallah, 1930s–40s.**
Silk with machine embroidery. Veils such as this were at first imported from Japan and Germany, and later made in Ramallah and Bethlehem.
Collection: Widad Kawar

Headdresses

The outstanding feature of Palestinian women's headdresses is their heavy ornamentation with silver and gold coins. These coins, acquired at marriage, were essential to married women's attire and, together with a variety of silver or gold jewellery, were financially and symbolically linked to the 'brideprice' (*fayd*) the groom was obliged to pay to the bride's father or guardian at marriage.[6]

Brideprice

The term 'brideprice', as used here, reflects Palestinian terminology and poetic rhetoric, and is not, of course, meant to imply that marriage was a commercial transaction.[7] Far from being devoid of social repercussions or meaning, the payment was a strong statement of social commitment and values. As the largest and most important of the gift exchanges at marriage, it bound the members of both families in a strong chain of reciprocal obligations; it was a powerful expression of the high social value of women, marriage and the institution of the family; and it conferred prestige on family and village in proportion to their ability to pay a substantial sum. As Granqvist states: 'The value of a woman is something very real. They say proudly ... "Artas brides are expensive!"'[8]

The amount of brideprice varied according to a range of social and economic factors. It was higher for virgins and lower for widows and divorcees; and it was lower if bride and groom were from the same kinship group (*hamuleh*), and higher if they were unrelated, or from different villages. For example, in Artas in the 1920s, the brideprice demanded for a girl marrying into the same *hamuleh* as the groom's was P£50, into a different *hamuleh* £100, and into another village £150.[9]

Girls from rich, high-ranking families could also command higher brideprices than those from humble backgrounds, and brideprices were higher, overall, in wealthy villages than in poor ones. For example, in the 1920s the brideprice in relatively poor Artas was far less than in prosperous Lifta near Jerusalem: 'It was said that no one in Artas had given such a high brideprice (P£100) as was given for Hamde Mhammad who went to Lifta; but this was nothing like the sum which is required for a brideprice in Lifta itself (£700–1000).'[10]

Brideprice was always large in relation to income. In the 1920s, when these brideprices were paid, the average daily wage for labourers was less than half a pound. So for poor men without land, cash crops or paid employment, it was hard to accumulate the money for the brideprice and wedding expenses to marry off a son. Many were only able to do so after receiving the brideprice for one or more daughters.

The provision of a girl's headdress coins and jewellery at marriage was the responsibility of her father,[11] and they were regarded as representing a girl's rightful share in her brideprice – because 'it was the price of her neck', as Beit Dajan women put it. Her father was therefore generally expected to spend what remained after meeting other wedding expenses. This was often half or more of

Headddress (*smadeh*), Beit Jann, Galilee, Mandate period or earlier.
The horseshoe-shaped padded roll (*saffeh*) is sewn with a variety of silver coins of different periods and divided in the centre by a piece of watch strap. The cap is of green and black cotton of recent origin, lined with the original blue *durzi* cotton. This headdress, collected in 1967, had been passed down through the family for several generations, and was lent to other families for brides to wear at their weddings. *H 36cm Museum of Mankind: 1968 AS12 25*

the brideprice.[12] As brideprices varied, so also did the value and quantity of women's headdress coins and jewellery. The pressure was always, as with the brideprice, towards conspicuous expenditure; it was important for the prestige of both families that the bride be as well-adorned as the next girl, and, physically and figuratively, hold her head high among her fellow women.

A woman's ostentatious coins and jewellery were therefore status symbols for her father and husband and, by extension, and through their evaluation, for herself. The status aspects of brideprice and jewellery are clearly expressed in the song quoted at the beginning of this chapter, in which a woman's high social value is metaphorically equated with her high-value ornaments, and her father and husband are praised for their appreciation of her worth.

A woman's bridal jewellery and coins were entirely her own property, and she could dispose of them (or add to them) as she wished; they were like a portable bank account, except the contents were flaunted. Women might sell pieces to help with improvements in the home or on the farm, or exchange their silver for gold when it came into fashion and they could afford it. Women sometimes gave their jewellery away during their lifetimes, or it was shared between their children when they died.

Galilee villagers

In the nineteenth century, Galilee women wore a headdress which comprised a bonnet (*smadeh*) with coins attached, surmounted by a padded horseshoe-shaped cylinder sewn with closely overlapping coins, called a *saffeh*. Sometimes, as in the south, a piece of fabric with a row of coins, called a *shakkeh*, was attached to the *smadeh* above the forehead, and a chain (*iznaq*) was suspended from each side to hang below the chin.

This headdress was customary daily wear over a wide area of Galilee in the mid-nineteenth century, as described by Tristram who was there in 1863–4. He first encountered it in the village of Al-Bussah north of Acre:

The head-dress ... baffles my powers of description ... It is called the semadi, and consists of a cloth skull-cap, with a flap behind, all covered with coins – silver, but sometimes gold, and a fringe of coins suspended from it on the forehead. Round the face, from chin to crown, are two stout pads, by way of bonnet-cap, fastened together at the top. But outside of these pads are attached a string of coins, not lengthwise, but solidly piled one little girl ... had 30*l*. worth of silver round her cheeks. Many had frontlets of gold coins, and I saw one centre-piece on the forehead of a sheikh's wife consisting of a Turkish 5*l*. gold piece. All the young ladies pieces of the size of sixpences at the forehead. The weight is no trifle, and one little girl ... had 30*l*. worth of silver round her cheeks. Many had frontlets of gold coins, and I saw one centre-piece on the forehead of a sheikh's wife consisting of a Turkish 5*l*. gold piece. All the young ladies thus carry their fortunes on their heads; and this jewellery is the *peculium* of the wife, and cannot be touched by the husband.[13]

Later Tristram saw a similar headdress in the Druze and Christian village of Esfia on Mount Carmel south of Acre, where '... the semadi and roll of coins on the head [were] somewhat smaller' than they had been at Al-Bussah, and '... Though not rich, all the women here wear gold bracelets, sometimes three on a wrist, of solid metal, twisted in the pattern of a rope, and the ends not meeting, so that the ornaments can be easily taken off'.[14] He also noted the 'rolls of silver coins' fringing the faces of women at the well in Nazareth.[15]

Coin headdresses went out of use for daily wear in Galilee at the beginning of this century, but continued to be worn by brides for their weddings. This demotion to purely ceremonial wear was also the fate of certain southern Palestinian headdresses.

Southern Palestinian villagers

Young girls went bare-headed, but as they approached puberty and marriageable age they began to wear a simple home-made head cover (*wuqayeh*) beneath a veil. Often this was a simpler version of the headdress they would wear after marriage, and sometimes even had a few coins attached; in the Hebron hills a single Maria Theresa dollar or other large silver coin was suspended from the front edge, a simultaneous expression of social value and readiness for marriage.

The most common headdress in central Palestine and the coastal plain comprises a rectangular piece of material with two flaps at the back, and two long hairbands attached to the sides or back after marriage. The material is usually red *dendeki* cotton, often embroidered with mainly red silks, or patched with red *atlas* satin; this is formed into a bonnet by gathering the material at the back, then wrapping the hair in the bands. The use of red cotton in preference to equally available blue or white cottons, the predominantly red embroidery and patchwork and the hairbands, all have sexual significance. This headdress goes by different names: *smadeh* (as in Galilee) in the Jaffa area, *shatweh* around Nablus (where coins are not usually attached), and *wuqa* or *wuqayeh* in the Ramallah district and the coastal plain. Hairbands, though, are universally called *laffayef* or *laffalef*.

Coins are usually attached directly to the sides, back or crown of this style of cap, and sometimes also on a band (*shakkeh*, or *qudleh* south of Ramleh) suspended over the forehead as in Galilee; and in most areas a silver chin-chain (*iznaq*) is suspended from each side, with a large particularly valuable silver or gold coin hanging under the chin; this chain is less for functional than display purposes.[16]

In Ramallah a horseshoe-shaped padded roll (*saffeh*) with a row of large silver coins attached was placed on top of the *wuqa*; this slopes forward at the front and is joined at the back by a heavy pad which, though it no longer functions as such, derives from bundled hairbands, and acts as a counterweight to the *saffeh*. To secure the headdress, a ribbon is threaded through two small rings ('*erweh*) behind the *saffeh* at each side, and tied at the back of the head. A simple chin-chain with flat links is usually suspended from each side of the headdress, with an ornamental bobble and large coin hanging beneath the chin.

Girl from the Hebron hills, probably 1920s or 1930s.
The single Maria Theresa dollar over her forehead signifies her single status, and the fact that she is wearing a headdress and veil, her readiness for marriage. *Photo: American Colony, Jerusalem*

Refugee woman from Falujeh, southern plain, photographed in Amman, 1970.
Her headdress (*wuqa*) is decorated with red *atlas* satin on the crown and bundled hair bands, and Maria Theresa coins (*abu risheh*, literally 'father of feathers' because of the wings on the obverse). *Photo: Shelagh Weir*

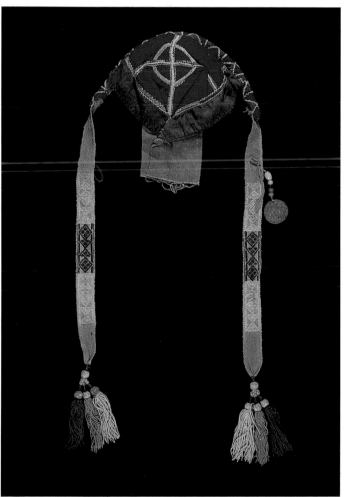

Above **Headdresses (*wuqa* or *wuqayeh*), central hills of Palestine, late 19th or early 20th century.**
These are probably girls' headdresses. They have been opened out to show the basic shape. When worn the coins lie above the forehead, and the fabric is gathered at the back of the head. Both have imitation brass coins, and are made from *dendeki* cotton.
Left: red broadcloth panel embroidered with Bethlehem-style couching and satin-stitch, bordered with taffeta appliqué. Made in Bethlehem or Beit Jala.
Right: embroidered in cross-stitch, bordered with cotton appliqué. *W 30cm and 40cm Museum of Mankind: 1966 AS1 89 and 88*

Left **Headdress (*shatweh*), Nablus area, early 20th century.**
Imported green and red cotton, red *dendeki* cotton lining, cotton stitching and embroidery. The rectangular panel has been drawn together to make a bonnet. The narrow padded roll with triangular patches framed the face, and was not usually ornamented with coins as in other regions. The hair was bound at the nape of the neck in the long bands (*laffayef*), which are simply embroidered in cotton. This type of headdress was worn in Deir Istia and Rafidiah, among other villages. *Museum of Mankind: 1966 AS1 102*

During the Mandate period, the silver *shakkeh* coins were replaced by gold, and *saffeh* coins ceased to be worn. However the padded roll, covered with white lace, was retained, and this form of *wuqa* is still worn today.

A row of *saffeh* coins was once attached to the basic bonnet in many villages, either for everyday wear, or for festive occasions – especially by brides at their weddings. For example, in Beit Dajan and Yibna, brides wore a *saffeh* during the wedding ceremonies.

Jerusalem-Bethlehem area

The headdress (*shatweh*) of the Bethlehem area was in striking contrast with those of other villages. In shape and colour it resembles a man's *tarbush*, another example of women copying men's clothing. The *shatweh* was made from red, or red and green, broadcloth, stiffened by layers of padding between its outer covering and lining, and crowned by a horseshoe-shaped padded roll (*harbeh*) with the gap at the back. Small triangular ear-flaps (*dan*) were attached at each side. The front is covered with rows of coins, beads and coral.

The *shatweh* went through various transformations before going out of fashion in the 1940s. In the nineteenth century it was low and wide in shape, and sometimes surmounted by an ornamental silver disc (*qurs*). (Similar hats with silver discs, and probably also made in Bethlehem, were worn by boys in the Hebron area for their circumcision ceremonies.[17]) These early *shatwehs* are sparsely embroidered, and have relatively few coins, all silver on those preserved.

Later *shatwehs* are narrower and higher, similar in shape to the tall *tarbush* worn by upper class townsmen (effendis) in the late Ottoman and early Mandate periods. Their embroidery is more lavish, and they have more coins, often including gold. Some rich women had two *shatwehs* for different occasions, one with mainly silver coins for everyday wear, and another with gold for celebrations.[18]

Consistent with Bethlehem's status and wealth, most Bethlehem women did not make their own headdresses; they were made by a few women in Bethlehem and Beit Jala for sale to women of their own villages, and others surrounding them. *Shatweh*-making was complex and labour intensive, involving several specialists, hence its cost and prestige. One woman embroidered the broadcloth, another shaped, padded and lined it, another made and stuffed the crown and ear-pieces, and the last attached the beads, coral and coins. The chin-chain (*iznaq*) worn with the *shatweh* was also more elaborate and costly than the single or double-stranded chains worn elsewhere. It had five or seven chains, as well as floral or star-shaped ornaments at their junctions.

The *shatweh* was only worn by married women and widows. Unmarried girls and single women, however old, wore instead a small, circular embroidered cap (*taqiyeh*) similar to those worn in the Jerusalem area. Widows covered the coins and embroidery of their *shatwehs* with dark blue or black fabric as a sign of mourning, and women whose husbands were away for long periods, for

Imm Munir Salih in 'Aboud, 1979.
Her bonnet (*wuqa*) is decorated with gold coins. *Photo: Shelagh Weir*

Woman in Ramallah, late 19th or early 20th century.
Ramallah women wore a particularly large halo of coins (*saffeh*) on their headdresses. *Saffehs* were once worn in many parts of Palestine. *Photo: Matson Collection, Library of Congress*

Ramallah woman in traditional dress, 1987.
In the wealthier villages like Ramallah (which is now a town), gold jewellery and coins replaced silver during the 1920s. In other villages gold coins and jewellery were increasingly adopted during the 1930s and 1940s, depending on family means and the wealth of the village. Today gold jewellery has almost entirely replaced silver among Palestinian villagers and bedouin, including refugees. *Photo: Shelagh Weir*

example in America, removed the coins from their *shatwehs*, or stopped wearing them altogether, until they returned.

Until the 1920s the *shatweh* was the customary headdress of married women in several villages in the Bethlehem and Jerusalem areas, including Beit Jala, Beit Sahur, Lifta and Qubeibeh.[19] Each village had a distinctive style of *shatweh*, with the wealthiest villages, as always, the fashion leaders. By 1918 the new taller *shatweh* had been adopted in Bethlehem and Beit Jala, while the older, lower *shatweh* was still in fashion in Lifta and other villages.[20] In Artas and other villages in the Bethlehem area too poor to afford their own, a borrowed *shatweh* was worn by brides up to the 1920s.[21]

In the villages round Jerusalem, the *shatweh* was replaced as the married woman's everyday headdress by small, embroidered caps (*taqiyeh*) sewn with sequins or gold coins, up to forty quarter pounds depending on wealth – a sign of the relative affluence of these villages. The *shatweh* was, however, retained as a ceremonial headdress, worn on top of the cap (*taqiyeh*) by brides.

Left **Headdress (*shatweh*), Bethlehem and Jerusalem area, 19th century.**
Red broadcloth; sides embroidered with crude gold cord couching with satin-stitch filling; a silver disc (*qurs*) with a stamped pattern on the crown; brass coins on the front; pendant white metal chains, coins and ornaments. The inferior workmanship of this headdress suggests it might have belonged to, or been commissioned by, a relatively poor family for a bride to wear during her wedding ceremonies. Similar headdresses were worn by boys for their circumcision ceremonies.
H (excl. chains) 11cm; D 17cm (at base) Museum of Mankind; 1966 AS1 30

Above left **Disc on the crown of the headdress on the left.** *D 12cm*

Below left **Headdress (*shatweh*), Bethlehem area, 19th century.**
Outer covering of woollen broadcloth, with zig-zag appliqué (*tishrimeh*) at the sides; sides, padded roll on the crown and ear-pieces embroidered with silk cross-stitch; silver coins, metal ornaments, and coral and glass beads at the front. This low, wide type of *shatweh* was worn by married women in Bethlehem, Beit Jala, Lifta and Beit Sahur in the last century. *H 12cm D 17cm at base Museum of Mankind: 1967 AS2 13*

Right **Headdress (*shatweh*), Bethlehem or Beit Jala, 1930s or 40s.**
The sides embroidered in herringbone (*sabaleh*) and gold cord couching; ear-pieces and roll at the crown embroidered in cross-stitch; silver and gold or gold-plated coins and coral attached to the front. This is the tall, narrow type of *shatweh* which had replaced the wider, lower *shatweh* of the 19th century by around 1920 in these villages. This is a particularly elaborate headdress; earlier versions of the tall *shatweh* were embroidered mainly with *sabaleh* stitch and had less couching. *H 15cm D 15cm at base*
Collection: Julia Dabdoub

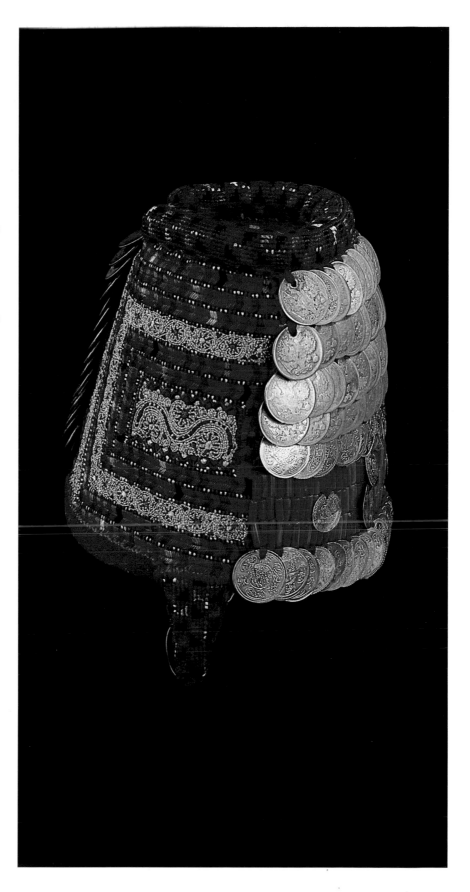

Left **Drawing of a Christian Bethlehem woman, Rufka Gregory, circa 1860.**
The subject was a schoolteacher for a Christian mission in Beirut. Note her low, wide *shatweh* and plain chest panel with zig-zag appliqué borders. *From: Jessup, 1873:5 (the drawing has been reversed)*

Below left **Woman, Bethlehem, late 19th or early 20th century.**
She is wearing the tall, narrow *shatweh* and an elaborate chin-chain (*iznaq*). *Photo: American Colony, Library of Congress*

Facing page, above **Women in Bethlehem, 1925–31.**
This photograph shows four distinctive styles of headwear, from the left: black veils of Palestinian city women; white veils of villagers; European hat; and white veils over the distinctively shaped *shatweh* of Bethlehem. *Photo: Hilma Granqvist*

Facing page, below **Caps (*taqiyeh*), Jerusalem area.**
Two embroidered in cross-stitch, one with couching; brass sequins imitate gold coins which would have been worn by wealthy married women. *D 13cm Museum of Mankind: 1967 AS2 18, 19, 20*

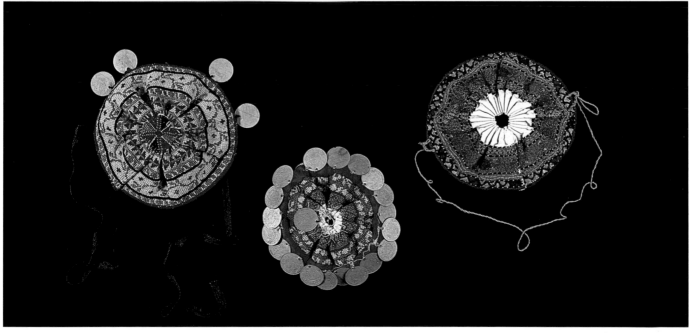

Hebron hills and south east plain

The married woman's headdress of the Mandate period (still worn today in the Hebron hills) is a heavily embroidered circular cap (*'araqiyeh*) gathered into a point at the crown, padded with wool and lined. Encircling the crown is a band (*saffeh*) of Maria Theresa dollars, and more dollars or other large coins are attached at the back. Some recent *'araqiyehs* have gold coins in addition to, or instead of, silver.

In the Mandate, the hairbands (*laffayef*) attached to the back of the *'araqiyeh* were made from plaited wool and were over 150 cm long. Later, *dendeki* hairbands became more common, similar to those of the villages further north but embroidered, and sometimes terminating in narrow plaited woollen bands and tassels, similar to the earlier bands but narrower. Beneath the *'araqiyeh* a small white cotton cap (*taqiyeh*) with an embroidered edge is worn.

In the nineteenth century and up to the Mandate, brides in the southern Hebron hills and their western foothills wore a spectacular ceremonial headdress, called a 'money hat' (*wuqayat al-darahem*), which was made commercially in Bethlehem. Few examples have been preserved, but it is known to have been worn in Beit 'Ummar, Halhul, Bani Na'im, Dura, Dhahariyeh, Samu'ah, Tarqomiyah, Idna, Dawaimeh, Qubeibeh Ibn 'Awad and Beit Jibrin – all villages in which the *'araqiyeh* was the everyday headdress. This headdress was for restricted ceremonial use. It was worn only during the wedding ceremony, sometimes for the first, wedding-day procession, but always for the second 'going out' ceremony, when it was balanced on top of the *'araqiyeh*.

The *wuqayat al-darahem* was usually the property of the patrilineal kin group (*hamuleh*): groups which did not possess one borrowed it for weddings, paying a few piastres, or returning it filled with sweets. This headdress therefore displayed the pride, status and value of the kin group, like the Bethlehem *shatweh* and the Galilee *smadeh* when they were borrowed for weddings. Some informants claimed the *wuqayat al-darahem* was owned by individual women, and that daughters inherited them, in which case they would have passed out of the *hamuleh* when women married into other *hamulehs* or villages. Possibly both accounts are true, for different periods.[22]

Similar dramatic headdresses, dating from nineteenth-century Palestine, but of unknown provenance, were presumably used in the same way as the *wuqayat al-darahem*.[23]

In villages where the *wuqayat al-darahem* was worn, another striking coin ornament, called a *miqlab*, was worn by brides. This was a rectangle of material, covered with coins and often beads and other ornaments, and sometimes fringed all round with silk. It was placed on the backs of brides during the first wedding-day procession, and on their chests for the final 'going out' procession.[24]

Refugee woman from Dura, southern Hebron hills, in Amman, 1970.
She is wearing an *'araqiyeh* decorated with gold coins. *Photo: Shelagh Weir*

Hairband (pl. *laffayef*) for *'araqiyeh*, Samu'ah, southern Hebron hills, probably 1940s.
Dendeki cotton and *atlas* satin, cross stitch embroidery, plaited wollen band (*sfifeh*).
W 8cm L 254cm Museum of Mankind: 1971 AS1 33b

Woman wearing an ʿ*araqiyeh*, Samuʿah, southern Hebron hills, 1967.
Photo: Shelagh Weir

Girl wearing an ʿ*araqiyeh*, Yatta, southern Hebron hills, 1967.
The crown and coins have been covered with black because she is in mourning. *Photo: Shelagh Weir*

Headdress (ʿ*araqiyeh*), Hebron hills, pre-1960s.
Embroidered in cross-stitch; embroidered hairbands (*laffayef*) of cotton (*dendeki*) are bundled at the back; coins Maria Theresa dollars (*abu risheh*) and Turkish coins. The embroidered edge of the undercap (*taqiyeh*) projects from the edge. *H (of cap) 10cm Museum of Mankind: 1971 AS1 30*

Left **Front (above) and back (below) of a headdress (*wuqayat al-darahem*), Hebron hills and their western foothills, circa 1845.**
Light indigo-blue cotton (*durzi*), with remnants of a brown cotton (*dendeki*) lining; silk cross-stitch embroidery. The small silver coins (over 1600 in number) in densely overlapping rows are Ottoman Turkish paras dating from the reign of Ahmad III (1703–30) to that of Mahmud II (1808–39). About 30 other 18th and early 19th-century Ottoman coins are sewn on with thick, undyed cotton thread, and were clearly attached when the headdress was first made. In 1844 a new type of milled currency (the *mejidiyeh*) was introduced in Palestine, and it is unlikely that large quantities of paras were available for long thereafter. Headdresses of this type were therefore probably made shortly after 1844 when paras were abundant but becoming obsolete. About 50 more valuable gold and silver coins, attached to the front and back of the cap, cover an extraordinary range of periods and nations: ancient Greek and Roman, Byzantine, Crusader, medieval Italian, Hungarian, Polish, Danish and Spanish from the 16th to 18th centuries, and Islamic coins dating back to AD 708. These could have been attached at any time.

This headdress was collected in Palestine, purportedly in Bethlehem, by General Sir Charles Warren while excavating for the Palestine Exploration Fund between 1867 and 1870. See Weir, 1973. *Pitt Rivers Museum: 1952.5.86*

Facing page, left **Bride wearing a *wuqayat al-darahem*, Qubeibeh ibn 'Awad, southern plain, 1932–3.**
The wrapped hairbands of her *'araqiyeh* headdress, worn beneath the *wuqayat al-darahem* at the wedding, can be clearly seen at the back of her head. On her chest is a panel of coins (*miqlab*) worn by brides on the back during the wedding procession, and possibly on the front (as here) for the 'going out ceremony', for which this bride is dressed up. *Photo: Olga Tufnell*

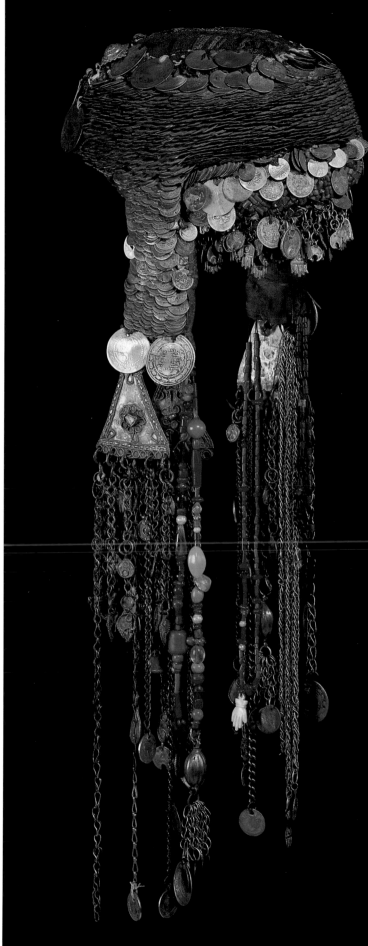

Right **Headdress (*wuqayat al-darahem*), Samuʻah, southern Hebron hills, circa 1840s with later additions.**
Blue (*durzi*) and brown (*dendeki*) cotton, with a later red satin lining. Original embroidery on the crown in similar colours and pattern to the headdress on page 186, overlaid with more recent embroidery. The most numerous coins are Ottoman Turkish paras attached with thick cotton, and dating from the reign of Mahmud I (1730–54) to that of Mahmud II (1808–39). Other coins include debased silver and copper piastres of Mahmud II, silver and copper coins from Selim II (1789–1807) to Muhammad V (1909–19), a silver coin or ornament of ʻAbd al-Aziz dated 1277:17 (AD 1893), and a Romanian 2-lei piece dated 1924. This headdress has clearly had many owners, each of whom added some coin or trinket. Other ornaments, attached to the cap or pendant from the ear flaps, include: two 16th-century German reckoning counters of brass, a regimental brass badge of the 19th or 20th century in the form of a four-pointed star, triangular white metal amulets (*herz*), various glass, plastic, imitation pearl and coral beads, a glass button, metal discs, crescents and ʻhands of Fatimah' (against the Evil Eye), and a pink plastic hand. Headdresses of this type were made commercially by Bethlehem women for brides in the villages of the Hebron hills and their western foothills. *D (of cap) 20cm H (incl. pendants) 60cm Museum of Mankind; AS4 5*

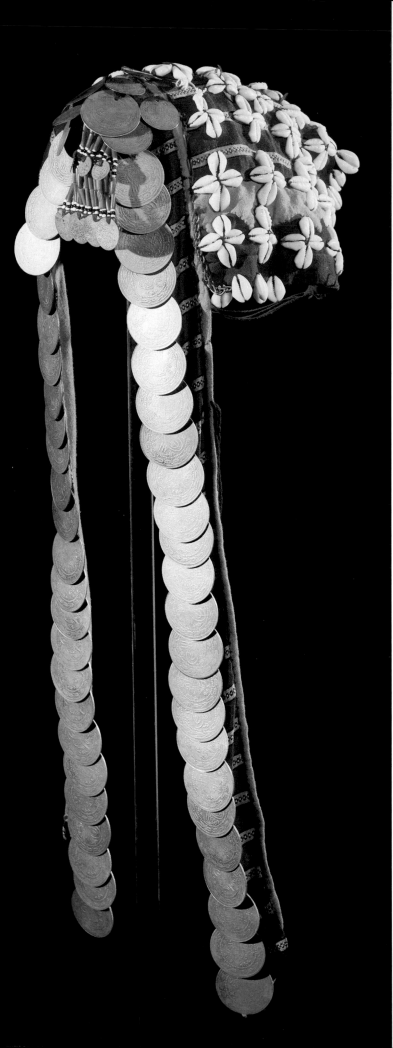

Southern bedouin

A common style of southern bedouin headdress (*wuqa*) consists of a long band of silver coins which hangs on each side of the face as far as the chest. Another has a wide flap which hangs down the back. Headdresses are often made from red and yellow striped *atlas* satin (like those of the villagers), embroidered with cotton cross-stitch, and decorated with coral, cowrie shells, buttons, stones and beads as well as coins.

Among some bedouin tribes, married women wear a striking coin-encrusted face ornament (*burqa*·); this comprises a band, sometimes embroidered, fastened round the forehead, and two rows of coins suspended from it on each side of the nose and looped up at the sides. An interesting variant of this ornament has polished stones instead of coins. Colourful plait ornaments (*karamil*) are also popular among the bedouin, either woven or embroidered, and decorated with tassels and often beads and coins.

Facing page, left **Headddress, Negev bedouin, bought in the Khan Yunis area, 1930s.**
Atlas satin and red and yellow *dendeki* cotton; ornamented with cowrie shells, Turkish coins, coral, beads and imitation gold coins. *H 60cm Dar al-Tifl Museum: 80.40*

Facing page, right **Girl of the Al-'Azazmeh bedouin, Negev desert, 1970s.**
Photo: Klaus-Otto Hundt

Right **Bedouin plait ornaments (*karamil*), 1938 or earlier.**
Embroidered in cotton cross-stitch, with woollen tassels, and attached to false plaits. Bedouin women decorated their hair (and false plaits such as these), while most village woman concealed it and bound it; in the former case women's allure was enhanced, in the latter concealed and controlled. *Dar al-Tifl Museum: 38.200*

Below right **Detail from the back flap of a bedouin headdress, Negev desert.**
Cotton cross-stitch embroidery; decorated with tiny beads, shells and shirt buttons (a popular substitute for cowrie shells). *Collection: Widad Kawar*

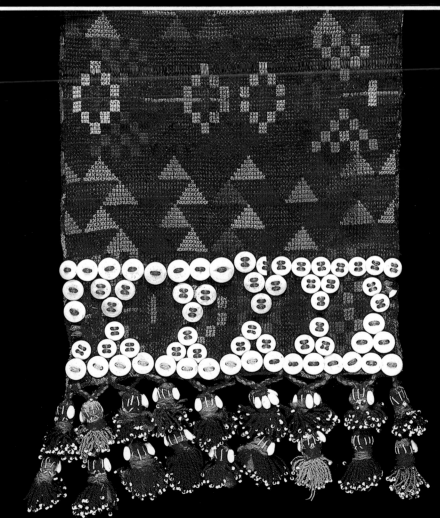

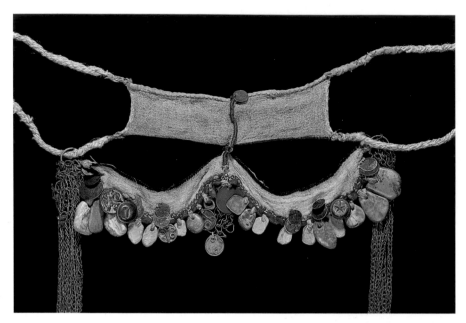

Left **Face ornament (*burqa'*), bedouin, Negev desert, probably 19th century.** Gauze ornamented with polished stones, buttons and coins. *Museum of Mankind: 1987 AS15 1*

Below left **Bedouin woman in Deir al-Balah, Gaza Strip, 1967.** She is wearing a *burqa'* face ornament, a nose ring (*shnaf*) and coral and bead pendants. *Photo: Shelagh Weir*

Right **Face ornament (*burqa'*), Negev bedouin, 1938 or earlier.** The coin-bearing bands are embroidered in cotton cross-stitch. *Dar al-Tifl Museum: 38.200*

Jewellery

Above **Negev bedouin woman, British Mandate period.**
She is wearing several types of silver bracelet, and a necklace of amber beads. *Photo: John Whiting*

A variety of silver bracelets, necklaces, chokers, hair ornaments and rings were worn by villagers and bedouin and made by silversmiths based in all the main towns. Like garments, Palestinian jewellery was subject to continual foreign influence. Silversmiths can easily travel with their craft, and many migrated to Palestine from other parts of Arabia during periods of Levantine prosperity or hardship in their own countries. Early this century, silversmiths from Syria, the Hejaz, Armenia, the Caucasus and Yemen were working in Palestine and Transjordan, as well as silversmiths of local origin. There was also local migration across the Jordan river. For example, Yaqoub Zakariyah (who signed his bracelets 'Hanna' after his father) moved during the First World War from Nablus to Al-Salt in present-day Jordan, where he learnt new techniques. In 1930 he moved to Jerusalem for three years, and then to Bethlehem where he stayed until 1967, when he moved to Amman.

Palestinian jewellery styles and techniques therefore have diverse origins. Black niello work was introduced by Armenian and Circassian silversmiths from the late nineteenth century; the technique of soldering and granulation was imported from the Hijaz in 1921 by silversmiths in the entourage of Emir Abdullah; and filigree work came from Yemen. Yemeni Jewish silversmiths migrated to Palestine and Transjordan well before the mass exodus of Jews from Yemen around 1950. Silversmiths were often members of religious minorities, either Christians or Jews, specialist skills and knowledge tending to be safeguarded in families.

Some silversmiths specialised in specific articles and styles, which were worn by the women in the catchment area of their town, leading to some regional differences in jewellery, but many articles were worn over much of the country. Bedouin in the eastern hills and Jordan valley tended to wear silver made in Nablus, Jerusalem and Bethlehem, while that worn by the bedouin of the southern Negev desert was made and purchased mainly in Gaza and Beersheba. Townspeople, villagers and bedouin living in the same areas bought their jewellery from the same shops and wore similar styles, the main difference being in the value of the pieces. The well-to-do bought jewellery of the highest grade of silver (made from melted-down Maria Theresa dollars mixed with about fifteen per cent of copper), while cheaper items made from coins of lower grade silver and brass were bought by the less well-off customers, especially the bedouin.

Certain jewellery was important for its beneficial physical effects as well as for decoration.[25] Cylinders (*khiyarah*, literally 'cucumber') often contained Koranic inscriptions on tiny paper scrolls, and oval or rectangular pendant amulets (*maskeh*) were often engraved with the name of Allah. Triangular packets containing inscriptions were also made from leather or beading. Among bedouin women, the wearing of stones, beads and other articles such as tortoise-shells and alum was thought to prevent specific illnesses or promote well-

Left **Silver and jewellery shop, place and date unknown.**
The main wares are silver or metal wire for the use of silversmiths, evil-eye beads (top left) and Hebron-made glass bracelets. *Photo: Library of Congress*

being. For example a smooth white bead (*kharzet al-halib*) is still believed to promote lactation, and a dark green bead (*kharzet al-kabseh*) to prevent post-natal diseases.

Blue beads, and glass beads with 'eyes' ('*owayneh*, made in Hebron), were considered particularly efficacious against the 'evil eye' – the jealous glance of certain malevolent persons which was believed to cause disaster, illness or death. Children were specially vulnerable to the 'evil eye', and were kept scruffy and unwashed to avoid attracting dangerous attention. Their caps were often covered with amulets, and beads and charms were attached to their clothing. Women's tattoos were also thought to ward off the evil eye.

Bracelets of blue and brown glass, made in Hebron,[26] were once widely worn, and necklaces made from coral, imitation pearls and cloves were popular among bedouin and villagers, cloves being specially associated with weddings.

From the late 1920s and 1930s, as people became better off, gold jewellery, mass-produced in Beirut and Damascus, gradually replaced silver; at first gold coins were strung on cords as necklaces; later mass-produced gold necklaces, bracelets and rings appeared in the shops, and new types of jewellery appeared, still fashionable today, such as earrings, hair-slides and brooches for fastening the necks of dresses. So jewellery of foreign origin replaced local products, and Palestinian villagers were drawn into the modern, international market, as happened with garments and materials.

Bedouin woman, southern Palestine.
She is wearing a silver choker (*kirdan*), worn by both bedouin and villagers. *Photo: John Whiting*

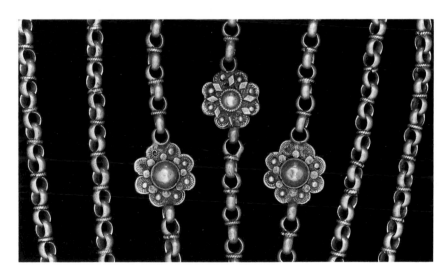

Above **Detail of the ornaments on the chin-chain on the right.**

Right **Silver chin-chain (*iznaq*), Bethlehem, Mandate period.**
Most villages wore *iznaqs* with single or doubled chains; the seven chains and elaborate ornaments of the Bethlehem area *iznaq* proclaimed their superior wealth. It was suspended from the sides of the tall headdress (*shatweh*). *L 50cm Collection: Widad Kawar*

Silver necklace or chin-chain (*iznaq*), southern Palestine, British Mandate period.
The chain with flat links is typical of the chin-chains worn in the Ramallah area. Silver Turkish coins, and a Maria Theresa coin (*abu risheh*, 'father of feathers'). *L 38cm Museum of Mankind: 1966 AS1 346*

Silver choker (*kirdan*), southern Palestine, British Mandate period.
Made mainly in Nablus, in different qualities and prices depending on the number of ornaments.
L 46cm Museum of Mankind: 1966 AS1 347

Detail from a silver necklace (*sha'riyeh*, literally 'noodles'), mainly worn in the Hebron area.
More expensive versions were gilded.
H 2·5cm Museum of Mankind: 1971 AS1 105

195

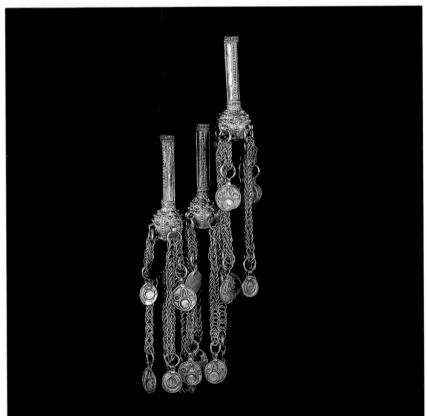

Above left **Silver pendants worn by the wealthier villagers and townswomen.**
Left: the 'almond' pendant (*lozi*)
Right: a cross (*salib*) worn by Christian Arabs, for example in Bethlehem. *Collection: Widad Kawar*

Above right **Silver pendant (*maskeh*).**
Filigree-work chain and pendant, with Arabic inscription. *Collection: Widad Kawar*

Left **Silver hair ornaments (*karamil*), Galilee or Nablus area villagers.**
One of two sets of three attached to false plaits. *H 17cm Museum of Mankind: 1984 AS10 14*

Facing page, above **Girls dancing in festive dress, Sebastiyeh near Nablus, 1926–35.**
The girls have obviously dressed up in their mothers' jewellery. Two are wearing chokers (*kirdan*), and all have silver hair ornaments (*karamil*) dangling from false plaits.
Photo: Grace Crowfoot

Facing page, below **Silver bracelets worn by the southern (Negev) bedouin, Mandate period.**
Left: hammered silver.
Centre: niello work.
Right: plaited pattern (*masriyeh*), made in Egypt and Gaza. *Museum of Mankind: 1988 AS6 8; 1988 AS6 7*

197

Ramallah woman wearing *habbiyat* and *haydari* bracelets, 1900.
Photo: Library of Congress

Silver 'lentil' bangles (*habbet 'adaseh*).
Worn (often in sixes) in the towns and in
the wealthier villages such as Bethlehem
and Ramallah. *Left: Museum of Mankind: 1971
AS1 90; right: Collection: Julia Dabdoub*

**White metal (*left*) and brass (*right*)
hinged bracelets.**

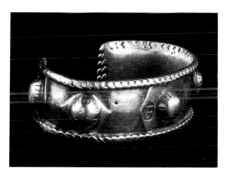

Above **Bracelet (*haydari*), southern
villagers.**
High-quality silver; inscribed 'Khalil'
after its maker. Other silversmiths who
made and inscribed *haydaris* were
Hanna, Samur, Al-Ghawi and Ya'qub.
Worn in pairs, one on each wrist, or two
per wrist.

Right **Silver bracelet (*aswareh habbiyat*),
made mainly in Nablus.**
Worn by villagers in the central hills, usually
in pairs, one on each wrist. *H 6·5cm Museum of
Mankind: 1971 AS1 90*

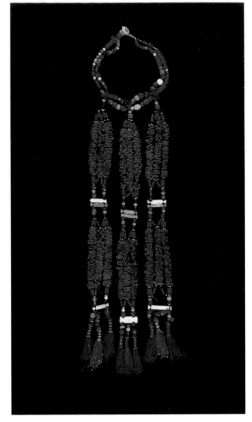

Above **Woman, Al-'Azazmeh bedouin, Negev desert, 1974.**
She is wearing bead necklaces, a gold nose ring (*shnaf*), a hair slide with gold coins, and a machine-embroidered dress. *Photo: Shelagh Weir*

Above right **Necklace, Negev bedouin.**
A variety of beads, cloves, and mother-of-pearl spacers. Clove necklaces were associated with weddings. *Museum of Mankind: 1975 AS3 31*

Right **Bead necklaces, worn by bedouin and villagers.**
The beads are of coral, imitation coral, amber, glass and silver. The necklace on the right includes a black bead apparently made from a broken ancient spindle whorl. *Museum of Mankind: 1975 AS3 34, 35*

200

Talismanic necklace, probably Negev bedouin.
Various amulets worn to promote well-being or avert illness: blue beads against the evil eye, alum, a tortoise-shell, and a triangular cloth amulet (triangles being efficacious) probably containing a Koranic inscription. *Museum of Mankind: 1966 AS1 379*

Detail of glass necklaces, made in Hebron, Mandate period or earlier.
Blue and green beads were believed to protect the wearer against the evil eye; so also were small hands (the two lower rows), which represented the hand of Fatimah, the daughter of the Prophet Muhammad, and 'eyes' ('*owaynah*). *Museum of Mankind: 1966 AS1 363, 368, 382, 378*

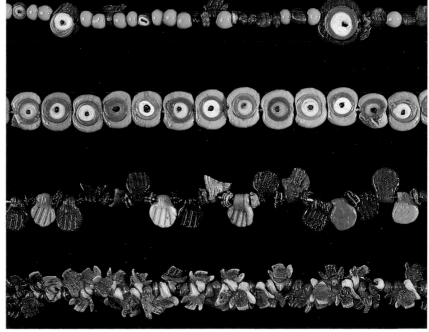

Child's cap with beads and amulets against the evil eye and to promote well-being.
Museum of Mankind: 1966 AS1 244

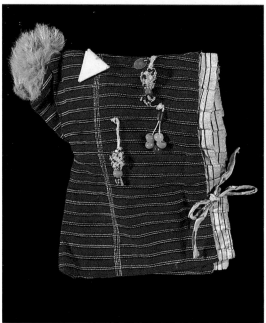

Child's bonnet with blue beads against the evil eye, and an inscribed amulet.
Museum of Mankind: 1966 AS1 329

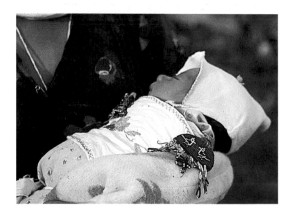

Swaddled baby with amulets, Galilee bedouin, 1967.
Photo: Shelagh Weir

5 Changing Fashions in Beit Dajan

we are the Na'ani dresses in the wardrobe
with our men riding horses before us
we are the Na'ani dresses inside the room
with our fashionable men in the lead
we are the Na'ani dresses on the hangers
and our men going before us are chauffeurs
we are the Na'ani dresses inside the room
with our men in the lead 'à la mode'
we are the Na'ani dresses in the upper room
and our men going before us are brave

Beit Dajan wedding song

A 'black' *Na'ani* dress, Beit Dajan, 1930s.
Collection: Widad Kawar

This chapter will attempt a deeper understanding of the language of women's costume, and of the way village fashions reflected social and economic change, by focusing on the evolution of the Beit Dajan wedding trousseau between roughly 1920 and 1940.

The trousseau (*jihaz*) is a useful and illuminating context for interpreting changing fashions; trousseaus contained the most up-to-date articles of dress and adornment, making it possible to compile a chronology of costume changes (women vividly recall the contents of their own trousseaus); and, as structured sets of clothing and jewellery, trousseaus provide an important framework for understanding the significance of their constituent items, and of their replacement and transformation through time.

First the social and economic background of the village of Beit Dajan will be described, followed by an analysis of the changes which took place in the bride's (and her father's) contribution to the trousseau, on one side, and the groom's (*kisweh*) presentation, on the other.

Social background

Beit Dajan

The village of Beit Dajan was situated on the maritime plain of Palestine, about twelve kilometres south-east of Jaffa and close to Lydda and Ramleh. It was a large village by Palestinian standards. In 1895 its population was estimated at 2500;[1] it was 2661 in 1931[2] (about four times the average population of a Palestinian village at that time); and in 1945 it had risen to 3840.[3]

Around 1920, villagers lived in the single-storey mud brick houses typical of the plain, and cultivated cereals and a variety of fruits and vegetables. The soil was fertile, and there was abundant sweet water from wells; the main well (*bir*) in the west of the village figured prominently in wedding celebrations.

Beit Dajan boasted Roman remains, and in the late nineteenth century it had five mosques, one said to have dated from the seventh or eighth century.[4] The villagers define their wider regional identity – the coastal area around Jaffa[5] – as 'conquered' (*ftuh*), which to them means 'conquered by the armies of Islam' in the seventh century. They contrast *ftuh* with the factions or alliances, 'Qays' and 'Yaman', to which the hill villagers (*jabaliyeh*) belonged: 'We were neither *Qaysi* nor *Yamani* like the *jabaliyeh* – we were *ftuh*.'

The village was divided into three main quarters (*harah*),[6] each containing several patrilineal kin groups or extended families (*hamuleh*), of which thirty-two were recorded around 1930.[7] The *hamuleh* and the village were the primary sources of social identity, and most people married within the village, and many within the *hamuleh*, marriage between close relatives, particularly paternal cousins (*awlad ʿamm*), being the ideal as elsewhere in Palestine. Most marriage outside Beit Dajan was with the neighbouring villages of Safriyeh, Kheriyeh, Saqiyeh and Kufr ʿAna. The range of women's everyday social interaction, based on kinship, marriage and neighbourhood, was therefore limited, as in all rural Palestine, to a cluster of neighbouring villages with adjoining lands.

Above **Ashdod, on the coast south of Jaffa, probably British Mandate period.**
Beit Dajan was a similar village of mud-brick houses with thatched roofs, but was further inland, and surrounded by fields and orange groves. *Photo: Library of Congress*

Above right **House in Ashdod, British Mandate period.**
Photo: Library of Congress

Right **Ramleh, the market town south of Beit Dajan, 19th or early 20th century.**
Church's Ministry Among the Jews

Women working in orange groves, south west Palestine, pre-1918.

Photo: Imperial War Museum

The nineteenth century

It is unlikely that conditions in the coastal plain were sufficiently stable or prosperous in the early nineteenth century to have stimulated or sustained the production of expensive or richly ornamented costumes. The region suffered greatly from Napoleon's invasion of 1799; after capturing Jaffa, the French army was defeated at Acre, and retreated southwards to Gaza leaving a trail of devastation; Jaffa and many villages were destroyed, and 'the plain looked like a sea of fire from the burning crops'.[8] A century later an olive tree on the outskirts of Beit Dajan was said to mark the spot from which Napoleon had surveyed his troops during his disastrous campaign.[9]

The 1830s were also turbulent years, with revolts against Ibrahim Pasha who had occupied Palestine in 1831 and was driven out in 1840.[10]

During the second half of the nineteenth century, economic conditions improved. Various visitors remarked on the thriving agriculture in the Jaffa region. For example, Van de Velde, who visited in 1851–2, observed lush gardens and fruit trees around Jaffa, Ramleh and Lydda, and the exportation of oranges to Europe (as well as the importation of manufactured goods from England and Holland);[11] and Tristram, who visited in 1863–4, remarked on the expansion of orchards around Jaffa since his previous visit six years earlier, and the town's 'broad belt of two or three miles of date palms and orange groves'.[12]

In the 1860s and 1870s, a radical change took place in the economy with the implementation of the 1858 Turkish land code, which allowed registration of land ownership by individuals.[13] Many villagers sold their land at this time to avoid taxation; one third of Beit Dajan land was sold to townsmen (effendis) from Jaffa, one third remained in individual ownership, and one third in joint ownership (*musha'*).[14] In *musha'* tenure, specified quantities of land were jointly owned by *hamulehs*, but the actual land cultivated was periodically redistributed, discouraging investment and development.

This change brought secure tenure to landowners and stimulated citrus cultivation. It also exaggerated social inequalities by expanding the landless class, and by replacing relatively egalitarian joint tenure by individual ownership of parcels of variably appointed land.

Among the people who acquired large landholdings in Beit Dajan as a result of these changes were Christian families from Jaffa and Bethlehem,[15] and the local family of Sheikh Yusef Darwish al-Dajani. By the 1920s, Sheikh Yusef was the largest landowner in the village, and a powerful local leader with influential family connections among officials in Jaffa. His wife and daughters were leaders of fashion in Beit Dajan, with the richest, most ostentatious costumes and jewellery in the village.

The changes in land tenure also facilitated Jewish colonisation, and in 1882 one of the first Jewish settlements in Palestine, Rishon le-Zion, was founded by Russians on land adjoining Beit Dajan (called 'Ayun Qara').[16] Beit Dajan people advised the new immigrants, who were townspeople, on farming methods, and later some of the poorer men and women of Beit Dajan found employment in Rishon as labourers or maids.

In the late nineteenth and early twentieth centuries, further opportunities for wage labour were created for the villagers by nearby road and railway construction. In 1888 work started on the first Palestinian railway line between Jaffa and Jerusalem, and railway work continued during the First World War and Mandate period.[17] The first surfaced roads were built during the same period, and a road connected Jaffa and Jerusalem by 1896.[18] Beit Dajan was well placed to benefit from these developments, lying about a kilometre from the Jaffa–Jerusalem railway and the cross-roads between Jaffa, Jerusalem, Gaza and Haifa. In 1895 Baldensperger noted about Beit Dajan:

The inhabitants are very industrious, occupied chiefly in making mats and baskets for carrying earth and stones. They own camels for carrying loads from Jaffa to Jerusalem, cultivate the lands, and work at building etc., in Jaffa or on the railway works. The women flock every day to Jaffa, and on Wednesdays to Ramleh – to the market held there, with chickens, eggs and milk ... The Jewish colony of Rishon l'Zion also affords the Dejanites plenty of work, in planting vineyards and as domestic servants.[19]

Two years earlier (in 1893), the same author gave a tantalising glimpse of Beit Dajan women's costume:

... Beit Dajan women wear gaudy dresses, and put scent on themselves, whilst those of Ibn Ibrak [Kheriyeh] have plain blue clothes, and are never allowed to flirt like their neighbours of Beit Dejan.[20]

It can be gleaned from this that (at least some) Beit Dajan women were better off than those of neighbouring villages, and could afford more ostentatious clothing. This sartorial contrast must have related to the larger landholdings of some Beit Dajan families, or to the greater involvement of Beit Dajan people in a money economy through cash cropping and wage labour. For 'gaudy' (i.e. expensive and highly-decorated) dresses are always associated with disposable income.

The British Mandate period

The First World War period is recalled as a time of hardship; most young men were away fighting for the Turks, and only old men remained to tend the fields, together with a few young men exempted from conscription by marriage to a girl from another village.[21]

With the ending of the War and the establishment of the British Mandate for Palestine, economic conditions greatly improved. The opening of British army camps, first at neighbouring Sarafand, and later at Deir Terif and near Lydda, increased opportunities for wage labour, and the influx of cash into the village further increased after the implementation, in about 1930, of the 1928 British Land Settlement Ordinance.[22] Settlement Officers partitioned and registered the remaining jointly owned land (*musha'*) in the names of (male)

The mosque of Nabi Rubin south of Jaffa, 1978.

Photo: Shelagh Weir

individuals,[23] stimulating agricultural investment, particularly the development of orange groves. Former landowners say: 'After the Land Settlement (*taswiyeh*) we all worked harder because we knew exactly what we owned for the first time; everyone who could do so planted trees and dug a well.'

Citrus cultivation greatly increased the incomes of both landowners and labourers, especially during the 1930s. The daily wage rose from about 10 piastres a day around 1920, to about 50 piastres (half a pound) in the 1930s, and P£1 in the 1940s.[24] In 1935 men could earn £60–100 in four months for unskilled work, such as wrapping and carrying oranges, and £100–150 for a similar period of skilled work. The villagers say: 'After the British came, we had money in our pockets for the first time.' Though not strictly true, there was certainly much more cash in circulation.

This increase in disposable income stimulated ostentatious expenditure as people vied for prestige and status in an increasingly individualistic, mobile and competitive social environment. Much new money went into building and furnishing more impressive dwellings; the richer villagers built two-storey houses of cement or sandstone, the more expensive having balconies and arches, and the simple village furnishings of rugs, mattresses and storage chests were replaced in many homes by carpets, beds, sofas and wardrobes.

As this chapter describes, improved economic conditions were also dramatically reflected in brideprice inflation, more costly jewellery, and larger, more expensive trousseaus.[25]

The other major change in village life was the introduction of motor transport in the 1920s, bus and car travel replacing laborious journeys on foot or by donkey. With improved transport, security and incomes, all Palestinian villagers travelled more widely, and more frequently encountered people from far afield.[26] Hill villagers came more often to buy in the coastal markets, to sell their olives, to graze their cattle on the plain and to feed their bees off the orange blossom (paying the tree owners later in honey). And the Beit Dajan people also travelled more – to Jaffa, to the Monday market in Lydda and the Wednesday market in Ramleh, and to religious shrines, especially Sayyidna Ali north of Jaffa and Nabi Rubin to the south. Nabi Rubin was the site of an annual pilgrimage lasting one or two weeks, attended by male and female villagers from a wide area of southern Palestine. The villagers say: 'There was much more mixing'; this widening of social horizons meant that Beit Dajan women were more exposed to, and influenced by, the fashions of other villages.

Another important external influence on Beit Dajan costumes, especially from the 1930s onwards, was the influx of foreign materials into the markets of Jaffa, Ramleh and Lydda, to all of which the villagers had easy access. Outside influence on local costume and embroidery also increased with the opening of the first village school for girls in 1935 (the first boys' school having opened in 1920).

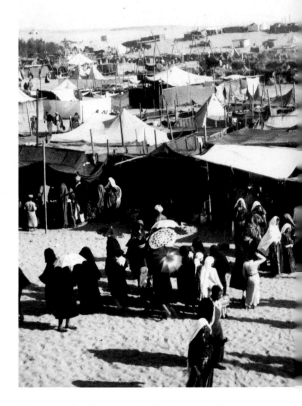

The camp for the annual pilgrimage to the shrine of Nabi Rubin south of Jaffa, 1930.
Photo: Library of Congress

Above right **Men packing oranges for export, south west Palestine, pre-1918.**
Photo: Imperial War Museum

Centre right **Ruin of a two-storey house with arcaded balcony in Beit Dajan (renamed Beit Dagon), 1978.** The house probably dates back to the 1930s or 1940s. *Photo: Shelagh Weir*

Below right **The shrine of Sayyidna Ali north of Jaffa, 1978.**
Photo: Shelagh Weir

Villagers watching the annual procession to the shrine of Nabi Musa south of Jericho, pre-First World War.
In the foreground are Turkish soldiers.
Photo: Matson Collection, Library of Congress

The exodus of 1948

During the war of 1948 the entire population of Beit Dajan, by then about 5000, fled the village, in fear of the surrounding Jewish forces and of neighbouring Rishon le-Zion which was heavily armed. Though they expected to return in a few days, they never did, and most have lived in refugee camps in Gaza, the West Bank and Jordan for the past forty years.

Village identity and pride remain strong among the refugees. Much intermarriage still takes place between fellow villagers, the older women still wear costume which proclaims their village origins, and there is a Beit Dajan Society in Amman which organises welfare, educational and cultural activities for over seven hundred fee-paying members.

Beit Dajan still exists, since 1948 within the State of Israel, and re-named Beit Dagon after an ancient site about three kilometres west of the village. Its inhabitants are now Jewish, many of Yemeni origin.

In the following sections the structure and meaning of the bride's and groom's (*kisweh*) contributions to the Beit Dajan trousseau (*jihaz*) will be examined in turn – first in the early 1920s, then around 1935.

The bride's contribution to the trousseau: early 1920s

Classification and ranking

The most important articles the bride prepared for her trousseau, as elsewhere in Palestine, were a number of dresses heavily embroidered in the style of the village.[27] These dresses formed a system or set in which each was named, classified and ranked according to its cut, fabric colour and embroidery. How and why dresses and their embroidery changed during the period considered here can only be fully understood in the context of this structured system.

Up to the early 1920s the trousseau (*jihaz*) contained two types of southern Palestinian dress: the coat-dress (*jillayeh*) with short sleeves and an opening in the front of the skirt, and the dress (*thob*)

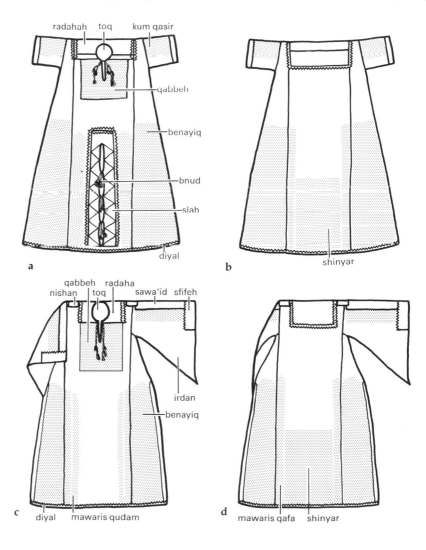

Back and front of a *jillayeh* (a, b) and *thob* (c, d), with the Arabic names of the main parts.

Jillayeh, **Beit Dajan, circa 1920.**
Museum of Mankind: 1968 AS4 31

Thob, Beit Dajan, circa 1920.
(The couched embroidery on the yoke, sleeves
and skirt is a later addition). *Collection: Widad
Kawar*

with long winged sleeves, both heavily embroidered in cross-stitch
with similar patterns.

Jillayehs were always made from 'black' (*asmar*) linen, and the
festive *thobs* of this early period were always of undyed 'white'
(*abiadh*) linen, never black. The skirt opening of the *jillayeh* was
patched with taffeta (*heremzi*), and the yoke panel was normally of
red and yellow striped *atlas* satin.

The *jillayeh* was defined as the 'chief' (*shaykh al-thob*) of the Beit
Dajan dress hierarchy, because of its more costly indigo-dyed
fabric, its lavish patchwork embellishments and its starring role at
the wedding, as the dress worn by the bride for her 'going out'
ceremony when she appeared in public for the first time as a
married woman.

Jillayehs and *thobs* each came in two versions or sub-types, called
'big' and 'small'. The full set of Beit Dajan-style dresses at this
period therefore comprised:
– a 'big *jillayeh*' (*jillayeh kabireh*);
– a 'small *jillayeh*' (*jillayeh saghireh*);
– a 'big white *thob*' (*thob al-abiyad al-kabireh*);
– a 'small white *thob*' (*thob al-abiyad al-saghireh*).
These terms bear no relation to the size of the dresses, but derive
from the embroidery on the back skirt panel (*shinyar*), which
functioned as a kind of name-tag or identification mark for the
whole dress. (This was first revealed during research when a group
of Beit Dajan women were invited to identify the sub-types of
various dresses from their village; their immediate reaction was to
turn the dresses over, and examine their *shinyars*.)

The back skirt panel on the 'big' version of each type of dress is
called 'the panel of solid embroidery' (*shinyar binaqleh talis*) (because
the embroidery completely conceals the fabric), and that on the
'small' version 'the necklace panel' (*shinyar qelayed*) (because certain
motifs are strung together like ornaments on a necklace). The terms
for these two contrasting types of back skirt panel are often used to
refer to the whole dress. For example women often refer to 'the big
white dress' as the *thob binaqleh* for short.

The sub-types of *jillayehs* and *thobs* are not only identified by their
shinyars, but are also ranked by them, the 'big' versions being
superior to the 'small' because they required greater amounts of
embroidery silk, and more of a girl's time, to execute.

Possibly because the *shinyar* had this important classificatory
function, and stood for the whole dress, it was more resistant to
change than other embroidered sections. This is also the case in
other areas of southern Palestine, and suggests the possibility of a
common embroidery 'grammar'.

The full weight of the *shinyar's* significance in the Beit Dajan
costume language was amply conveyed by one woman when I
asked why it was so important. The astonished reply was 'a *shinyar*
is a *shinyar*!', as though I had failed to learn a fundamental fact of life
(as indeed I had). And when asked why the *shinyar* was not at the
front where it would be more visible, she intoned 'from the day the
world was created the *shinyar* was behind!'[28]

213

The classification and ranking of dresses served the purpose of conspicuous display by facilitating the assessment of the size and quality of each woman's collection. It was essential that brides have a *jillayeh* in their trousseaus to wear for the 'going out' ceremony, but it could be either the 'big' or the 'small' version, or she could have both; and 'the small white dress' was an optional extra, the possession of which indicated even greater financial resources. (The remaining dress, the 'big white dress', was presented by the groom in the *kisweh*.)

The bride therefore prepared a minimum of one and a maximum of three dresses for her trousseau at this period, depending on her father's means, and her spare time:
– a 'big' *jillayeh*;
– a 'small' *jillayeh*;
– a 'small' white dress (*thob al-abiyad al-saghir*).

The size and quality of her collection after marriage was likewise determined by her husband's means, and how heavy her workload was. If she entered marriage with only one or two festive dresses in her trousseau, she might or might not be able to add any missing dresses.

Village identity

The most striking embroidery pattern on early festive dresses is the bold repeat-pattern of triangles and upside-down trees, called 'pockets and cypress trees' (*jiyab u srau*), on the skirt sides. Variations on this pattern were typical of the Jaffa region at this period, and no doubt gave the villages which shared it a sense of regional identity; but for the older Beit Dajan women, who now boast the pattern was 'theirs', it was primarily an expression of village identity and pride in the excellence of Beit Dajan embroidery. When asked whether other villages could embroider as well as hers, a Beit Dajan woman replied fiercely: 'Never! Never! Not a single village embroidered as well as ours, or better. They didn't know our designs. They didn't put the pockets and cypress trees!'

Sexual identity

The opening at the front of the skirt (called *slah al-jillayeh*, the 'armour' or 'weapon' of the *jillayeh*), non-functional since it was joined at the hem and only extended to the waist, was an overt sexual symbol. Women describe the opening with its patchwork decoration as 'a picture of a woman' (*rasmet al-hurmah, taswiret al-hurmah*), and as having 'a double meaning', or give more explicit explanations. The villagers' strict code of sexual behaviour did not impose a corresponding reticence about sex as a subject of public concern and celebration, and it was proper and acceptable, until the early 1920s, for this important subject to be depicted in costume.

Back skirt panel (*shinyar*) 'of solid embroidery' (*binaqleh talis*) on a 'big' *jillayeh*, circa 1920.
Collection: Widad Kawar

**'Necklace' back skirt panel (*shinyar qelayed*)
on a 'small' *jillayeh*, circa 1920.**
The 'necklace' is the first row of small, upside-
down trees suspended between triangles.
Museum of Mankind: 1968 AS4 31

Detail from the leg of a pair of pants (sirwal), Beit Dajan, 1930s.
Cotton material with machine embroidery imitating couching.
Collection: Widad Kawar

Changes in Beit Dajan-style dresses: 1920s–1930s

The demise of the *jillayeh*

Between the 1920s and early 1930s, radical changes took place in the Beit Dajan dress system, the most striking of which was that *jillayehs* went out of fashion. Beit Dajan women attribute this to the changed outlook of village men after the First World War. When they returned to the village from fighting in the Turkish army 'they began to differentiate between traditions which were shameful (*'ayb*) and those which were not. It was men's attitudes which changed, not women's'. As one woman put it, 'You only had to look to understand the meaning of the *slah* – so it became shameful (*'ayb*)'.

Men apparently saw the front opening (*slah*) in the skirt of the *jillayeh* with new eyes, initially as a result of their experiences in the army, with pressure for more modest dress increasing on their return because of greater contact between the villagers and the outside world. Women, repository of family honour, were increasingly exposed to the view of male strangers from outside their village cluster, and their reputations had to be protected by more modest dress. For similar reasons, women began to wear ankle-length black pants (*sirwal*) beneath their dresses at this period.

Women portray the discarding of the *jillayeh* as an advance from innocence to sophistication: 'We stopped wearing the opening in the *jillayeh* because the world developed', said one old lady. 'Long ago people were simpler and trusting, then they changed. Every generation gets more enlightened', explained another.

So strong were the forces of change that even Sheikh Yusef's daughters failed to withstand them; they sewed up the openings of their *jillayehs* and patched them with velvet 'so that from a distance they would still look like openings', but though they paraded their dresses at feasts and weddings, their modifications failed to catch on.

The *jillayeh* therefore disappeared from the bridal trousseau during the early 1920s, though it continued to be worn by older women who already owned it, their maturity and secure roles as wives and mothers probably diluting its impact, or increasing their resistance to male pressure.

With the disappearance of the *jillayeh*, only dresses in the *thob* style remained; these retained the same basic shape and arrangement of embroidery, but they increased in number, and major changes took place in their colour schemes and embroidery patterns.

Classification and ranking

The new generation of dresses which had developed by the early 1930s were classified into three principal types, named and ranked as follows:
– Na'ani dresses (*thob al-Na'ani*);
– 'moon' dresses (*thob abu qmar*);
– 'lamp' dresses (*thob al-fanayir*).

Above **The 'moon' (*qmar*) pattern.**
This appeared above the 'solid' panel (*shinyar binaqleh talis*) of the 'big' dresses of circa 1920, but then had no classificatory significance.

Right **The back skirt panel (*shinyar*) of a Na'ani dress (*thob al-Na'ani*), 1930s.**
Note how the 'necklace' of the older 'necklace' *shinyar* has been replaced by a recently-introduced copy-book pattern.
Collection: Widad Kawar

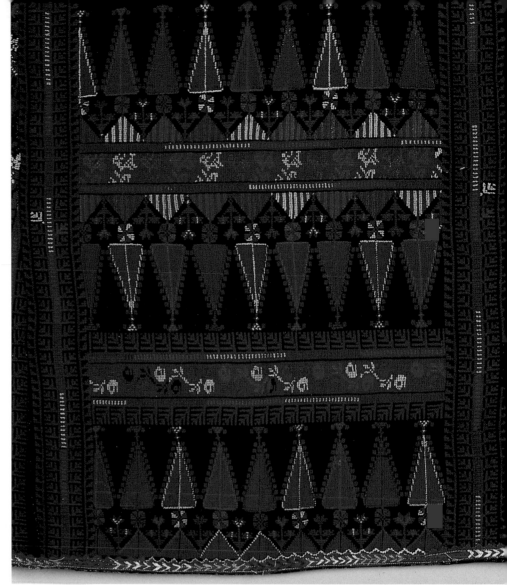

Above **The 'lamp' (*fanayir*) pattern.**

Right **The 'lamp' *shinyar.***
The 'lamp' pattern appears in the same position (below the first row of trees) as the 'necklace' on the earlier panels, and as the 'moon' pattern on 'moon' *shinyars*.

Above **A white Naʻani dress, Beit Dajan, early 1930s.**
Museum of Mankind: 1969 AS8 19

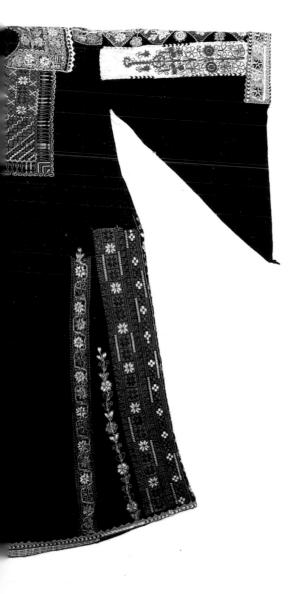

Below **A 'lamp' dress (*thob al-fanayir*), Beit Dajan, 1930s.**
Note the difference in the number of the narrow vertical bands of embroidery (*lohah*) on the sides of the skirt, and in the quantity of couching, between this dress and the Na'ani dresses opposite and on page 203. (Each *lohah* comprises a 'branch' of variable motifs bordered by the 'feather' motif).
Museum of Mankind: 1969 AS8 18

Because all three of the main types of dress were *thobs*, they could not be distinguished by their cut. Nor, as there were three, could they be distinguished or ranked by the binary opposition black/white with its useful intrinsic inequality. This classification problem was solved by elevating the *shinyar* to be the primary defining feature of the dresses.

To accommodate the need to distinguish between an increased number of dress types, the embroidery on *shinyars* changed. The panel 'of solid embroidery' (*binaqleh talis*), which had defined the 'big' versions of the older dresses, disappeared, and the 'necklace' panel (*shinyar al-qelayed*), which had defined the 'small' versions, also disappeared in name, while its basic structure of horizontal rows of motifs was modified to make several alternative types of panel.

The Na'ani *shinyar* is similar to the 'necklace *shinyar*' of the 'small' versions of the earlier dresses, having rows of horizontal motifs prominent among which are 'cypress trees'. The *shinyars* on the other two main types of dress have a similar format, the 'necklace' being replaced in one *shinyar* by a row of motifs called 'moons' (*qmar*), and in the other by 'lamps' (*fanayir*). Each *shinyar* is therefore named after one of its embroidery motifs, and each type of dress is named after its *shinyar*.

These new *shinyars* were more significant as labels or markers, and less intrinsically important for ranking the dresses, than the earlier ones; none used significantly more embroidery silk than the others. Instead the superiority of the Na'ani dress was marked by its having three or more panels (*lohah*) of embroidery on the skirt, the other dresses having only two, and by its richer and more elaborate embellishment with Bethlehem-style couching.[29]

Another radical change in the dress system of this later period is that festive *thobs* could now be black, which they had never been before, as well as white. This made fabric colour available for the classification of each new type of dress into two sub-types. Thus the Na'ani, 'moon' and 'lamp' dresses could be white *or* black, the latter being superior to white as before. Only the white versions tend to be described as such, a dress being assumed to be black by default.

Black and white dresses were further distinguished by their yokes. The yoke of red and yellow striped *atlas* disappeared with the *jillayeh*, and was replaced by a red velvet yoke on black dresses, and blue velvet on white dresses. With the adoption of these new luxury materials, the red and yellow striped satin *atlas* ceased to be used for the *jillayeh* yoke. This meant the disappearance of another sexual symbol from women's dress (as will become clear in the following chapter).

There was a further, tertiary level of classification in the new dress system: both the black and white versions of each type of dress were subdivided into two sub-types, classified according to whether they had full or 'half' versions of their *shinyars*. 'Half' *shinyars* were simply smaller versions of the Na'ani, 'moon' and 'lamp' *shinyars*, with one or more horizontal rows omitted. The dresses also had less embroidery on their sides. As before, these dresses were named after their back panels, for example 'the half Naʿani dress' (*thob nuss shinyar al-Naʿani*). So dress ranking was, as before, expressed in a size idiom: full/half instead of big/small.

'Half' *shinyar* dresses, in contrast to the others, were not festive but everyday working dresses; in contrast to festive dresses, they had tight sleeves and were without tasselled ties at the neck. For such dresses to be decorated with more than token embroidery was an innovation which reflected both increased prosperity and the reduction of the dirtier kinds of women's work in the fields and orchards.

To summarise, the named dresses at this later period were as follows:
– 'Naʿani' dress: full and 'half' versions, each in black and white;
– 'moon' dress: full and 'half' versions, each in black and white;
– 'lamp' dress: full and 'half' versions, each in black and white.

Between the early 1920s and the mid 1930s, then, the number of named dresses in the Beit Dajan dress system increased from four to twelve, and the hierarchy became more elaborate, with three levels of ranking.

With this change, the structure became more extensible. At the early period, the system only allowed binary classification at each of two levels, so was limited in size. At the later period, however, the system had the potential to extend indefinitely because the first order classification was based on individually named dresses, not on the contrast between dark *jillayehs* and white *thobs*. The changed structure of the dress system therefore facilitated its expansion, as well as the differentiation and evaluation of its constituent dresses.

This transformation of the dress system mirrored social and economic change. As people became more widely differentiated, so too did the dress system. And, as disposable income increased, the number of dresses in the system also increased, and their ornamentation became more ostentatious and expensive. At the same time, the aspects of costume which had 'naively' and safely expressed aspects of female sexuality when the village was more insulated from the potentially critical or dangerous gaze of strangers and foreigners, disappeared.

The Naʿani dress

The dress which replaced the *jillayeh* as 'chief' or 'leader' of dresses (*shaykh al-thob*) at the summit of the new Beit Dajan dress hierarchy, as the principal trousseau dress and as the dress worn for the 'going out' ceremony at the wedding, was the black Naʿani dress (with the full *shinyar*).

The dress was named after the village of Al-Naʿani to the southeast of Beit Dajan; a girl from Al-Naʿani married into Beit Dajan, and her dresses were so admired they named their chief dress after her village.

What they particularly admired was the way her back skirt panels (*shinyar*) were executed. Perhaps because of the importance of the *shinyar* in the classification of dresses, it was considered particularly important to plan and execute its motifs correctly, especially the

Above **A small *shinyar* worn by a Beit Dajan woman, Amman, 1978.**
Only the 'cypress trees', the most important motif on *shinyars*, has been retained on this modest panel, worn by an old woman.
Photo: Shelagh Weir

Facing page, above **Cypress trees in the orange groves near Beit Dagon, formerly Beit Dajan, 1978.**

Facing page, below **The 'airy-fairy' or 'dainty' pattern (ʿerq al-nafnuf).**

'cypress trees' (*saru*) which were supposed to be 'tall and straight, like the cypress trees in the orange groves' (where they were planted as windbreaks). And they had to be bordered by the right number of little squares, called 'seeds' (*bizr*), neatly done. 'Oh what awful cypress trees!', exclaimed one Beit Dajan connoisseur when shown a *shinyar* with only ten *bizrs* instead of thirteen. When the *shinyar* contained two horizontal rows of trees, one upside-down, they had to be equal in number. And the trees had to be mounted on a row of triangles (*shakhat*), otherwise 'they would look ugly – as though they were floating in the air'.

The Na'ani embroidery was admired because it achieved and even surpassed the highest aesthetic standards of Beit Dajan embroidery: its stitches were tiny and neat, its designs were well-organised, and its 'cypress tree' motifs were well-executed on the *shinyar*: 'They did such neat and systematic seeds (*bizr*), and they fitted more cypress trees into each row!'

Village pride and sense of superiority were preserved, however, despite copying from another village: 'We copied the dresses of Al-Na'ani, but we did our own versions', said one woman; another added 'We copied the *idea* of their *shinyar* and its rows of motifs, but we did it better'.

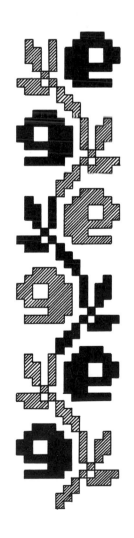

Outside influence on cross-stitch embroidery

On the new generation of dresses the distinctive 'pockets and cypress trees' pattern which had been a marker of regional identity and source of village pride on the earlier dresses, disappeared. Women say they discarded the pattern because 'it reminded us of the bad times under the Turks'; but the younger women were also eager for innovation and change.

The 'pockets and cypress trees' pattern was replaced by 'branches' (*'erq*) – parallel, vertical rows of repeated small motifs arranged in two or three panels (*lohah*) on each side of the skirt. These were similar to the vertical rows ('furrows', *mawaris*), which had bordered the 'pockets and cypress trees' pattern, but now they entirely covered the skirt sides.

The 'branches' style of embroidery included new motifs derived from European pattern books, and the Beit Dajan women called this new fashion *jabaliyeh* embroidery because the hill villages (*jabaliyeh*) were the first to get the pattern books and use the new motifs. One of the first new motifs to be imported was called 'the airy-fairy branch' (*'erq al-nafnuf*), a floral pattern quite different from the indigenous, predominantly geometric motifs. This was incorporated into the skirts, back panels and chest panels of the new dresses, and the chest panels were called 'hill panels' (*qabbeh jabaliyeh*) when they included the *'erq al-nafnuf*. The introduction of this popular motif was celebrated in the following little ditty:

look girls look!
she who brought the *nafnuf* branch
Ruqiyeh Abbas with the beautiful eyes!

However, Ruqiyeh Abbas (now Imm Ibrahim), a noted Beit Dajan

Right **The 'pockets and cypress trees' pattern (*jiyab u srau*) (left) and the 'mountain' (*jabaliyeh*) patterns which replaced it, including the 'airy-fairy' pattern (*'erq al-nafnuf*).**

Facing page **Chest panel of the Na'ani dress illustrated on page 203.**
This is the *qabbeh jabaliyeh* because of the inclusion of the *'erq al-nafnuf* motif. The yokes on 'black' dresses are always of red velvet. The *qasab* couching here is particularly dense and beautifully executed. Pearl neck ties (*bnud lulu*) with silk tassels are typical of Beit Dajan dresses, and were also used to tie the opening of the *jillayeh*.

embroideress, does not accept credit for this innovation; possibly she was just responsible for its popularity, for her embroidery was greatly admired.

The spread of 'branches' from the hills to the coast reflects both the greater mobility and mixing of villagers from different areas after the advent of motor transport, and the eagerness for innovation. One professional embroideress told how 'every bride begged me to put a new pattern on their dresses so they would be different from their friends, so I kept my eyes open for any outsiders in the village to copy new designs from'. The admission that these new patterns were copied from outsiders contradicts the frequent assertion that 'other villages copied from us, but *we* never copied from *them*'. However this is glossed over by the claim that although techniques or ideas may have originated elsewhere, they were modified locally to conform to local standards and give them a uniquely Beit Dajan character.

Apart from expressing the villagers' modernism, and contact with the wider world, 'branches' may have also caught on because of their greater intrinsic potential for incorporating new motifs. In contrast to the 'pockets and cypress trees', which are large, relatively immutable patterns, 'branches' are easily modified, one 'branch' of motifs simply being exchanged for another. At a period when new embroidery patterns were appearing in the markets, and it was prestigious to innovate, this could have been an important factor.

Detail from the skirt of the Na'ani dress illustrated on page 203.
Four new patterns introduced in the 1930s are shown, each bordered by 'feathers' (*rish*): three of these are, from left to right, 'the almond branch' (*'erq al-loz*), the 'airy-fairy branch' (*'erq al-nafnuf*) and 'stories' (*'alali*). The embroidery colours are typical of Beit Dajan at this period.

During the early 1930s new motifs copied from the hill villagers were increasingly incorporated into the 'branches' on the skirts of the Beit Dajan dresses; then, around 1936, the first teacher of the new school for girls, Sitt Naziha,[30] who taught embroidery among her subjects, brought the village its first pattern books. Sitt Naziha stressed how eager her first pupils were to learn the new designs, begging her to obtain pattern books, and visiting her even after they had left school to obtain new designs. She associated eagerness to learn and innovate in embroidery with a general longing for education and change: 'The girls of Beit Dajan were so keen to learn they had been attending the boys' school before I came; they were the keenest in the whole area.'

Which motifs were selected from the copy-books was probably relatively arbitrary, whereas the names given to them sometimes had significance. While the older patterns were named mainly after familiar things in the natural world, several new patterns were given names which reflect the material and economic changes taking place in the village at that time: for example 'storeys' (*'alali*), a reference to the new, prestigious two-storey houses; and 'sofas' (*kanabayat*), a new, European-influenced piece of furniture bought by the better-off at that time.

Village identity
With the disappearance of the 'pockets and cypress trees' pattern, the Beit Dajan women lost their main symbol of village identity; the 'branches' patterns could not replace it in significance because of

their admitted outside origin, and because the 'branches' were in a constant state of flux as new motifs were incorporated and old motifs lapsed.

The symbolic responsibility for proclaiming village identity therefore shifted onto another feature: the embroidery colours. The embroidery of this period was done in a distinctive combination of colours: a specific shade of dark maroon red, animated by discreet touches of green, orange and mauve (which they call 'blue', *azraq*). This shift was probably facilitated by the appearance on the market of DMC perlé cotton threads, which meant that 'the Beit Dajan shades' could be precisely identified by matching them against the numbers of the DMC threads. (Later, when floss silk became too expensive or difficult to obtain, DMC threads were used instead.)

The concept of the uniqueness of Beit Dajan embroidery colours is expressed in the saying 'all the Beit Dajan colours were on the spool (*milwah*)'. A dress can be otherwise identical with those of Beit Dajan, but if it has too high a proportion of pink, green or yellow, Beit Dajan women will disclaim it. If it conforms with Beit Dajan standards in other respects, they assume it was made on commission for another village with silks provided by the client. They say 'other villages were less fussy', but probably they developed their own distinctive colour codes.

It seems likely that colour became the main marker of regional or village identity throughout southern Palestine because of its stability and contrastive potential; the same pattern book motifs were widely diffused, and constantly changed as people strove for innovation, so they were less suitable for this purpose.

Bethlehem influence

From the late 1920s, Bethlehem influence on the costumes and embroidery of Beit Dajan greatly increased, as it did throughout the Jaffa area.

Beit Dajan women had long been familiar with Bethlehem couched embroidery through the trousseau dresses presented in the *kisweh* since before the First World War; also the *jillayeh* had, scattered among the cross-stitch patterns, small motifs (*shibrik*) which women claim were inspired by Bethlehem couching. However, it was not until the late 1920s that proper Bethlehem-style couching with silk (*rasheq*) and silver (*qasab*) cord appeared on the trousseau dresses embroidered in cross-stitch by the bride.

The most elaborate, beautiful and expensive *qasab* work was done on the best black Na'ani dress; the other trousseau dresses were also couched with *qasab* or *rasheq*, but usually more loosely and cheaply. Couched embroidery was also applied at this period to older dresses (including the *jillayehs* still being worn by older women), so it is now difficult to find any Beit Dajan-style dress without at least some couching.

This decorative innovation came about mainly through the influence of the Bethlehem embroideress, Maneh Hazbun, who went to live in Beit Dajan around 1920 when her brother Anton bought orange groves there. One year in the 1920s, their farm

The late Maneh Hazbun in Bethlehem in 1975, when she was in her nineties.
Photo: Shelagh Weir

Left **The sleeve of the Na'ani dress illustrated on page 203, viewed from above.**
The beautiful *qasab* and *rasheq* embroidery is arranged in five panels, and is densely executed. 'Moon' and 'lamp' dresses have less couching, and narrower embroidered sleeve panels. Note the small, square 'pip' (*nishan*) at the shoulder.

manager's wife asked Maneh to add some *qasab* work to the Na'ani dresses she was preparing for her daughter's trousseau. Maneh recalled: 'I agreed and made some *qasab* branches, and my mother said "don't leave them empty, fill them with colours", so I did.'

However, the fashion for couching swept the village after Maneh embroidered the trousseau dresses of Sheikh Yusef's daughter, Halimeh; this was so magnificent that everyone wanted to copy it; as ever, they also wanted to emulate the richest girl in the village.

These embellishments to local-style dresses were not normally 'home-made'; they were commissioned from Maneh, or from other specialists who learnt the technique from Maneh and started doing it professionally, some employing other women to help as demand grew. The commercial production of *rasheq* and *qasab* was sustained by the custom that grooms paid for both the materials and the work as part of the *kisweh*. This could amount to as much as P£10, or about half the total cost of the dress. The fee added to the expense and prestige of couching, already a status symbol because of its association with Bethlehem.

At first, no doubt, this couched decoration differentiated between those whose future husbands could afford to foot the bill and those who could not; but as incomes rose and it became a widespread fashion, finer distinctions and evaluations emerged. Loose, open couching was inferior to dense couching which needed more cord and work; imitation silver cord (which came on the market at this period) was inferior to that of real silver; and single cord couching was inferior to doubled. When one professional embroideress and connoisseur was shown a dress from this period shoddily couched with imitation silver cord, she immediately recognised it as the work of a particular woman and exclaimed: 'How silly of Amneh to spend all that time and money embroidering her best dress, then put imitation *qasab* (silver cord) on it! We *told* her to use real *qasab*!'

Status and display

The Na'ani dress was the supreme status symbol in the trousseaus and dress collections of the 1930s. It displayed the new wealth with its rich, finely-executed embroidery, especially its lavish embellishment with expensive silver *qasab* couching; and it witnessed to the widening networks of the Beit Dajan people, and their ability, as connoisseurs of excellent embroidery, to copy what was best from elsewhere.

The status connotations of the Na'ani dress are evident in the song, quoted at the beginning of this chapter, in which women, personified as Na'ani dresses, are associated with other symbols of wealth, progress and modernity: upper rooms, fashionable men driving cars, and wardrobes – the latter being also potent symbols of large clothing collections, for earlier, smaller clothing collections were kept in chests.

With the changes which took place in the trousseau, dresses became a more effective medium for displaying gradations of wealth; superiority of means, both time for embroidering and money for materials or for paying professional embroideresses, could be demonstrated by having a greater number of the higher-ranking dresses than other women, or if possible the total possible complement of twelve. The social pressure for large, impressive trousseaus, was graphically expressed by one woman when asked how brides decided which dresses to make: 'It wasn't a matter of choice – you *had* to have a black and a white Na'ani dress, or only one if you couldn't afford two. And you *had* to have two "moon" dresses, or only one if you couldn't have two. And you *had* to have one or two "lamp" dresses.' Of course this was true only to the extent that the bride's father could afford to pay for the materials or for the work to be farmed out – for, with the great increase in trousseau size, it became more difficult, even for the leisured and wealthy, to make every dress they wanted in time for the wedding.

Women who were caught up in the competitive necessity to keep abreast of fashion in the 1930s boast how busy it kept them: 'We embroidered while we waited to see the doctor. We embroidered at the well. We even embroidered at the orange groves while we waited for the water to fill the irrigation channels. Everyone was always embroidering!'

Since only one dress could be worn at a time, and prestige attached to quantity as well as quality, occasions were needed for displaying the size of one's collection. This was partly achieved by the public, communal activity of embroidering which was, as it had always been, a form of display. The henna night was another occasion for showing the trousseau dresses to female friends, and the various trousseau dresses were worn by the bride during the week of seclusion after the wedding night when she was visited by female relatives. In addition to these traditional occasions, new customs developed to enable girls and women to flaunt their enlarged dress collections.

On the evening of the first day of the wedding celebrations, after the bride had arrived at the house of the groom, it became customary for her to change into each of her trousseau dresses in turn, and sit on a high chair to be admired by the women of both families. Women also displayed their collections on religious feast days when they congregated in the mornings at the cemetery and in the afternoons in the orange groves to swing from the trees, and sing and dance the *dabkeh*. On these days of rejoicing they went home several times to change into different festive dresses.

Annual pilgrimages to religious shrines, attended in greater numbers than before at this period, provided further opportunity for dress displays. The pilgrimage to Nabi Rubin was especially important to the Beit Dajan women; they and their families often camped there for a week or more, and decked themselves out in different Beit Dajan-style festive dresses on different days. This display self-consciously proclaimed their identity, superiority and wealth to other villagers as well as to one another: 'Wherever we went in our dresses, they knew we were from Beit Dajan. Girls and women from Beit Dajan – Jaffa!'

Halimeh and Ruqiyeh, the daughters of Sheikh Yusef al-Dajani, in Hussein refugee camp, Amman, 1974.
Photo: Shelagh Weir

The *qasab* couching on the yoke of a white Na'ani dress, 1930s.
White dresses always had blue velvet yokes. The repeat curved pattern which borders the rows of rosettes is called 'waves' (*mlawlaw*), and became popular at this period. *Collection: Widad Kawar*

The headdress and jewellery

The increase in disposable income, and the desire for innovation, were also reflected in the changes which took place in brideprice, headdresses and jewellery.

The early 1920s

In the 1920s, when a labourer's daily wage was between 10 and 30 piastres, the Beit Dajan brideprice ranged from around P£50 to £90,[31] of which between £20 and £50, that is a quarter to over a half of the brideprice, was spent on jewellery and coins.[32]

With this the bride's father bought her some or all of the following items of jewellery, depending on what he could afford:
– glass bracelets (*ghwayshat*) made in Hebron;
– a pair of amber bracelets (*khsur*);
– a pair of blue bead bracelets (*kharaz azraq*);
– a choker with pendant chains and coins (*bughmeh mshanshaleh*);
– a necklace (*zaybaqah*) of three cylindrical containers (*khiyarah*, literally 'cucumbers') suspended on a chain;
– a pair of wide silver bracelets (*asawir 'iradh*);
– four narrow silver bracelets with a twisted pattern (*mabrumeh*);
– finger rings (*khawatim*);
– a chin-chain (*iznaq*) for suspending from the headdress, with a pendant high value coin, often of gold (*mkhammasiyeh* or *ftireh*[33]);
– Maria Theresa dollars and other silver coins for attaching to her bonnet (*smadeh*).
Rich men also bought their daughters the extra headdress components, the horseshoe-shaped *saffeh* and the *shakkeh* forehead band, but most borrowed them from within the kin-group (*hamuleh*) for wearing during the wedding celebrations.

With the exception of the beads and glass bracelets, the gold coin of the *iznaq*, and the coins of the (usually borrowed) *shakkeh* (which sometimes included gold), the jewellery and coins most women owned at this period were all made from silver.

The 1930s

The social pressure to spend and display wealth in connection with marriage, and on the person of women, drove up the brideprice and expenditure on jewellery as economic conditions improved and disposable wealth increased. By the early 1930s, the brideprice had risen to between P£80 and £150, and at least £50 and often much more was spent on the bridal jewellery.

The inflation in brideprice, and the desire for modernity and fashions with a foreign flavour, were reflected in radical changes in headdresses and jewellery; the *smadeh* with its coins, the other headdress ornaments (the *saffeh* and *shakkeh*) and silver jewellery, all went out of fashion, and were replaced by items which continued to fulfil the dual functions of modesty and display, while accommodating the desire to demonstrate increased expenditure.

THE HEADDRESS The *smadeh* became less fashionable around 1935, and was replaced by a cap of crocheted brown or blue cotton

A simple *zaybaqah* necklace with 'cucumbers' (*khiyarah*).
Museum of Mankind: 1966 AS1 354

Above **Halimeh Jabr of Beit Dajan in Nablus, 1978.**
She is wearing the gold *ftireh* coin attached to the chin-chain
(*iznaq*) of her headdress (*smadeh*). *Photo: Shelagh Weir*

Above right **A Beit Dajan woman in Amman, 1969.**
She is wearing a horseshoe-shaped row of coins (*saffeh*) on her
headdress (*smadeh*). *Photo: Shelagh Weir*

Right **Bracelets (*mabrumeh*) of twisted and plaited silver.**
Collection: Widad Kawar and Museum of Mankind 1971 AS1 91B

**The 'bead net' cap (*shabakat al-kharaz*),
1930s.**
The small silver coins are a faint echo of the
heavy coin decoration of the *smadehs* which
this style of cap partially replaced. *Museum of
Mankind: 1971 AS1 29*

decorated with small glass beads, 'the bead net' (*shabakat al-kharaz*). This innovation came about as a result of the opening of the first school for girls. This event increased the feeling of change and progress already in the air, and its pupils, the first girls in the village to receive a formal education, regarded themselves as more modern and advanced than the older women. In this spirit they rejected the *smadeh* as old-fashioned, and cast about for a more 'modern' alternative to cover their heads and preserve their modesty.

The first solution was to wear European hair-nets then on sale in the shops, but these were rejected 'because they did not conceal the hair well enough'. About this time the craft of crocheting had spread in southern Palestine through the influence of English teachers and religious institutions, and had been adopted by village women for making gloves to create henna patterns, by a kind of resist technique, on the hands of brides. Using the same technique, the girls took thick cotton yarn and crocheted thicker, more acceptable versions of hair-nets.

Gradually many women copied the fashion of the teenage girls and put aside their *smadehs*, but others, especially the more conservative older women, kept on wearing them. Some were afraid of the headaches they would get if they removed the weight of the coins (girls gave the fear of headaches as additional justification for *not* wearing the *smadeh*); others disapproved of the radical break

Beit Dajan woman in a refugee camp in Gaza, 1978.
She is wearing the *mshakhleh* gold necklace, and the *zunnar maqruneh* girdle which has remained fashionable among Beit Dajan women for over sixty years. Women past the menopause wear white dresses with simple embroidery. *Photo: Shelagh Weir*

with tradition 'that fashion began with *schoolgirls*, and imagine, married women put aside their *smadehs* too!'.

The decision to discard the *smadeh* was no light matter, and some women felt obliged to obtain the sanction of men, some of whom condoned and even encouraged the change. One man, who disliked the cold hard coins, begged his wife to remove her *smadeh* at night, saying 'may God break the head of whoever made this hat!'; so she wore a scarf instead, but continued to wear the *smadeh* during the day. Another man, with 'advanced' ideas through working outside the village as a driver, asked his wife to stop wearing the *smadeh* because it was 'old-fashioned'. Uncertain of the propriety of doing so, she consulted her brother, a religious sheikh; he assured her it was all right to stop wearing it 'because nowhere in the Koran was it written that a woman had to wear a *smadeh*'. Later, when her husband built a new house, she sold her *smadeh* to help with the expenses.

JEWELLERY During the 1920s, the better-off began to wear gold jewellery instead of silver. The first to sport gold were the wife and daughters of wealthy Sheikh Yusef. His wife is said to have sewn five gold coins onto the shoulders of her dress, and his daughters wore nine Turkish gold coins (*osmanliyeh*) as a necklace, and had gold coins on the tasselled ties (*bnud*) which closed the opening (*slah*) of their *jillayehs*. Later, when *jillayehs* went out of fashion, they attached a large gold coin (*mkhammasiyeh*) to small shoulder patches on their Na'ani dresses. These patches, called 'pips' (*nishan*), which were attached to all Beit Dajan-style dresses in the 1930s, were interesting miniature status symbols; they were made from luxury materials, velvet decorated with a *qasab* rosette, and were imitations of the pips, symbols of military rank, on the uniforms of British soldiers.

Others were not wealthy enough for such ostentation, but most, except the poor, were able to substitute some gold jewellery for silver during the 1920s – some made from Turkish or British gold coins, other pieces manufactured and imported from abroad.

By the early 1930s, brides were therefore presented with some or all of the following jewellery, according to the size of their bride-prices, and their fathers' and husbands' means:
– one or two large gold coins (*ftireh* and *mkhammasiyeh*), for attaching to the chin chain of their *smadehs*, if they still wore them, and to the chest-panels of their dresses (as in the song below). (Halimeh, Sheikh Yusef's daughter, who married in 1936, claims to have had seven *mkhammasiyeh* coins);
– a 'gold necklace' (*qiladeh dhahab*) of between 20 and 40 Turkish gold coins (*osmanliyeh*) or British gold sovereigns sewn onto a black ribbon. (Halimeh claims to have had 72 of these coins in her dowry);
– a pair of twisted gold 'snake' bracelets with small gold coins (*asawir dhahab hayayiyeh*) (about P£15 each);
– a gold necklace (*mshakhleh*) (about £8, rising to £30 by 1940);
– gold coin earrings (about £1.5);
– gold finger rings.

Imm Ibrahim of Beit Dajan in Amman, 1974.
She is wearing the *zunnar kashmir* below her
waist, in the Beit Dajan style. *Photo: Shelagh Weir*

In the following songs, the splendour and value of this new
generation of jewellery is equated with the high social worth of
women (who wore it) and men (who paid for it):

We Dajani women are like coins
of choicest, purest gold
We Dajani women have no tarnished reputations
Let the rider dismount from his horse
Oh Beit Dajan girl! Oh one hundred per cent perfect!
Walk with honour, and hold your head high!

We are the gold on the chest panel
you can count our men
if it comes to a fight
our men will protect us
We are the gold on the head
our men are good marksmen
if it comes to a feud
our men will defend us.

With the adoption of gold jewellery, it became even less common
for brides to own their own ceremonial headdress components
(*shakkeh* and *saffeh*).

The substitution of gold jewellery for silver was accompanied by
changes in the way a bride received her jewellery. Increasingly, a
girl's jewellery was given to her directly by the groom, instead of by
her father (using the money received from the groom as
brideprice). At the same time, the occasions on which the groom
was expected to give his fiancée gold jewellery proliferated.

During the engagement period the groom had previously made
modest gifts to his betrothed on formal visits called *nafakah*; this
period was now extended, and he was expected to give a far more
valuable present, for example a gold bangle, on each occasion. One
such occasion, when girls expected to receive a pair of gold
bracelets, was called *khashet al-dar*. Men were also expected to give
their fiancées presents of gold on special occasions, such as the
annual pilgrimage to the shrine of Nabi Rubin, and on 'egg
Thursday' (*khamis al-baydhuh*) – the equivalent of Easter. Some
women admit they deliberately prolonged their engagements to
reap the maximum harvest from such occasions.

**Details of the two ceremonial girdles
presented in the *kisweh*.**
Above: the *zunnar maqruneh*, which older Beit
Dajan women still wear in the late 1980s as a
sign of their regional origins; below: the
zunnar kashmir, worn widely in southern
Palestine in the Mandate period, and by older
women up to the 1980s. *Museum of Mankind: 1977
AS10 3; 1971 AS1 124*

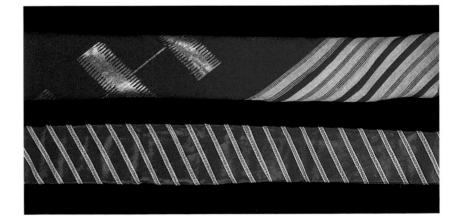

The *shunbar asmar* ceremonial veil.
Black silk crepe with a panel (*naqleh*) of silk
embroidery, band with fringe (*dikkeh*) and
tassels (*sharashib*). In the 1920s the bride wore
this veil with the *jillayeh* for the 'going out'
ceremony at the end of the wedding week.
Collection: Widad Kawar

The *kisweh*

The changes which took place in the *kisweh*, like those in the rest of the trousseau, also reflected the increase in disposable wealth, the urge for innovation, and the desire and financial ability to imitate prestigious Bethlehem-style couching.

The early 1920s

In the early 1920s, the groom was obliged to present the bride with the following articles in the *kisweh*:

– the 'big white dress' (*thob al-abiyad al-kabir*). This was embroidered by one of the groom's female relatives, and was the only Beit Dajan-style item in the *kisweh*. In the context of the trousseau, this dress balanced the principal dress, the *jillayeh*, provided by the bride. They say 'the big white dress was opposite to (*nid*) the *jillayeh*'.

– the materials for making three Bethlehem-style dresses: *thob malak*, *thob ikhdari* and *thob jiljileh*. These were ranked in the order given, and in the context of the trousseau, the *malak* dress was equivalent in status to the 'big white dress' and the *jillayeh*.

– two girdles: *zunnar maqruneh* and *zunnar kashmir*. These were ranked in the order given, the *maqruneh*s being further differentiated by the 'teeth' in their brocade 'combs'.[34]

– materials for two ceremonial head-veils: *shunbar asmar* of black crepe with red embroidery and fringe; *shunbar ahmar* of plain red crepe.

In addition the groom provided or paid for the following prior to the wedding:

– a length of red and yellow striped satin (*atlas*), for making into a coat (*kiber*) for the bride to wear on the wedding day.

– a length of white cotton material (*bayt al-sham*), for making into an underdress, also for the wedding day.

– the satin (*atlas*) and taffeta (*heremzi*) for the patchwork decoration on the *jillayeh*, and the fee for having it applied.

In contrast to the bride's contribution to the trousseau, which comprised home-made dresses in the style of the village, the *kisweh* comprised articles of non-village origin purchased in the market – with the notable exception of the 'big white dress'. This contrast reflected men's greater identification with the outside world, their involvement in the cash economy, and the status-conferring aspect of earning money and having disposable income. The bride's contribution, on the other hand, reflected women's greater identification with, and confinement to, the village, and a female value system in which status and prestige derived from women's investment of time and energy in creative work.

The 1930s

DRESSES By around 1930 the groom no longer provided the 'big white dress', the only garment in the *kisweh* which had been in the local, Beit Dajan style. This dress with its 'pockets and cypress trees' on the skirt, and its back panel (*shinyar*) of solid embroidery, went out of fashion, like the *jillayeh*, during the 1920s, but unlike the *jillayeh*, was not replaced in the trousseau by a locally-made

Detail of the *zunnar maqruneh* illustrated on page 234.
This girdle came in different qualities and prices according to the number of teeth in its brocade 'combs' (*mushut*).

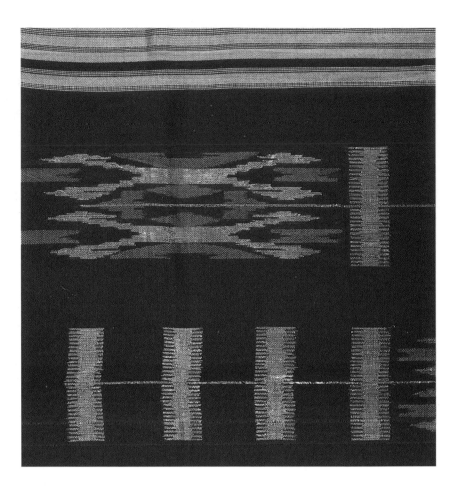

dress with the new 'branches' embroidery. By the 1930s, therefore, no articles of village origin remained in the *kisweh*, reflecting the groom's increased identification with the outside world.

Around 1935, a fashionable new dress, 'the blue velvet dress' (*thob mukhmal azraq*), similar in style to the three Bethlehem-style dresses, became an obligatory *kisweh* garment. The idea for this is said to have developed from an earlier innovation of the late 1920s: a simple blue velvet underdress (*fustan mukhmal*) which replaced the white cotton underdress (*bayt al-sham*) worn by the bride during the procession from her father's to her husband's house on the wedding day. The 'blue velvet dress' (*thob mukhmal*) may have caused the demise of the lowest ranking of the three Bethlehem-style dresses in the *kisweh*, the *thob jiljileh*, which disappeared from *kiswehs* at this time.

A similar dress of red velvet also had a brief life in fashion, but was soon discarded 'because the blue provided a better contrast to the *malak* dress' (which was predominantly red). Contrast was always important to make the size of collections obvious.

The introduction of the blue velvet dress coincided with an increase in Bethlehem-type couching on the *thob malak* and *thob ikhdari*, as happened on the village-style dresses. Their chest panels continued to be imported from Bethlehem, but the couching applied to the skirt, sleeves and yokes of dresses was increasingly done by specialists in Beit Dajan. Later they also began to make their own couched chest panels, in competition with Bethlehem products.

Although the number of dresses contributed by the groom remained the same, at first, and was then reduced from three to two, their combined value increased because of the greater expense of imported velvet, and their more lavish *qasab* and *rasheq* couching.[35]

VEILS The other main change in the *kisweh* was the disappearance of both the red and black veils. The red veil (*shunbar ahmar*), for covering the bride's face during the wedding procession, was

The 'blue-velvet dress' (*thob mukhmal azraq*). This dress was sometimes called 'the almond velvet' (*mukhmal abu lozi*) after the almond-shaped motifs woven into the selvedge by the (German) manufacturer. The chest panel was embroidered in Bethlehem, and the yoke panel, the taffeta (*heremzi*) sleeve and skirt inserts, and the vertical 'branches' on the front and back of the skirt, were embroidered with Bethlehem-style couching by Beit Dajan specialists. *Collection: Widad Kawar*

replaced, first by a muslin scarf (*mandil*) printed with flowers – a fashion which came in with the blue velvet underdress (*fustan mukhmal*) she wore on the same occasion. Then during the 1930s, both these garments were replaced by an all-white European-style wedding outfit (*badleh baydhah*).

The black veil (*shunbar asmar*) was replaced in the *kisweh* by one or two European-manufactured rayon veils (*lefhah*), in pink or maroon. Just as the black *shunbar* had been the ceremonial veil for wearing with the *jillayeh*, the chief dress of the trousseau in the early 1920s, so the maroon *lefhah* went with the dress which replaced the *jillayeh*: the 'black' Na'ani dress. The pink *lefhah* was worn with the white Na'ani dresses.

The daughters of Sheikh Yusef claim responsibility for introducing the *lefhah* to the village. They say they spotted it in a textile shop in Jaffa, and when the other women saw them wearing it 'they all wanted one', and the fashion swept the village. However the veil undoubtedly caught on because of its prestige as a luxury article of foreign origin, and it was widely popular in southern Palestine.

These changes resulted in the mid-1930s in a *kisweh* which consisted of:
– three dresses with Bethlehem-style embroidery: *thob malak* and *thob mukhmal* (ranked equally), and *thob ikhdari*;
– one or two veils (*lefhah*), one maroon, one pink;
– two girdles: *zunnar maqruneh* and *zunnar kashmir*.
The groom was also obliged to pay for the addition of velvet yokes and Bethlehem-style couching (*qasab* or *rasheq*) to the Na'ani and other dresses provided by the bride. This replaced his previous obligation to pay for patchwork on the *jillayeh*, but was more expensive in materials and labour.[36] Women therefore continued to ensure that their future husbands financed striking embellishments on their home-made dresses.

Facing page, above **Chest panel on a Beit Dajan *malak* dress, 1930s or 1940s.**
The Bethlehem-style couching was done by specialists in Beit Dajan. *Collection: Widad Kawar*

Facing page, below **Side skirt panel on the same dress as above.**

Left **Rayon veils (*lefhah*), 1930s or 1940s.**
These (or just the maroon one) replaced the *shunbar* in the *kisweh* in the 1930s. The bride wore the maroon veil with the 'black' Na'ani dress for the 'going out' ceremony. *Museum of Mankind: 1971 AS2 125, 126*

6 Wedding Rituals in Beit Dajan

Oh daughters of the wedding
trail your *jillayehs*
a wedding is here again
may it happen to your families!
Oh daughters of the wedding
trail your *shunbars*
a wedding is here again
may it happen to your sisters!
Oh daughters of the wedding
trail your *malakehs*
a wedding is here again
may it happen to your loved ones!
Oh daughters of the wedding
Oh mothers of 'white dresses'
a wedding is here again
may it happen to every beloved!

Beit Dajan wedding song

Women taking gifts to a wedding, Gaza, 1978.
Photo: Shelagh Weir

At her wedding a girl was transformed from single to married status, and from girlhood to womanhood. Both these aspects of her transformation were reflected symbolically in costume.

The transformation of single girl into married woman took place in a sequence of ritual events which extended over a period of one or two weeks. These rituals marked stages in the departure from one social identity and arrival at the next, and were filled with statements about marriage and womanhood.

Wedding rituals are of prime interest here because these statements were repeatedly and pointedly made in the language of costume. Indeed, costume was one of the most important symbolic components of the wedding rituals in all villages. Costumes are mentioned in many of the songs which women sang during the celebrations; costumes and jewellery were the most important gifts exchanged at marriage, next to the brideprice; and the bride wore various garments during the rituals, all of which were loaded with significance. Costume was a language which always expressed key aspects of social identity, but never so fully or eloquently as during the wedding.

This will be illustrated by analysing the meaning of costume in the context of the wedding rituals of Beit Dajan in the early 1920s, the period when the old women interviewed married. The rituals of other southern Palestinian villages were similar, in essence, to those described here, though only those of Artas have been described in any detail. In the absence of any photographic record of Beit Dajan weddings, this chapter is illustrated by photographs showing similar customs in Artas and other villages.

The events of the wedding

The following is the sequence of formal and ritual events which normally took place at marriage in Beit Dajan in the early 1920s:

– the negotiations (*tulbeh*): meetings between the bride's father and the groom to negotiate the marriage transaction, at variable times before the wedding.

– the betrothal (*mlak*): the signing of the wedding-contract (*'aqd*) containing the terms agreed at the *tulbeh*, usually shortly after the *tulbeh*.

– the trousseau celebration (*zaffet al-kisweh*): the celebration of the groom's purchase of trousseau gifts for the bride, shortly before the wedding.

– the henna night (*laylat al-henna*): the preparation of the bride and her farewell to her friends on the night before the wedding.

– the wedding day (*yom al-'urs*): the procession of the bride from her father's house (*tal'at min dar abuha*) to that of the groom; the groom's feast and money ceremony (*zaffeh* and *nqut*).

– the wedding night (*laylat al-dakhleh*): the consummation of the marriage.

– the bride's money ceremony (*nqut*): the presentation of money to the bride the following morning.

– the 'going out to the well' (*tal'at al-bir*): the bride's emergence from a week's seclusion, and procession to the village well.

Previous page **Women going in procession and singing to celebrate a betrothal, Artas, 1925–31.** *Photo: Hilma Granqvist*

Men at a wedding in Artas, 1925–31.
The man on the right, the bride's paternal
uncle (*'amm*), had refused to allow the
departure of the bride until he received a coat.
Photo: Hilma Granqvist

The negotiations (*tulbeh*)

The *tulbeh* was a private meeting between the male heads of the two families to decide how much the groom or his father should pay in brideprice, and to specify the articles of clothing (or materials for making them) he should present to the bride and her relatives. Some of these clothing presents were obligatory, others open to negotiation.

The groom was obliged to make the *kisweh* presentation to the bride, and to buy clothing for the bride's mother and eldest maternal uncle (*khal*). It was important these obligatory gifts of clothing conformed with current village custom, and enquiries were made among recently-married men to find out what the groom should buy. Gifts of clothing to other relatives of the bride were negotiable. For example her father might press for gifts for her other maternal uncles, her paternal uncles (*'amm*) and her male cousins (*ibn 'amm*), and if this was agreed the brideprice was reduced accordingly.

By means of these agreements and negotiations certain key relationships were affirmed and strengthened, largely through the medium of gifts of costume. Costumes were the material symbols of the social ties which bound people together, and of the importance of the relationships they mediated.

The obligatory gifts to the bride's mother and maternal uncle were, respectively, a heavily-embroidered 'white dress' (*thob al-abiyadh*), and a white silk coat (*qumbaz*); these symbolised, by their high quality and the fact that they were not voluntary, the permanent and absolute importance of these two persons in the bride's past and future life. Conversely, the negotiability of the gifts to the bride's other relatives meant that the continuing strength of her relationships with them was less automatic and more dependent on reaffirmation through gifts.

By his insistence that the bride's uncles or cousins receive gifts from the groom, the bride's father drew the groom into the bride's kinship network, and ensured the continuing support of her male relatives after she married. For the receipt of a gift implied the acceptance of a lifelong commitment to their female relative. This was symbolically expressed for the first time at the *nqut* ceremony on the morning after the wedding night, when all the male relatives of the bride who had received gifts from the groom were obliged to present her with a gift of money. Thereafter they presented her with gifts and visited her on every feast day, and whenever she gave birth, throughout her life.

The *kisweh* was much the most complex and expensive of the costume presents made at marriage, and its purchase and presentation were surrounded by public celebrations. For the trousseau, together with the brideprice, was far more significant than other gifts; it symbolised the establishment of a new, centrally important relationship, and, it was fervently hoped, the beginning of a new family.

Women singing to celebrate a betrothal, Artas, 1925–31.
They are on their way to the bride's village.
Photo: Hilma Granqvist

The betrothal (*mlak*)

The terms agreed at the *tulbeh* were recorded in a wedding contract (*'aqd*), formally signed on the betrothal day (*mlak*). After the families of the bride and groom had eaten a celebration lunch, provided by the groom's family but eaten at the bride's house, the groom, the groom's father and the bride's father, together with other male relatives as witnesses, gathered in the presence of a religious sheikh to sign the contract. Before this could take place, two members of the (all-male) gathering had to go to the bride to obtain her consent to the amount of her brideprice (*fayd*) and the contents of the groom's contribution (*kisweh*) to her trousseau. She was also asked for her formal approval of her father acting as her legal representative. The contract was then signed and became legally binding.

The signing of the wedding contract was a momentous and anxious occasion for the groom, for it irrevocably committed him to one of the two actions which were essential for the legitimisation of marriage, the presentation of the brideprice and *kisweh*, without the certainty that he could pull off the other, the consummation of the marriage on the wedding night. This insecurity was expressed in the fear and tension surrounding the contract-signing, and in the associated ritual. At the moment of signing the groom was believed to be especially vulnerable to being rendered impotent on the wedding night – a failure which would bring great shame to him and his family. This could be effected by anyone who wished him ill

Top **Women dancing at a wedding, Jerusalem area, 1926–35.**
Photo: Grace Crowfoot

Above **A bridegroom on his betrothal day, Artas, 1925–31.**
Note the white coat (*qumbaz*) he is wearing beneath his European-style jacket. The child may have signified the hope that the marriage would be fruitful. *Photo: Hilma Granqvist*

deliberately or accidentally clasping their hands, tying a knot in a piece of string or revealing the soles of their shoes. Small boys were therefore sent round the room to prevent this happening.

In addition to this important male *rite de passage*, another ritual took place on the betrothal day involving only women, and specially in honour of the groom's mother. At dusk, female relatives of the groom walked in procession to his mother's (and his) house, carrying torches (*mashu'il*) made from crossed sticks, with candles, oranges and orange branches attached, and singing as they went. In one of the songs for this ceremony, allusions to fine garments express admiration for the groom (personified as Sa'id):

I am singing for Sa'id
for his mother's sake
what a beautiful *ghabani* coat!
with such lovely sleeves!
I am singing for Sa'id
for his sisters' sake
how smart the groom's coat is!
well-fitting to his hands
were it not for you, dear precious one
we would not have come here
nor entered your house
and sung

The coat in the second line is a *qumbaz*, the tight-fitting long-sleeved village men's coat, which, for ceremonial occasions and for presentation purposes, was made of fine Syrian silks. The *qumbaz* in this song is made from white *ghabani* fabric, and the allusion to this white coat has significance in the light of the symbolism of another white coat on the wedding day.

Buying the *kisweh*

Once the brideprice was paid, the wedding could take place as soon as the groom had bought the *kisweh*, which involved an expedition by members of both families, but never the bride, to a trousseau merchant in Jaffa or Ramleh.

The *kisweh*-buying expedition usually included the groom, his close male relatives, his mother, the bride's mother, and often a female wedding specialist, called the *mashitah*, to provide expert advice on prices and what the *kisweh* should contain. If the cost came to more than the groom had anticipated, his relatives made up the difference.

The bride's relatives took part in the expedition to see she was not stinted of any article customarily included in the *kisweh* of her time. Often the contents of the *kisweh* were agreed at the same time as the brideprice was settled, but sometimes the two families would haggle in the shop about what should be bought.

In contrast with the preceding activities and transactions connected with arranging a marriage, which were private low-key affairs between the two families, the purchase of the *kisweh* was accompanied by a festive public ceremony, called 'the trousseau celebration' (*zaffet al-kisweh*), which joyfully heralded the imminent wedding.

Back in Beit Dajan, the women of both families and other village women gathered at the village well to sing and dance while they waited for the *kisweh* expedition to return. One of the songs boasts about two of the main *kisweh* garments:

God be with Abu Ibrahim
he has 'cut' for us *malak* dresses
Oh host of the *hamuleh*!
who makes all his sisters happy!
God is with Abu Ibrahim
he has cut for us *maqruneh* belts
Oh host of the *hamuleh*!
who makes all the loved ones happy!

The centrepiece of this merrymaking was a mock-bride (*zarafeh*) made by the groom's female relatives from a pitchfork (*midhrah*) with a piece of rolled cloth for the head and a cross-piece for arms, and dressed in similar clothes and jewellery to those the bride would wear on the wedding day.[1] The visual distraction of the *zarafeh* was intended to deflect the evil eye from the *kisweh*; it appeared again during the wedding, and also featured at circumcision ceremonies, which paralleled weddings as male rites of passage.

When at last the *kisweh* party with their bundles appeared on the horizon, the women advanced to meet them singing and trilling their welcome, led by a woman waving the *zarafeh* like a banner. The whole procession then filed through the village to the house of the groom. There the contents of the bundles were laid out on basketry trays (*tabaq*) for everyone to admire, and the groom's female relatives placed the trays on their heads and sang the

Above **The late Abu Subuh of Beit Dajan, Amman, 1970.**
Abu Subuh was famous for his songs and sense of fun, and was in great demand at wedding celebrations. *Photo: Shelagh Weir*

Above right **Two boys on horseback during their circumcision procession, Artas, 1925–31.**
On the left is a mock-bride (*zarafeh*), a pitchfork (*midhrah*) dressed up as a bride to avert the evil eye from the boys. The mock-bride has a pink face veil (because Artas was Qaysi), a white head veil, and a silver chin-chain (*iznaq*). Note the striped coats (*qumbaz*) of the boys, almost certainly of red and yellow striped *atlas* satin. *Photo: Hilma Granqvist*

Right **A bride in Ramallah, 1987.**
Possibly the doll is the modern equivalent of the *zarafeh*. *Photo: Shelagh Weir*

following song, celebrating the purchase of the *kisweh*, and praising the hospitality of the groom's father (personified as Abd).

The merchant has cut the cloth!
the merchant has cut the cloth!
a piece of good life
in your home, oh Abd
we will lay our mattresses and sleep.
The merchant has cut the cloth!
the merchant has cut the cloth!
a silver coin dress
in your home, oh Abd
life is so sweet!

The following day the *kisweh* was taken to the bride's home, and her mother and future mother-in-law took her for fittings to a village dressmaker. This was the bride's first direct involvement in the wedding preparations.

The henna night
The betrothal and trousseau celebrations mainly involved the groom's family; they marked the beginning of his change of status from single to married man, while joyfully and proudly displaying his family's intentions and generosity, and announcing their delight at the impending wedding.

Basketry tray (*tabaq*), Sinjil area.
Used for displaying the *kisweh*, for laying out meals, and as a wall decoration. At Beit Dajan weddings, the groom's female relatives danced with the *kisweh* displayed on such trays. *Museum of Mankind: 1968 AS12 34a*

There were no parallel celebrations prior to the wedding by the bride's family, for their pleasure at her marriage was tinged with sadness at her leaving them to live with her husband. This is reflected in the songs and activities of the henna night (*laylat al-henna*), preceding the wedding day. This was the first wedding ritual in which the bride took part, and like the betrothal ceremony for the groom, marked the first step in her change of status from single girl to married woman. However, whereas the essence of the groom's first step towards marriage was a binding financial agreement, the essence of hers was the parting from her family and friends, and the preparation for the wedding night. The betrothal ceremony was a rite of commitment, and the henna night was a rite of separation from one status and preparation for the next.

During the week before the wedding night the bride underwent various beautifying activities to enhance her allure. A key figure in these preparations was the female wedding specialist, the *mashitah*. The literal meaning of *mashitah* is 'hairdresser', but she did far more than dress hair. Several days before the wedding, so her skin would not be red on the day, the *mashitah* removed all the bride's body hair. She also prepared a special bridal necklace (*qiladet al-qrunful*) from cloves softened in water, imitation pearls (*lulu*), coral (*murjan*) and coins (*wazari*). Similar, smaller necklaces were made for the bride's female relatives and friends who attended the henna night.

Right **Embroidered cushions from various parts of southern Palestine, British Mandate period.** *Museum of Mankind collection*

248

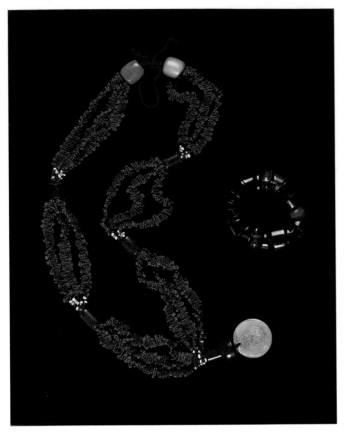 

The clove water was saved to bathe the bride on the wedding morning.

On the night before the wedding day, the bride's female relatives and friends gathered at her home for the application of henna, by the *mashitah*, to their hands, forearms, feet and legs. Special designs were reserved for the bride, similar to and with the same names as certain Beit Dajan embroidery patterns: 'palms' (*nakhleh*), 'arches' (*quwas*) and 'cypress trees' (*saru*). In other words, the bride was decorated like a dress.

All who attended the henna night were presented with a scarf (*mandil*) bought, like the clove necklaces, by the bride's father; in return they were expected to give the bride a money present at the *nqut* ceremony on the morning after the wedding night. A link of reciprocal gifts was therefore created to span the separation of the wedding. The bride's father also provided refreshments for the henna night. The groom's contribution was to pay for the *mashitah*'s services and for the henna. The bride's father thereby symbolically acknowledged the importance of her relationships with her female friends and relatives, and her desire that they should continue. Consistent with his concern for the success of the wedding night, the groom, for his part, took responsibility for her appearance.

The henna night was an occasion for girls and women to celebrate their companionship and lament the girl they were 'losing', while sharing in the elaborate preparation of the bride's body for the wedding night. Like the betrothal ceremony for the groom,

Above left **Clove necklace (*qiladet al-krunful*) and amber bracelet (*khsur*).**

Above right **A bedouin woman displaying the henna patterns on her hand, Negev desert, 1930s.**
Photo: Olga Tufnell

Facing page, above **The ceremonial version of the *kashmir* girdle (called *ishdad* in some areas).**
Red *atlas* fabric, and the fringed and tasselled band (*dikkeh*) had erotic significance. Old photographs show it tied in front of the dress, not at the side as here. *Collection: Church's Ministry Among the Jews*

Facing page, below **A kohl holder (*mukholeh*), Galilee, British Mandate period.**
The kohl (antimony) is in two small containers at each side, and is applied with the stick in the centre. The large padded holder, ornamented with red *atlas* fabric, coins, beads and floss silk, is entirely for decorative purposes. Kohl holders were often decorated with ostrich feathers (like the bride in the wedding procession). Beit Dajan brides danced for their husbands on the wedding night, holding a kohl holder. *H 30cm Museum of Mankind: 1968 AS5 7*

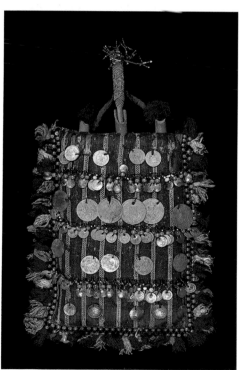

the ritual focused on relationships with the same sex, of such importance in this society, and on the central event of the wedding, the consummation – although the emphasis in the bride's case was on her desirability rather than her performance. These two principal aspects of the occasion are reflected in the following henna night songs, with key themes again symbolically expressed through costume. In this song, embroidering the panels for trousseau dresses represents the girls' long, close friendships.

we embroidered the side panels for such a long time
remember Halimeh when we were pals?
we embroidered the chest panels for such a long time
remember Halimeh when we were girls?

In the following song the bride appears as a young gazelle – a common metaphor in Palestinian poetry and song for female grace and beauty. She is pictured as tempting but elusive, being pursued and taken, and the song is clearly an oblique reference to the events of the wedding night.

what did you wear, little gazelle, on your henna night?
they clothed me in *atlas*, the clothing of kings.
what is this deer darting past our house?
his waist is dainty and his mouth drowned in honey
what is this deer which ran past our house?
his waist is dainty and girdled with *kashmir*
what is this deer which promises but escapes?
they laid nets and caught him
at the bottom of the valley

The coats of the second line are of *atlas* fabric (plural *atalis* in the song), striped red and yellow satin. In fact, the bride did not wear a coat of *atlas* fabric on the henna night, but it was an important garment in the wedding procession on the following day. The girdles of *kashmir* were also made from *atlas* fabric. This double reference to garments of *atlas* has a sexual significance to be explored below.

Other significant features of the song are the sexual inversion of the gazelle metaphor, a common device in Arab poetry, and the invocation of male authority figures – kings – to enhance the prestige of the coats and by association their female (portrayed as male) subject. As has been described, women's appropriation of status symbols from the male world is a common feature of their costume, and this is also the case in songs containing costume idioms.

The wedding day
On the wedding day the groom held a feast (*zaffet al-ʿaris*) for the male members of both families and other villagers. There was dancing and singing round the village well, and afterwards the groom was playfully beaten and goaded by his friends 'in order to arouse his desires'. He also received small money presents from his guests in a ceremony (*nqut*) similar to that which the bride would have the following morning.

The groom's *nqut* ceremony on the wedding day, Ramallah, 1900.
After a feast for the groom (*zaffet al-'aris*), his friends and relatives threw him presents of
coins. *Photo: Underwood and Underwood, Library of Congress*

The bridegroom (left) at his wedding-day celebrations, Ramallah, 1900.
Photo: Underwood and Underwood, Library of Congress

Meanwhile the bride was prepared for the evening wedding procession when she would be led on horseback through the village (or to a neighbouring village) to her new home. She was bathed in the clove-scented water which had been saved, and her eyes were lined with kohl. She was then dressed in special garments, some of which she would never wear again. These embodied symbolic statements about the bride's ritual status as she took part in the procession, and about her imminent transformation into a married woman.

Her undergarment was of white cotton (*bayt al-sham*) from the *kisweh*. This the bride or her mother had patched on the chest and cuffs with red silk appliqué (*tishrimeh*), probably symbolising the blood of defloration. The hem was left raw to ensure the bride would be fertile, and was only sewn up after she became pregnant.[2]

Over this dress she wore a long-sleeved man's coat in the *qumbaz/hidim* style called 'the *atlas*' after the satin from which it was made. This was the same material from which the 'coats of kings' and the *kashmir* girdle were made in the henna night song, and, though red striped yellow, was defined as 'red'. It was evident this coat had special significance from the way women referred to it. When describing the wedding procession, they would say in meaningful tones 'she wore the *atlas*', as westerners might say of a widow 'she dressed in black'; and they used the phrase 'she who wore the *atlas*' to refer to a bride, much as bishops are referred to as 'taking the purple'. So the fact that the *atlas* was a powerful symbol is explicit,

Above **A circumcision ceremony at the shrine of Nabi Rubin, British Mandate period.** The two small boys to be circumcised are seated beneath the umbrella on the back of the camel. The dark stripes of their red *atlas* coats can just be seen. *Photo: Matson Collection, Library of Congress*

Above **Front of a *malak* dress, Artas south of Bethlehem, late 19th or early 20th century.**
Note the red and yellow striped *atlas* patches.
Collection: Widad Kawar

Facing page, below **The *smadeh* of the late Imm Sa'id of Beit Dajan, 1974.**
Note the patch of red *atlas* satin, and the Maria Theresa coins (on the right). *Photo: Shelagh Weir*

but what precisely it symbolised is not. This can only be revealed by looking at other contexts in which it makes an appearance.

The other main ritual occasion when an *atlas* coat was worn was at circumcisions; it was worn by the boy about to be circumcised while he was paraded round the village on horseback like a bride. (In fact, if the groom had failed for some reason to supply the *atlas* fabric in the *kisweh*, a coat would be borrowed from a recently circumcised boy.) The boy wore the *atlas* again for his first annual pilgrimage to the shrine of Nabi Rubin south of Jaffa, which took place after he was circumcised and was expected to start participating in Muslim rituals. Like the wedding ritual, which marked the graduation from girlhood to womanhood for a girl, circumcision marked an advance in social status for the boy – from a state of childish irresponsibility to one of adult-like religious responsibility. The villagers articulate the obvious parallels between the two ceremonies by saying 'circumcision was like a wedding'.

The specific feature which the circumcision and marriage rituals shared was that the transition from childhood to adulthood was effected in both by an irreversible genital transformation involving the shedding of blood. It is this fundamentally important, and greatly emphasised, element of the rituals which was symbolised by the 'red' *atlas* coat. Further support for this interpretation is provided in the poetic account of the wedding night encounter and defloration in the henna night song above, in which the attractive and finally possessed gazelle/bride is twice portrayed as clothed in *atlas*. The metaphorical association can therefore be extended further, so that *atlas* = red = henna = blood.

Red *atlas* satin made several subsequent appearances during the wedding rituals, and was an important feature of women's costumes in Beit Dajan after marriage. It continued to be worn as a girdle, married woman's headdresses were patched with it, and it was used for the yoke of the most important and highly embroidered Beit Dajan dress, the *jillayeh*. In all these cases it was a symbolic reminder of the most important moment of the wedding ritual, when girl was irrevocably and physically transformed into woman by defloration.

Red *atlas* fabric was used in similar ways in village and bedouin women's costumes throughout southern Palestine, as has been described; and at weddings among bedouin of the Negev desert, an *atlas* coat was sometimes hung like a banner on the front of the bridal tent in which the newly-married couple were secluded. It is therefore probable that the symbolic significance of *atlas* was widespread, and was not confined to one village or district. This, of course, is what we would expect for a symbolic feature of universal significance, as opposed to a symbol of regional identity which, by definition, had more restricted significance.

The remainder of the bride's wedding procession outfit comprised head coverings and a final overgarment. Her head was covered by the embroidered bonnet (*smadeh*) adopted at puberty as a sign that she was of marriageable age, and which therefore marked the first step (menstruation) in her transition to woman-

Above **A Beit Dajan *smadeh*, 1969.**
Note the bundled hair-bands (*laffayef*)
decorated with red *atlas* satin. Unusually, this
smadeh also has a *saffeh* of coins attached;
saffehs were usually reserved for ceremonial
occasions. *Photo: Shelagh Weir*

Below **A village notable in Artas, 1925–31.**
The horse of Sheikh Yusef of Beit Dajan was
also white. Horses were highly prestigious
possessions, and Sheikh Yusef's was the only
one in the village in the early 1920s, and was
borrowed by every bride for her wedding.
Photo: Hilma Granqvist

hood. This was made from red *dendeki* fabric, often patched with *atlas*, and embroidered mainly in red; attached at the back were two long red hair bands (*laffayef*). At puberty a girl started conforming to the female modesty code, and had to cover her hair in public, and bind it up in the *laffayef* at the back of her head. This binding signified that the exciting yet dangerous aspect of women's nature, symbolised by loose, visible hair, was curbed and controlled. This was necessary once she was sexually mature in order to protect her reputation and the honour of the family.

Attached to the bonnet were a number of Maria Theresa coins (*abu risheh*), over the crown was placed a horseshoe-shaped padded band of coins (*saffeh*), and a band of coins (*shakkeh*) was attached over her forehead. The Maria Theresa coins were bought by her father from the brideprice, and if it was large enough or he was rich, he also bought her the *saffeh* and *shakkeh*. If he could not afford them, they were borrowed from relatives. The *smadeh*, with its valuable silver coins, was the headdress she would wear as a married woman for the rest of her life, even in bed, whereas, even if she owned them, the *saffeh* and *shakkeh* were usually only worn after the wedding for special celebrations.

Over the bonnet with all its coins was draped a red veil (*shunbar ahmar*) which completely covered the bride's face – the only occasion in her life when her face was concealed by a veil – and on her wrists and round her neck were placed her silver bridal jewellery and the clove necklace made by the *mashitah*. Finally a second man's coat (*qumbaz*), made from white silk *rozah* or *ghabani*, was draped over her head and body like a veil. This coat belonged to the groom, and was returned to him after the wedding.

These overgarments also had significance. The covering of the bride by the white silk coat signified the transfer of responsibility for the bride's protection and support from her father to her husband. However, neither the face veil nor the coat had the political significance they had in other villages, where their colour indicated whether they were Qaysi or Yamani, for Beit Dajan people disclaim allegiance to either faction.

So other explanations have to be sought for the red face veil and white coat which covered the bride. The red face veil probably related, like the use of red elsewhere, to the blood of defloration. The significance of the coat being white, rather than any other colour, will emerge when the entire set of wedding rituals is considered.

The first bridal procession

At dusk the groom's male relatives left the merrymaking at his home, and set off with a horse to fetch the bride. The groom stayed behind, but the groom's mother or other female relative went with them, carrying the mock bride (*zarafeh*). The horse (owned by Sheikh Yusef at this period) was specially decorated 'for the groom' with articles of clothing identical to some of the bride's. On the horse's head was placed a *saffeh* coin headdress ornament, tied on with a green, yellow and red silk girdle (*zunnar maqruneh*) like the

Above **Front (left) and back (right) of the bride's outfit for the wedding-day procession in Artas, 1925–31.**
The outfit comprised a dress (the *thob malak* from the drawing), a coat (*qumbaz* or *hidim*), a deep pink girdle (*hizam*) worn as a face veil, a headband (*'asbeh*), a string of coins, sprigs of citron leaves, and ostrich feathers.
From Granqvist, 1935: 67

Right **Men's coats (*qumbaz* or *hidim*).**
Left: the type of coat, of 'red' *atlas* material, worn by Beit Dajan brides on their bodies during the wedding-day procession.
Right: a white coat similar to that worn by Beit Dajan brides over their heads during the wedding-day procession. *Museum of Mankind: 1984 AS10 1; 1966 AS1 192*

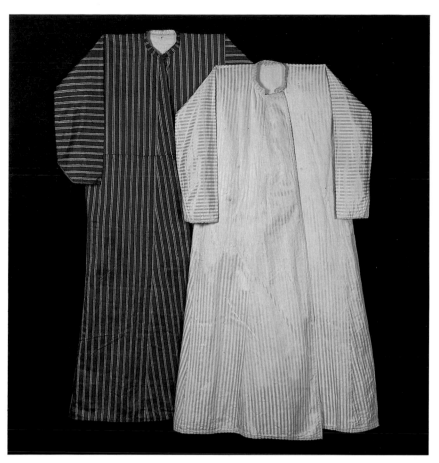

best girdle of the trousseau, and on its back was draped a red *atlas* coat (*qumbaz*). The joy of those going to fetch the bride was expressed in the song, quoted at the beginning of this chapter, in which the most important trousseau garments (*jillayehs*, *shunbars*, *malakahs* and 'white dresses') become banners of jubilation.

When the escorts arrived at the bride's house, she mounted the horse wearing the outfit described above: a white underdress, the red *atlas* coat, the coin headdresses, her silver jewellery, a red face veil and, over her head and body, a white coat. As she sat on the horse's back, a pair of shoes belonging to the groom were placed on her feet, and a sword was placed in her hands. A prickly-pear leaf (*sabr*) was stuck on the point of the sword, and candles were stuck on its spines. The procession of members of both families and other villagers then set off for the house of the groom led by female relatives of the bride who walked in front of the horse, one carrying her trousseau in a box (*sanduq*), others the mattress, quilt and bridal cushions stuffed with straw.

This procession was the second wedding ritual in which the bride took part, and the first in which she appeared in public. The first ritual was the henna night gathering on the previous night, a rite of separation from her female friends and relatives and from her girlhood, and a rite of preparation for her wedding night and womanhood.

Right **Procession to fetch the bride from another village to Artas, 1925–31.**
The children riding the bridal camel were chosen according to whether the groom wanted his firstborn to be a girl or a boy.
Photo: Hilma Granqvist

Below **Woman carrying the trousseau box (*sanduq*) in a wedding procession, Artas, 1925–31.**
Photo: Hilma Granqvist

This second ritual was her rite of transition. Not only was she transported physically from her father's home to her husband's, but she simultaneously departed from her status as a virgin girl, and moved towards her new status as a married woman. This transition was not complete, however, until the marriage was successfully consummated that night. During the wedding procession she was therefore betwixt and between her old status, which she had shed, and her new status, which she had not yet acquired. As in most cultures, this marginal inter-state of a *rite de passage*, when the principal was temporarily devoid of status, was inherently dangerous, and in Beit Dajan and other Palestinian villages this danger was expressed as a threat from the evil eye – the envious, malevolent human glance which could cause illness and accidents. The bride therefore needed protection during the rite of transition when she was especially vulnerable.

The dominant themes and concerns of this procession were all reflected in the bride's costume. Her entire body was enveloped in clothes which completely concealed her face and body, and deprived her of sexual and individual identity. She was an anonymous, shapeless bundle which did not even move of its own volition, but was passively transported from one status to another on the back of a horse. The white outer coat, which belonged to the groom, represented, as stated, the transfer of responsibility for her protection and support from her father to the groom at marriage. During the wedding procession this coat, and the groom's shoes on her feet, were explicitly believed to shield her from danger and the evil eye. Thus, as in many cultures, special attention was paid during the rite of transition to insulating the extremities of the body from harm.

The possible significance of the outer coat worn by the bride being *white* can be explored by the same method used to reveal the meaning of the *atlas* coat – by searching for a common denominator in the different contexts in which it was worn and alluded to in song.

In the song at the women's ritual on the betrothal day, the groom is portrayed as wearing a beautiful white coat (although it is not clear whether he actually wore one during the *mlak* ceremony). The betrothal day marked the departure of the groom from his single status, by the act of signing the marriage contract, and his entry into a marginal state preceding his achievement of marital status on the wedding night. So in both the *mlak* ritual and the wedding day procession, the white coat is associated with transition between statuses. This is similarly the case at burial, the transition from this world, to the next, when (in Beit Dajan) the dead body was clothed in a white dress (in the case of a woman) or wrapped in a white shroud. Furthermore, mourners often wore a piece of white clothing, and white turbans and dresses were favoured by old men and women in transition to their own deaths.

So white probably carried connotations of transition, as well as protection, in the case of the coat which the groom was obliged to give to the maternal uncle (*khal*) of the bride, for the gift marked the uncle's transition from a warm, informal relationship with his niece to a more formal relationship which carried responsibilities towards the married couple and their future children.

If white signified transition and the associated indeterminacy of status, then we might expect to find the opposite, black, and bright strong colour worn to signify the acquisition and celebration of *new* status. This is exactly the case in the final ritual of the wedding celebrations, as will be described.

Below **A wedding-day procession, Artas, 1925–31.**
A camel loaded with the box (*sanduq*) containing the trousseau goes first, followed by the camel bearing the veiled bride seated on the various furnishings she is taking to her new home. Note the white outer coat of the bride, perhaps signifying that she is from a village of the Yamani faction such as Bethlehem. *Photo: Hilma Granqvist*

Above **Wedding-day procession, Artas, 1925–31.**
Note the sword carried by the bride. Artas brides wore a striped outer coat and a dark pink face-covering to signify the Qaysi affiliation of their village. *Photo: Hilma Granqvist*

Left **Wedding-day procession, Qubeibeh ibn 'Awad, south east coastal plain, 1932–3.**
The bride's face is veiled in white, possibly indicating her Yamani affiliation, although her coat is dark, perhaps red, which could mean she was Qaysi. In the foreground a woman waves the bridal sword decorated with beads and coins. *Photo: Olga Tufnell*

A groom and his mother awaiting the arrival of the bridal procession at their house, Artas, 1925–31.
The groom is holding a twig of greenery to ensure that his bride brings prosperity to his home. *Photo: Hilma Granqvist*

When the wedding procession arrived at the house of the groom, the *mashitah*, the female wedding specialist who had prepared the bride at the henna party, again had a part to play. The bride was helped down from the horse, and the *mashitah* took the sword from her hands, removed the white coat from her head, and lifted the red veil to reveal her face. The groom's mother handed the bride a pitcher of water to drink from, and she placed it on her head. It was said that it would be unlucky for anyone else to drink from this pitcher before the groom. A mulberry leaf (*tut*) or some other green leaf containing yeast (*khamireh*) (prepared by the groom's mother) was then placed in the bride's hand and, still carrying the pitcher, she crossed the threshold into the house, pressing the yeast onto the door lintel as she entered.

The hope that the bride would bring good fortune to her new home is expressed in the song sung by the women as she performed this ritual:

fold up your *shunbar*, maiden, put it aside
let the good fortune in your face fill [the house]
fold up your veil and arrange your chains
let the good fortune in your face radiate [through the house]

The *shunbar* referred to is the red veil which covered the bride's face during the wedding procession, and the chains are those of the choker (*bughmeh mshanshaleh*), usually part of the wedding jewellery, which had long pendant chains with coins. The belief that luck and well-being could flow from someone's face is the logical opposite of the belief in the harmful effects of the evil eye.

Once inside the house, the bride sat serenely on her cushions, and the *mashitah* completed her adornment by painting her face with red and white make-up and pressing gold leaf all over it. This occasion was called the 'transformation' (*jalweh*), because the bride's appearance was 'transformed' (*titjalla*) into something more beautiful than before, and probably also because the transform-

The bride's arrival at the house of the groom, Ramallah, 1900.
The bride (to the left of the gateway) has a dark coat over her head, probably of red
atlas material signifying the groom's Qaysi affiliation, and carries a sword in front of
her face. *Photo: Underwood and Underwood, Library of Congress*

A bride and groom at the entrance to his home, Bethlehem, probably 1930s.
They are pressing leaves containing yeast (*khamireh*) over the door to express the hope that the bride will bring good fortune to the house and be fertile. The urbanised and sophisticated Bethlehemites probably started wearing European-style white wedding dresses earlier than elsewhere, but they were common throughout Palestine by the 1940s.
Photo: Matson Collection, Library of Congress

ation of her status was about to take place. A similar term is used by Christian Palestinians to refer to the transfiguration of Christ, and the term *jillayeh* is also related.

In one of the songs sung by the close female relatives present during the bride's 'transformation', alternating allusions to high-status trousseau items and high-status men are a device to emphasise prestige and pride.

by the life of my father, I will only wear a *malak* dress
we are the chiefs whose fame has been recorded
by the life of my father, I will only wear a coin of gold
we are the chiefs whose fame is legion
by the life of my father, I will only wear an *ikhdari* dress
we are the chiefs whose reputation is high

how lovely to hear the compliments when we wore our *jillayehs*!
we the elders are in our upper rooms
how lovely to hear the compliments when we wore our *malak* dresses!
we the elders are under our arcades

The second part of the song probably dates to the period from the late 1920s when the village grew increasingly prosperous from orange growing and working for wages, and the wealthiest villagers began to build two storey houses with balconies and arches. This song therefore combines and juxtaposes four categories of status symbol: costume, money, male leaders and architecture.

When it was time for the groom to come to his bride, she was again covered by the red veil (*shunbar*), and his first act was to lift it to reveal her radiant golden face, and place a small gift of money in her lap. This was the first of the money gifts (*nqut*) which would be continued by relatives the following morning. If the bride's heavy coin headdresses were secured by a headband, the groom untied it. This action, called 'untying the knot' (*infakat al-'oqdeh*), was thought to 'solve any problems', and can be seen as the opposite of the belief

Above **A Bethlehem bride's newly washed underdress is displayed as proof of her virginity, Artas, 1925–31.**
This was not the custom in all villages, including Beit Dajan, but the events of the wedding night were everywhere the focus of intense interest because the marriage had to be nullified if it was not consummated.
Photo: Hilma Granqvist

Facing page, above **The groom on his way to the men's club on the morning after his wedding, Artas, 1925–31.**
By his confident manner he showed that he had successfully deflowered his bride. Note the luxurious headropes, with long sections of gilded cord. *Photo: Hilma Granqvist*

Facing page, below **A young bride 'going out to the well', Artas, 1925–31.**
In Artas this ceremony took place on the morning following the wedding, and was explicitly stated to be so that she would, like her water container, become full (of children). Note her exceptionally wide, flamboyant girdle which she wore as a face veil on the preceding wedding day. *Photo: Hilma Granqvist*

that if a knot were tied when the wedding contract was signed, the groom would be rendered impotent on the wedding night. After she was unveiled, the bride sometimes loosened her hair and performed a slow dance, waving her kohl holder (*mukholeh*) with its special ostrich feather decorations. The following song refers to this dance and its effect on the groom:

sway beauty sway
you flower in the garden
when your pearls cause a sparkle
then loosen your tresses!

When the women left, the couple shared a meal of special delicacies prepared by the groom's mother, 'so that they would become more comfortable together'. Both families hoped and expected that the marriage would be consummated that night, called 'the night of entering' (*laylat al-dakhleh*) in explicit reference to the sexual act. As the foregoing descriptions have made clear, great emphasis was placed on the defloration of the bride as the central and most important act of the wedding rituals, the event which transformed girl into woman, and sealed and legitimised a new marriage. The wedding night was therefore the focus of great tension and concern for both families (not to mention the groom).

As soon as the sexual act had taken place, the groom's mother brought water for the ritual cleansing of the bride and groom, for at that transitional moment they were considered specially vulnerable to evil spirits, the great fear being that the bride might be rendered infertile.

The bride's *nqut* ceremony
In the morning, the successful consummation of the marriage was publicly announced to the whole village with ululations and song. This moment of celebration and happy relief was not without its humour, as shown in this song the groom's mother sometimes sang from her window to announce her son's success to the village:

this is not the blood of a bedbug
nor the blood of a flea
but the blood of a virgin
whose reputation lifts up our heads!

It was important that the sexual act produced blood as visible proof that it had taken place, and that the bride had been a virgin, and the blood was supposed to be spilt onto the bride's white underdress (*bayt al-sham*) which, it will be recalled, was patched in red; they say 'the *bayt al-sham* was specially for the wedding night to show her blood'. While the groom went to the coffee house to announce his success to the men, the bride's mother and close female relatives, including, as one informant put it 'any nosy aunts', gathered at the groom's house to inspect the bloodstained dress. The bride took great pride in displaying it, and the women rejoiced at the happy outcome. (In Artas the bride's mother took the dress to the well to wash it as a sign that the marriage had been successfully consum-

mated, and it was a Bethlehem custom to hang it on a line outside the house.[3])

Later that morning the bride received formal visits from her female friends and relatives 'who were indebted to her and her family', and her close male kin on both her father's and mother's side. Each visitor threw a small money present of about a pound into her lap in a ceremony known as the *nqut* (from the verb 'to drip'). The gifts from her female friends exactly reciprocated the sums of money she and her family had made to them at their *nqut* ceremonies, if they were married, or would be expected to make when they did marry, and a careful tally was kept. The first of her male kin to make his presentation was the maternal uncle (*khal*) to whom the groom had been obliged to give a coat (*hidim al-khal*), and was an acknowledgement of the responsibilities entailed in accepting it.

For the *nqut* ceremony the bride wore most of the same clothes she had worn for the wedding procession the previous day: the white underdress (*bayt al-sham*), from which the spots of blood had been washed, the red and yellow striped *atlas* coat, her coin headdress and its ornaments, her jewellery, and the red crepe face veil which was pinned to the centre of her headdress so as to reveal, not cover, her face. The significant omission was the white coat (*qumbaz*) thought to shield her from malevolent onlookers during the wedding procession, which had symbolised the transfer of responsibility for her protection and support from her father to her husband, and the indeterminacy of her status during that rite of transition.

The *nqut* ceremony could not take place until the marriage had been consummated, and therefore marked the bride's successful transformation from girl to woman and her safe arrival at her new marital status. It is therefore consistent with the interpretation of the symbolism of the white coat that she did not wear it for the *nqut* ceremony, and it is also confirmation of the symbolic association between her virginal blood and the various red garments she wore on the wedding day, that she donned them again for the ceremony directly associated with her defloration. This was the last occasion on which she wore the red crepe veil and the red *atlas* coat.

The 'going out to the well' (*tal'at al-bir*)

For the week following the wedding day, the bride and groom stayed at home receiving visits from those close to them, and each day the bride changed into different trousseau dresses to show them off to her friends.

At the end of the week the final ritual of the wedding celebrations took place, the 'going out to the well'. This exclusively female ceremony marked the bride's emergence from seclusion and first appearance in public as a married woman.

The bride left her husband's house and walked in a joyful procession of women, all decked out in their most beautiful costumes and jewellery, to the village well. All carried water pitchers, the bride's specially painted with red designs and decorated with

A *bughmeh mshanshaleh*.
This was part of the bridal jewellery, and it is these chains which made the *khush* sound when the women processed to the well.
Museum of Mankind: 1966 AS1 347

sprigs of greenery. At the well she presented its guardian with a tray of sweets 'to ensure the good fortune of her new home', and filled her pitcher with water. Old people, recalling this important and colourful event, referred nostalgically to the lovely *khush khush khush* sound of all the silver chains as the procession went by.

This ceremony was both an announcement and display of the bride's new status, and a rite of incorporation into the fellowship of womanhood, and it could not take place unless and until the crucial act of sexual transformation on which her new status depended had also taken place. If it had not, the bride was returned to her father's home and the marriage was annulled. If it had, then it was not only possible but essential that the ceremony take place. The fact of consummation was not enough; it had to be publicised with the proper ceremonial. Occasionally when a girl married before puberty, the consummation did not take place for months or years – a situation which could be tolerated and did not threaten her honour because of her immaturity – and the 'going out to the well' was deferred. One woman related how, as soon as her young daughter-in-law menstruated, she sought opportunities to leave the couple alone, and when she returned from market one day she was relieved to find they had slept together. She said 'When I saw the blood, I immediately rushed to prepare for *tal'at al-bir'*.

The 'going out to the well' was the second procession the bride took part in, and her appearance and demeanour were in striking contrast to the first. In the first procession from her father's house to the house of the groom she was in a marginal state of transition between statuses, passively transported on the back of a horse, a shapeless bundle devoid of identity. By the second procession she had successfully achieved her new status. She was no longer in transition; she had arrived. Far from being anonymous and immobile, she now strode along on her own two feet, her face revealed, her head held high, her newly-acquired status loudly proclaimed by the jangling jewellery and ululations of her brightly dressed female companions, and by her own dramatic, ostentatious costume with its bright, bold patterns and colours.

As we would expect, the costume worn by the bride for this important ceremony reflected and celebrated essential aspects of married womanhood – the payment and gifts which legitimised marriage, the sexual act which transformed girl into woman, the dual and contradictory aspects of female sexuality, the value of female fertility, and women's role in expressing village identity and family wealth and status.

On her head was the red bonnet (*smadeh*) which had marked her arrival at puberty, and at the nape of her neck her hair was neatly bound up in its long red bands (*laffayef*). This headdress was a prime symbol of her sexual maturity, her marital status (by its large silver brideprice coins), and her compliance with the female modesty code, according to which heads should always be covered and hair bound and controlled (just as the sexuality it symbolised should be safely contained within the sanctuary of marriage). She would wear the *smadeh* daily for the rest of her life.

Above **A bride dancing at her 'going out to the well' ceremony, Qubeibeh ibn 'Awad, 1932–3.**
Photo: Olga Tufnell

Above right **Front opening of a coat dress (*jillayeh*) from the Jaffa area, 1920s.**
Note the taffeta (*heremzi*) borders, and the red *atlas* patch surmounting the opening. In Beit Dajan the opening was closed with tasselled ties (*bnud*) which were considered enticing.
Collection: Widad Kawar

Attached to the *smadeh* she again wore the coin ornaments (*saffeh* and *shakkeh*) which she had worn for the procession from her father's house, and which she would henceforth only wear for special occasions. These represented brideprice, not hers in particular like the coins on the *smadeh*, but brideprice as a symbol of the social worth of women and as an expression of family and village prestige and pride. This is why, if there had not been enough brideprice money to buy her these items, they were borrowed from relatives and returned after the ceremony. It was important to put on a good show. Over her headdress she wore, for the first time, the black crepe veil (*shunbar*) with the panel of red embroidery and colourful silk fringe which had been among the groom's trousseau gifts. This also symbolised her new sexual and marital status. They say 'She could wear this now because she was no longer a virgin'.

Her dress, as befitted this important ceremonial occasion, was the chief dress she herself (or her mother) had prepared for her trousseau, the heavily embroidered *jillayeh* with the silk-patched opening on the front of the skirt. Beneath this she wore the white *bayt al-sham* underdress with the red patchwork trimming which she had worn for the first wedding procession, the wedding night, and the *nqut* ceremony the following morning. The *bayt al-sham* had long pointed sleeves which were pulled through the short sleeves of the *jillayeh*, and it was also visible through the skirt opening. This

A procession of women, Beitunia near Ramallah, 1938/9.
The women singing and clapping are probably taking part in a 'going out to the well'
procession. *Photo: Matson Collection, Library of Congress*

underdress, it will be recalled, was closely associated with the blood of defloration, and contained an overt fertility symbol in the loose threads of its hem. Once the bride became pregnant or gave birth, this frayed edge was properly hemmed. Her outfit for the procession to the well was completed by the better of the two girdles (*zunnar maqruneh*) presented by the groom in the *kisweh*.

The most complex and interesting garment worn by the bride to display her womanhood was the *jillayeh*, for, as described, it incorporated symbolic statements about a woman's village identity, economic status and sexuality. The 'pockets and cypress trees' (*jiyab u srau*) pattern on the sides of the skirt showed she came from Beit Dajan, the type of embroidered panel (*shinyar*) at the back of the skirt gave some indication of her father's means, and the opening in the front of the skirt symbolised her sexuality.

In the context of the wedding, the decorated skirt opening should perhaps be seen as a celebration by women of their essential difference from men, for it is a deliberately flamboyant, eye-catching feature, placed in a strategic position, framed with bright taffeta patches in red, green and yellow, sprinkled with sequins, and with its edges joined by swinging tasselled ties.

There may be further significance in the name for the taffeta frame of the opening. As mentioned, it was called *slah al-jillayeh*, meaning the 'arms' or 'weapons' of the *jillayeh*, and the specialist needlewoman who sewed the taffeta onto the dress was said to 'arm the *jillayeh*' (*taslah al-jillayeh*). This nomenclature helps make sense of a song which was sung by the women waiting in the village for the return of the *kisweh*-buying expedition from Jaffa:

they loomed up from the west
the Tarabin bedouin
their arms are taffeta
and their spears are decoration

The Tarabin are bedouin of the Negev desert who sometimes pastured their flocks in the Jaffa area, and at times probably raided the settled farmers of the villages. The song was sung as the *kisweh* party appeared over the horizon with their bundles of trousseau cloth, including the *heremzi* taffeta, and its members are jokingly compared with bedouin warriors whose 'arms are taffeta' (*heremzi*).

So the opening in the *jillayeh* encapsulates the inherent ambiguity of female sexuality, its alluring attractiveness, and its potential for causing harm; the capacity of women to uphold the honour of their fathers, brothers and husbands, and benefit them, or to bring them misfortune and disgrace. This dual aspect of femininity could explain the threshold ritual on the wedding day. The removal of the sword from the bride's hands is the symbolic removal of the bride's potential for harming her new home, the counterpoint to the pressing of dough on the lintel, the carrying-in of water and the song for the occasion, all of which express the longing that she will bring the house good fortune and produce many children.

Postscript

There are many aspects of this large and detailed subject which I have been unable to explore within the constraints of this book and of my own knowledge. Many interesting questions remain to be answered and many avenues of enquiry to be explored.

There is still much to be discovered about the production and trade in costume textiles (Palestinian, Egyptian and Syrian) at different periods, and about the penetration of the Palestinian, Israeli and Jordanian markets by clothing textiles from Europe and eastern Asia. This is not only of economic interest, but also relates to costume as a system of communication, for fabrics and garments are accepted or rejected by the consumer according to whether they conform to local costume codes and can be used to convey meanings of local significance. These meanings can of course be old, leading to conservatism, or new, leading to innovation.

The various 'dialects' of the Palestinian costume language, past and present, would also repay further investigation – especially the language of women's costume, symbolically so rich, and capable of so many renewals and transformations. Similar analyses of the meaning of costumes within specific temporal and ritual contexts as attempted in the final two chapters could be applied to other villages and regions. Specific topics, such as colour and sexual symbolism, could also be examined across a wider spectrum of

Coat dress (*jillayeh*), Beit Dajan, 1920s.
Worn by the bride for the 'going out to the well' ceremony with the black veil (*shunbar*) with red fringe and embroidery. *Museum of Mankind: 1968 AS4 31*

Fetching water in Artas south of Bethlehem, 1979.
Patterned dresses (*fustan*), some in western style, are worn within the village, but many women wear an embroidered *thob* over them when they leave the village. *Photo: Shelagh Weir*

Women in Ramallah market, 1987.
Some young women, like the one on the left, have adopted undecorated 'Islamic dress', while others, like the woman in the centre, continue to wear the traditional embroidered dress. Note the narrow embroidered belt worn over the chest panel, a popular fashion among younger women. *Photo: Shelagh Weir*

space and time, and compared with other cultures.

The focus of this book has been mainly retrospective, but there is also much of interest to be studied about the contemporary versions of 'traditional' costume, especially that of women. Surprisingly, perhaps, despite all their hardships and dislocations, many women of village origin, including those still living in their villages in the West Bank, and those living in refugee camps in the West Bank, Gaza Strip and Jordan, still wear embroidered dresses and flowing white veils, either for everyday wear or for special occasions. This not only includes the older women, who might be expected to be more conservative in dress and cling more tenaciously to village styles, but also younger women, many of whom have not lived in a village since they were children, or have never done so. At a period when alternative clothing styles are readily available to younger women – western dress, and 'Islamic' dress of varying degrees of modesty and concealment – it would be interesting to know why some young women choose to wear the 'traditional' embroidered costumes, while others reject them.

There is no doubt that the survival of highly decorated dress is closely related to the fact that it continues to be a medium for a variety of statements about women's identity, as it has always been; the question is, what are they? Some messages have not changed;

flamboyant embroidery is still a form of conspicuous consumption
– of money and time – and proclaims and flaunts wealth, now more
than before, the money to commission the embroidery as well as
pay for the materials, for fewer women appear to embroider for
themselves, and more do so professionally. Dress embroidery
therefore remains a good barometer of disposable income, the
expansion of the vertical 'branches' on West Bank dresses in the
1980s, for example, specifically reflecting the remittances of men
working in the oil-rich countries of the Gulf, just as in the past the
sumptuous embroidery of Bethlehem reflected the remittances
from men working in the Americas.

Some elements of women's costume still self-consciously indicate regional identity, not only among those living in their villages,
but also and more intriguingly, among refugee women who have
lived in camps for twenty or forty years. A variety of features can
signify regional origins, including the precise shade of embroidery,
the type of seam stitching, veil fabrics, dress colour and the method
of wearing a belt or veil. For example, the older Beit Dajan women
in the refugee camps of Amman say proudly 'wherever we go in our
white *thobs*, people know we are from Beit Dajan!'. It would be
interesting to know whether such regional indicators among
refugee women are mainly confined to the dress of the older
generation of women who were already married when they left
their homes, and have perhaps become living memorials of villages
now inaccessible or disappeared, but which remain a focus of
nostalgia and longing. Or does the dress of younger women also
sport some detail, a motif or colour perhaps, which provides some
vestigial visual reminder of the village they feel strongly they
'belong to', but have never seen?

Whatever regional markers have survived (or been created),
'traditional' women's costume and embroidery have certainly
acquired a new political significance as expressions of Palestinian
national identity – a symbolic role for which the other styles of
Palestinian dress are unfitted because of their wider associations
with western fashion or Islam. This new meaning has apparently
emerged from a desire for expression both on the part of those who
wear the clothes concerned, and those who do not. The richly
embroidered costumes worn by women of village origins have not
only become an increasingly self-conscious statement of their own
Palestinian identity and national aspirations, but are also, in
various modifications, performing the same task on behalf of
Palestinians generally, whatever their place of residence, social
background or usual modes of attire.

This phenomenon is to be understood in the context of a
beleaguered, fragmented society which has seen its land occupied
and appropriated, its villages and institutions destroyed, and its
people dispersed. In these circumstances, culture and tradition
become suddenly more precious, and intense efforts are made by
the educated to study, preserve and reproduce what comes to be
defined as the 'national heritage', as has happened most markedly
in the Occupied Territories. At the same time, visual symbols are

Girls wearing the *shawal* style of dress, 1985.
Note the scarf (left) in the form of the
Palestinian national flag, and the belt in the
same colours. The scarf on the right is made
from black-and-white *keffiyeh* material, which
has become a symbol of Palestinian
nationalism, and ends in a miniature flag. The
girls have dressed up specially for a film, and
would only wear these dresses for parties.
Photo: Shelagh Weir

The *shawal* style of dress.

needed which can condense and assert potent sentiments such as attachment to territory, the right to statehood, continuity from the past, present existence, cultural and social merit, and so on. Material culture has special qualifications for this symbolic role because it can be seen, because of its incontrovertible presence and tangibility, and in the case of old things, because it existed in the past and has survived into the present. Palestinian village women's costume and embroidery have the added advantages that they are colourful and beautiful, so are noticed and admired, and are also associated with the sector of Palestinian society, the *fellahin* peasantry, which was most deeply rooted in 'the land'.

The use of 'village' costume and embroidery as a medium for expressing national identity has taken several forms. Costume collections have been made and exhibited in the Occupied Territories and Jordan, some of which were initially motivated by love of the costumes for themselves, but all of which have inevitably taken on nationalistic significance. Chief of these are the Dar al-Tifl Museum in Jerusalem which grew out of the Palestine Folk Museum founded in the 1930s, the In'ash al-Usrah Museum in El-Bireh, the Village Home Museum in Bethlehem, the Folk Museum founded by Sa'adiyah Tall in Amman, and the private collection of Widad Kawar of Amman, an exhibition of which toured European Museums in 1988 and 1989. A number of catalogues and other publications on Palestinian costume have also been produced in connection with these collections and museums.

Village costume has also taken to the stage. The various dance troupes which have developed in the Occupied Territories in the past few years dress in versions of village costume (and perform dances and songs explicitly rooted in village or bedouin traditions), though their predominantly urban and middle class members do not wear such costumes in everyday life. Costume and embroidery symbolism was also used to dramatic effect by the Hakawati theatre group of Jerusalem in their play *The Story of Kufur Shamma*,

Right **'Ornaments' by Palestinian artist Nabil Anani.**
Village women's costumes and embroidery are popular images among Palestinian artists.

Below **Imm Ibrahim of Beit Dajan in Amman, 1985.**
Imm Ibrahim runs a successful business employing women to embroider cushion covers for sale. *Photo: Shelagh Weir*

performed in London in 1988, which chronicled recent Palestinian history. In one scene the interminable limbo of refugee camp existence was vividly portrayed by three faceless women in white veils, embroidering in unison with balletic movements of their arms. Images of village costume and embroidery are also popular motifs in Palestinian art.

Thousands of dresses, cushions and other household articles embroidered with village patterns are produced by welfare organisations in the Occupied Territories, Lebanon and Syria for sale to foreign visitors and urban Palestinians living outside their homeland. A few businesswomen in Jordan also sell dresses and jackets decorated with Palestinian embroidery on a commercial basis. Embroidering these articles provides many refugee women with significant income, while exploiting the desire of the members of the Palestinian diaspora to help their less fortunate compatriots, and to display on their persons or in their homes a beautiful artefact which expresses their national identity.

These artefacts are a step removed from what a museum curator would normally consider 'authentic specimens' because they are not made or worn by the villagers for their own use, but modified for external consumption. The dresses are tailored in the western style with bust darts and set-in sleeves, and the cushions are square rather than oblong like village cushions, and differently embroidered. Nevertheless, they have their own brand of authenticity as products of the desire of non-villagers to express their nationalism, solidarity and concern in a medium which conforms with their own urban fashions of dress and domestic decoration, while retaining stylistic features which are obviously derived from an older Palestinian tradition. This is an interesting reversal of the usual historical process, whereby it was villagers who copied the fashions or stylistic features of the dress of their social superiors – and could only have happened in the specific political context of recent years.

There has been interesting feed-back from welfare organisations into the costumes women still make and embroider for themselves. The *shawal*-style of dress almost certainly began life as the product of an embroidery centre, but is now widely popular among young village and townswomen in the West Bank and Jordan. Other fashions, such as the *malak* dress embroidered with lurex thread, may also have been copied from original versions exhibited in local museums.

Through the products of welfare organisations, the nationalistic significance of Palestinian costume and embroidery has become widely disseminated, even outside the international community of Palestinians, as evidenced by the British Foreign Office Minister, William Waldegrave, who found an embroidered Palestinian cushion a useful prop for important political assertions during his televised historic first meeting with Yasser Arafat in early 1989. The black and white checked *keffiyeh* and cravat almost invariably worn by Arafat has also become popular apparel among young people of many nationalities as an expression of sympathy with the Palestinian movement or perhaps with liberation movements generally, and due to its almost daily appearance in the media, its symbolism is now widely understood. Many people have thus unconsciously acquired a smattering of the rich language of Palestinian costume.

Girl embroidering for the Family Development (*In'ash al-Usrah*) cooperative, 1987.
Photo: Shelagh Weir

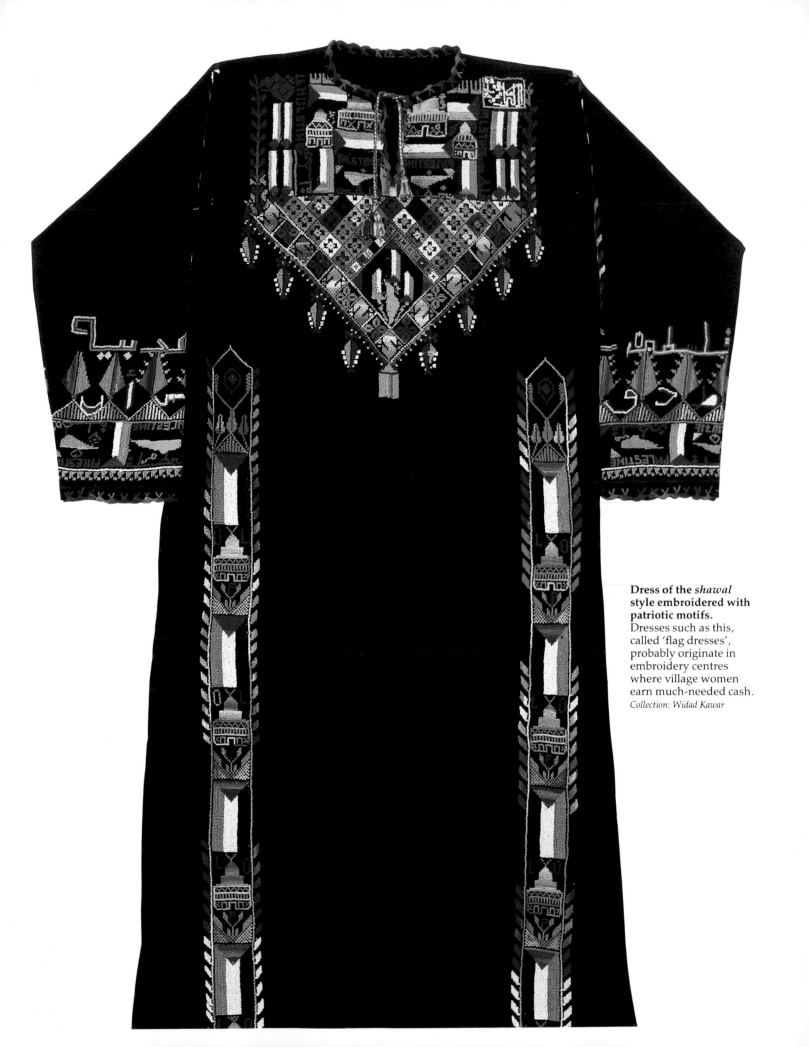

Dress of the *shawal* style embroidered with patriotic motifs.
Dresses such as this, called 'flag dresses', probably originate in embroidery centres where village women earn much-needed cash.
Collection: Widad Kawar

Notes

Introduction

1. I have drawn mainly on McDowall, 1987 and Morris, 1987, chapter 1, for this summary.

2. The map is based on several sources, mainly Morris, 1987, and the map of the Jerusalem Centre for Development Studies.

3. Gilbert, 1979: 49; McDowall, 1987: 10; Morris, 1987: xviii–xx, 1, 286, 298 and Map 2.

4. McDowall, 1987: 6, 31.

5. This approach derives from the seminal work of Ferdinand de Saussure, 1974 and is cogently summarised in Leach, 1976.

Chapter 1

1. See Dozy, 1845 and Stillman, 1979 for Arabic terms for costume in other countries.

2. Pococke, 1745, II: 61, who visited in 1697, noted that the plain near Acre was 'well-cultivated with corn and cotton.'

3. Robinson, 1860, II: 484, quoting from the memoirs of a relative of the French consul at Sidon, D'Arvieux; Pococke, 1745, II: 3, 4; Cohen, 1973: 259.

4. Maundrell, 1810: 149.

5. Volney, 1787, II: 302–8.

6. Burckhardt, 1822: 5. Burckhardt's travels were in 1811–12.

7. Ruppin, 1916: 220.

8. Owen, 1981: 20; Cohen, 1973: 11–17.

9. Owen, 1966: 417 and 1981: 178.

10. Tristram, 1865: 137, 139, 585.

11. Ruppin, 1916: 220.

12. In 1928 Palestine imported over 211 tons of cotton yarn for the local weaving industry, and over 2000 tons of woven fabric (479 tons of natural-coloured coarse material, 277 tons of bleached cotton, 1196 tons of dyed cotton, and 105 tons of printed cotton). Dalman, 1964: 160 quoting Gurevich.

13. See Weir, 1976.

14. Grant, 1921: 142.

15. *Indigofera argentea*. See Crowfoot and Baldensperger, 1932: 66–7. I am grateful to Jenny Balfour-Paul, who is an expert on the production and trade in Middle Eastern indigo, for commenting on this section.

16. Burckhardt, 1922: 392.

17. Robinson, 1860, I: 561; Tristram, 1865: 337, 339.

18. Warren, 1876: 509.

19. Dalman, 1964: 73. Dalman (p. 75) says kermes *Phytolacca decandra* was available locally, from the insect on the evergreen oak.

20. Dalman, 1964: 75.

21. Tristram, 1865: 153.

22. Dalman, 1964: 74–5, and Crowfoot and Baldensperger, 1932: 67 give sources for Palestinian dyes.

23. Naval Intelligence Division, 1921: 455; 1943: 167.

24. British Government, 1928: 42. The Subdistrict included Jaffa, Ramleh, Hebron and Beersheba, as well as Mejdel and Gaza.

25. Pococke, 1743: 174 describes an Egyptian fabric which sounds similar to Mejdel weaves.

26. Also called *mubarsam*, which probably derives from the word for clover.

27. Also called *abu hizz ahmar*.

28. Dalman, 1964: 55.

29. Dalman, 1964: 161 has *shurmbabi* for a yellow Egyptian fabric.

30. I am grateful to Widad Kawar for sharing her information on the Nasser establishment.

31. These veils were P£1.5 before the Second World War, and rose to P£10 during the War.

32. Jaussen, 1927: 284. Possibly the single weaving establishment recorded in the first census of industries of 1927 for the Northern District of Palestine (comprising Galilee and the Tulkarm–Nablus area) was in Nablus (British Government, 1928: 46).

33. Naval Intelligence Division, 1943: 167.

34. Crowfoot, 1943. I have corrected Surbahal to Surbahar. This article describes the plaiting technique, also called finger weaving, and the twined weaving, in detail.

35. See Crowfoot, 1944 and Weir, 1970b.

36. See Owen, 1981: 75–6.

37. *Ruhbani* cost 60 piastres the dress length (*maqta'*) in 1930–9.

38. Powdered pomegranate skins, and a crushed local pulse (*jahrah*). Crystals called *jazz* were added to give darker shades of red.

39. Or perhaps *qamakh*.

40. Khawlandi, a former *heremzi* manufacturer in Damascus, said that in the 1940s he sold *heremzi* in packets containing two rolls for 20 Syrian pounds (real silk), and 4 Syrian pounds (artificial silk).

41. Alternative terms encountered in Syria were *karmasud* and *karmasis*.

42. Weakley, 1966: 283.

43. Owen, 1981: 84–94.

44. Neale, 1851, I: 189.

45. Tristram, 1865: 114.

46. Britain had exported 'broadcloth' to Aleppo since the seventeenth century, but the term then meant literally cloth which was broad (about 1.25 yards), not necessarily wool with a felted surface as it has come to mean today. Davis, 1967: 96.

47. Jaussen, 1927: 64.

48. Amir, 1988 and Kawar, 1988 have *dubayt*.

49. Velvet was 12–15 piastres a *piq* in 1935 when it first came in (that is over P£8 for a dress length).

50. Winkelhane, 1988: 121.

51. They were sold by weight: 10 piastres the *wuqiyah* in the 1930s–40s.

52. Granqvist, 1935: 43–4.

Chapter 2

1. Dalman, 1964, Vol. V: 32.

2. De Thevenot, 1686 mentions bedouin wearing blue shirts, and Klein, 1881 also mentions blue *thobs* being worn by villagers.

3. Tristram, 1865: 131. As he notes, this style of *thob* was noticed by Holman Hunt, who dressed Jesus in it for his painting of the Finding of Christ in the Temple.

4. Wilson, 1906: 142–3 and Baldensperger, 1913: 54.

5. Klein, 1881.

6. Dalman, 1964, Vol. V: 241 mentions this garment, and it is illustrated in Macdonald, 1951: Plate XVI.

7. Granqvist, 1935: 54 mentions this evolution.

8. Granqvist, 1931: 126–7.

9. Two sayings encapsulated these sentiments: 'two thirds of a boy comes from his mother's brother', and 'before you cut the tree examine its roots, and before you betroth your son, find him a good mother's brother'. See Weir and Kawar, 1975.

10. See Spoer and Haddad, 1927.

11. Baldensperger, 1906; Granqvist, 1931: 14 and 1935: 86–91.

12. Thomson, 1867: 117–18, gives a list of mainly urban male garments with their Arabic names.

13. For example Oliphant, 1887: 114, who visited Palestine in the early 1880s, notes that Christian men in Haifa wore European dress combined with a red fez.

14. Macdonald, n.d.: 11.

15. Rothstein writing in 1910 says grooms in Lifta were just beginning to wear underpants.

16. Wilson, 1906: 140 notes this.

17. Ulmer, 1918.

18. These terms are given by Dalman, 1964, Vol. V: 234. General terms for belts are *hizam* and *zunnar*.

19. Baldensperger, 1913: 51.

20. Granqvist, 1935: 54 calls the type worn in Artas in the 1920s *hzam 'ajami*, which she translates as 'Persian girdle' although *'ajami* simply means 'foreign'.

21. These are described by Conder, 1880: 343.

22. Warren, 1876: 491–2 recorded no less than 230 shoemakers in Jerusalem in the 1870s, of whom 120 were Arabs, 83 Jews and 27 Armenians.

23. Klein, 1881.

24. Macdonald n.d.: 16.

25. Some of the terminology of male head wear has been taken from Ulmer, 1918, who provides very detailed descriptions.

26. Baldensperger, 1913: 51–2.

27. Ulmer, 1918 describes such a hypothetical case. Lutfiyya, 1966: 96 mentions (with regard to the village of Baytin) that the uncovering of the head of another in public was punishable in 'tribal' law.

28. Ulmer, 1918 gives a detailed description of such a headdress, which he says was called a *tase*, meaning the lid of a mug, after the metal disc on its crown. See also Granqvist, 1947: 192–4 for a description of the circumcision outfit.

29. Conder, 1880: 115.

30. Klein, 1881. My translation from the German.

31. The fact that green is reserved for descendents of the Prophet is mentioned in John Zuallardo's Travels in 1586, published in Rome in 1587, and

summarised by C. R. Conder in the *Palestine Exploration Quarterly*, January, 1902: 97–105.

32. Ulmer, 1918. Wilson, 1906: 141 also notes that the green turban was being adopted by 'people who have no real right to the title Sherif'.

33. Ulmer, 1918.

34. Tristram, 1865: 155.

35. Conder, 1880: 318.

36. Whiting, 1914.

37. Wilson, 1906: 141.

38. Conder, 1880: 262.

39. The role of the Ta'amreh in village life is described in Granqvist, 1931 and 1935.

Chapter 3

1. I heard of one man who embroidered, but in secret to avoid ridicule.

2. The following generalisations apply to southern Palestine, but are probably true for the Galilee area too.

3. Granqvist, 1931.

4. Canon A. Mansur (n.d.).

5. Canon Mansur provides a summary of the changes in Nazareth costume from the mid-nineteenth century to around 1920.

6. Tristram, 1865: 68.

7. These are in the Dar al-Tifl Museum, Jerusalem.

8. Ashkenazi, 1938 calls the dresses *thob*, but they were called *shirsh* in 1967 when I visited the area, and in the early 1980s, see Amir, 1984: 5.

9. It is probably bedouin women de Lamartine, 1835: 218 describes in the plain of Zebulon in Galilee in the 1830s as . . .

> robed in their long sky-blue gowns, wearing a large white girdle, the ends of which trail on the ground, and a blue turban ornamented with bands of Venetian sequins.

10. *Malas* simply means 'soft' or 'smooth', and is used for several different fabrics with this common feature.

11. See Amir, 1984 for a detailed description of Galilee bedouin costumes and embroidery in the 1980s. She points out that *malas* is the same material used by the Negev bedouin for their dresses, which they call *dubayt*.

12. Amir, 1984 provides detailed descriptions and diagrams of the

embroidery stitches used by the bedouin of Tuba in Galilee.

13. Ashkenazi, 1938.

14. Amir, 1984: 10–11.

15. An example preserved from the Ashdod area, in the Museum of International Folk Art, Santa Fe, no. 3356, is exceptional in having long sleeves.

16. There is a rare example from Ramallah in the Whiting collection at the Museum of International Folk Art, Santa Fe, no. 1716, described but unfortunately not illustrated in full in Stillman, 1979: 52.

17. There is an unusual white dress attributed to the Mejdel area in the Kawar collection, 1987: 317. This has winged sleeves, and is embroidered with large diagonal crosses on the skirt similar to those on the veil from Falujeh (east of Mejdel) in the Museum of Mankind collection. It is unlikely to come from the villages along the coast, since their dresses always had tight sleeves. In the Dar al-Tifl collection, no. 39.23, there is a tight-sleeeved dress said to be 'probably from Falujeh', which is white with vertical red stripes at the selvedge. The catalogue note suggests this is a nightdress worn by brides, and kept for burial.

18. Crowfoot and Sutton, 1935 claimed that white dresses were mainly worn in summer and for festive occasions, and dark blue in winter and for working in, but this is unlikely. As one Ramallah woman put it: 'White *or* black dresses could be worn for special occasions as long as there was a lot of embroidery on them'; the dresses with the richest embroidery tend, in fact, to be the 'black' ones.

19. The parallel between woven fabrics and embroidery structure was first pointed out by Ziva Amir, 1988.

20. Kawar and Amir have *dubayt*.

21. A beautiful old *jillayeh* from the Ramallah area in the Kawar collection, 1988: 162, plate 23 has this decoration.

22. Granqvist, 1965: 143.

23. Granqvist, 1965: 150.

24. See Weir and Shahid, 1988 for a detailed description of cross-stitch embroidery technique.

25. According to Amir's painstaking analysis (1988), Bethlehem women actually used

a double-rowed cross-stitch for the *sabaleh*, whereas true herringbone was used by other villages in imitation of Bethlehem.

26. I am grateful to Widad Kawar for this story.

27. 'The women generally are very fond of fancy needlework, and the teaching of it in mission-schools is one of the best ways of attracting otherwise unwilling scholars.' Wilson, 1906: 129. *See also* Jones, 1962.

28. The former leaders of Egypt and Israel, and the 1967 cease-fire line between the two countries.

29. Amir, 1988 describes the evolution of the Bethlehem chest panel in great and illuminating detail.

30. Bethlehem women's employment in the mother-of-pearl industry goes back to at least the seventeenth century, for it was noted by Pococke, 1745, II: 40 who travelled there in 1697.

31. Bailey, 1974.

32. Numbers 37.221, 37.301, 37.302, 37.271 (illustrated) and 38.76 in the Dar al-Tifl Museum.

33. There is an example in the Dar al-Tifl Museum: 37.296

34. Crowfoot, 1943 provides a detailed description of the making of the narrower of these two belt components among a branch of the Tarabin bedouin.

35. Alternative names are *saltah* and *furmaliyeh* (the latter given by Amir, 1984).

36. Amir, 1988.

37. Granqvist, 1935: 60.

38. Granqvist, 1935: 70. The woman was Louisa Baldensperger.

39. Granqvist, 1935: 53–4.

40. Granqvist, 1935: 122–3.

Chapter 4

1. Granqvist, 1935: 67.

2. Mansur describes it as being part of Nazareth dress around 1850, and going out of fashion in the early twentieth century.

3. In the Dar al-Tifl Museum: numbers 37.300 and 37.242.

4. Ashkenazi, 1938: 136–7.

5. In the Dar al-Tifl Museum: 37.290.

6. Brideprice payments were unnecessary in the case of exchange marriages. In Artas in the 1920s, 26.5% of marriages were exchange marriages

(Granqvist, 1931: 111), but marriage statistics undoubtedly varied according to village, period and economic conditions.

7. Some anthropologists prefer the term 'bridewealth' to avoid this possible misunderstanding.

8. Granqvist, 1931: 125.

9. Granqvist, 1931: 122.

10. Granqvist, 1931: 124.

11. Spoer and Haddad, 1927: 110 claim that in El-Qubeibeh near Jerusalem it was the groom's father who bought the jewellery, but this is unusual. Possibly some arrangement had been made between the two fathers in the case they describe, or they were close relatives.

12. See Granqvist, 1931: 128, Rosenfeld, 1957 and Weir, 1973 and 1975 for discussion of the amount of brideprice in various Palestinian villages, and the proportion which went to the bride.

13. Tristram, 1865: 68–9.

14. Tristram, 1865: 113–14.

15. Tristram, 1865: 416.

16. The village terms for silver coins commonly attached to headdresses and chin-chains include *abu risheh* (literally 'father of feathers', because of the wings on the obverse; these are Maria Theresa dollars), *abu 'amud* ('father of the pillar', because of the pillar-like decoration on the obverse), *wazaris* and *majidis* (Turkish coins); gold coins include *kheriyeh* (small coins used for *shakkehs*), and larger coins for *iznaqs*: *jhadi*, *mehnakeh*, *dobaliyeh*, *ftireh*, *mkhammasiyeh* and *othmanliyeh*.

17. There is an example in the Dar al-Tifl Museum, no. 36.161.

18. Widad Kawar, pers. comm.

19. Canaan, 1927: 149; Spoer and Haddad, 1927; Ulmer, 1918. Ulmer provides a detailed description of the coins on an elaborate Lifta *shatweh*.

20. Ulmer, 1918.

21. Granqvist, II, 1935: 66.

22. See Weir, 1973 for a more detailed description of the *wuqayat al-darahem*. Since that publication, I have confirmed that these headdresses were made on commission in Bethlehem.

23. There are examples in the Santa Fe Museum and the Royal Ontario Museum.

24. There is a beautiful example

of a *miqlab* in the Kawar collection.

Chapter 5

1. Baldensperger, 1895.

2. Mills, 1931.

3. Granott, 1952: 164–5.

4. According to informants, this mosque was inscribed with the information that it was built by the Caliph 'Amr Al-Khatāb. Baldensperger, 1895 names five mosques, but none named after Al-Khatāb.

5. Beit Dajan people claim the *ftuh* area extended to Yibna in the south and Qalqilya in the east.

6. Harat Shamiyeh, Harat Hawashi and Harat 'Ajajiyeh.

7. I am grateful to Khalid Muhammad, head of the Beit Dajan Society in Amman, for this and other information.

8. Naval Intelligence Division, 1943: 112.

9. Baldensperger, 1895.

10. Several Beit Dajan families, including the Bishtawis, Sawalhis and Santarisis, claim descent from Egyptians who settled in the village at that time.

11. Van de Velde, 1854: 18.

12. Tristram, 1865: 409.

13. Granott, 1952: 177.

14. Baldensperger, 1906: 193.

15. Including the Rok, Talamas, Dimiani and Tawaj families.

16. Granott, 1952: 253. Several other Jewish agricultural communities were also established in the Jaffa region in the early 1880s. Oliphant, 1886: 286.

17. Sawwaf in Himadeh, 1938: 315–17.

18. Sawwaf in Himadeh, 1938: 304.

19. Baldensperger, 1895.

20. Baldensperger, 1893.

21. This exemption rule may have increased extra-village marriage during the First World War.

22. Land Registration was completed at different times in different areas of Palestine. The Jaffa area as a whole was completed early, by 1932. Granott: 1952: 204.

23. Granott, 1952: 37, 108.

24. The economic effects of the national six-month strike of 1936, and the outbreak of the Second World War in 1939, were offset locally, to some extent, by the opening and enlargement of British army camps in the vicinity. P£ = a Palestinian pound.

25. The consequent increased demand for clothing materials attracted textile traders to Beit Dajan more often, some eventually opening permanent shops in the village.

26. Beit Dajan people mentioned people visiting from the following villages: 'Aboud, Deir Terif, Deir 'Ammar, Deir Qadis, Kharbatha, Beit Nabala and Na'lin.

27. As elsewhere in Palestine, her contribution to the trousseau also included simple, everyday dresses and veils, and household furnishings.

28. *min yom khilqat al-dunia al-shinyar lawarra.*

29. According to one informant, the Na'ani dress cost between P£30 and P£35, while the other dresses cost P£25 or less.

30. Sitt Naziha had kept the DMC copy-books from those days. They were: *Broderies Turqs, Motifs pour Broderies 5 ième Serie* and *Kreuzstich Neuw Muster IV Siècle*.

31. It was sometimes as low as P£25 for paternal cousins.

32. Most or all the remainder was spent on other wedding expenses: hospitality, trousseau materials for his daughter, and clothing gifts for other family members.

33. In the 1920s the *ftireh* was P£2.5 and the *mkhammasiyah* P£6.

34. The best *maqruneh* with twenty-toothed 'combs' cost P£8 in 1936.

35. In 1936, velvet cost around double the price of the *malak* dress, which was between P£2.5 and P£3.5 for the dress length. The velvet dress also had more couching, so was more expensive in material and labour costs to decorate. The work alone cost between P£1.5 and P£2.5.

36. Maneh Hazbun charged P£5 to do the *qasab* couching on the Na'ani dress, excluding the cost of the cord.

Chapter 6

1. A rare description of a *zarafeh* is provided by Grant, 1921: 54 in his account of trousseau celebrations in the Jerusalem area: '. . . the women had a stick dressed up with the bridal costume. This was the red striped dress and gay jacket on a cross-stick frame to hold out the sleeves. There were also a girdle, the heavy coin headdress and three small mirrors, one on each arm and one on the breast'.

2. This custom is mentioned by Wilson, 1906: 114 who says the threads at the frayed edge represent the many children it is hoped the bride will bear.

3. Granqvist, 1935: 127.

Arabic transcription of songs

Pages 23 and 247

qaṭaʿ al-kassā
qaṭaʿ al-kassā
ḥabb al-rumāni
fi dārak ya ʿAbd
nufrush u nāmi
qaṭaʿ al-kassā
qaṭaʿ al-kassā
thōb abū rīsheh
fi dārak ya ʿAbd
ṭabit al-ʿaysheh

Page 47 (see page 245 below)

Pages 73 and 251

yāmā khayyaṭnā ʿala al-benāyiq
saqā Allah yā Ḥalīmeh w-iḥnā rufāyiq
yāmā khayyaṭnā ʿala al-qabbāt
saqā Allah yā Ḥalīmeh w-iḥnā banāt

Page 150

iḥnā min al-jabal wa inti min al-saḥel
yalli zunnarik awastik saḥel

Page 159

Ṣafīyeh shakket al-dhahab
daqqat al-sāyigh
saʿdah illi ishtara
ʿawaḍ ʿala al-bāya
Ṣafīyeh shakket al-dhahab
la naḥū abūhā
saʿdah illi ishtara
ʿawaḍ ʿala abūhā
Ṣafīyeh imlīḥah
wa aysh bitūqulū fīhā
rakabah ṭawilah wa al-qelayed fīhā

Page 203

iḥnā al-naʿāniyyāt fil khazāneh
wa rijālnā qudāmnā khayāleh
w-iḥnā al-naʿāniyyāt juwwa al-ʿūḍah
wa rijālnā qudāmnā ʿala al-mōḍah
w-iḥnā al-naʿāniyyāt fil-ʿalāqah
wa rijālnā qudāmnā sawwāqah
w-iḥnā al-naʿāniyyāt juwwa al-ʿūḍah
wa rijālnā qudāmnā ʿala al-mōḍah
w-iḥnā al-naʿāniyyāt fi-l-ʿalīyyah
wa rijālnā qudāmnā nashmīyeh

Page 222

shūfi ya bint shūfi
min aṭlaʿ ʿerq al-nafnūfeh
Ruqīyeh Abbās imm al-ʿayūneh

Page 234

iḥna al-Dajanīyāt nqūd nqūd
zay al-dhahab al-ṣāfi al-manqūd
w-iḥnā al-Dajanīyāt ma finā danas
mintayyiḥ al-khayāl ʿan ḍahr al-faras
yā Dajanīyah ya miyah ʿalamiyeh
u imshū bi namūs walla timshū bi dhilīyeh

iḥnā al-dhahab ʿala al-qabbeh
wa rijālnā tinʿaddi
lamma tsīr al-ḥaddeh
wa rijālnā tiḥmīnā
wa iḥnā al-dhahab ʿala rāsī
wa rijālnā qawwāsi
lamma tsīr al-tawshī
rijālnā tiḥmīnā

Page 241

yā banāt al-faraḥ
jurrū jilālīkum
jadd al-faraḥ ʿandnā
ʿaqbāl ahālikum
yā banāt al-faraḥ
jurrū shunāberkum
jadd al-faraḥ ʿandnā
ʿaqbāl akhwātikum
yā banāt al-faraḥ
jurrū malakātikum
jadd al-faraḥ ʿandnā
ʿaqbāl aḥbabikum
yā banāt al-faraḥ
yā ummāt al-thiyāb al-bayḍā
jadd al-faraḥ ʿandnā
ʿaqbāl kull ḥabīb

Page 245

anā baghannī la-Saʿīd
kurmāl ummuh
ma aḥlā qumbāz al-ghabani
lābiq ʿala kummuh
w-anā baghannī la-Saʿīd
kurmāl khawātuh
ma aḥlā qumbāz al-ʿarīs
lābiq ʿala diyyātuh
lawlaki ʿazīzeh u ghāliyeh
ma jinā lahīna
wallā ʿabarnā lawaṣat al-dār
wa ghannaynā

Page 246

Allah maʿ Abū Ibrāhīm
qaṭaʿ linā malakāt
yā ʿazim al-ḥamūleh
yā mfarriḥ kull al-khawāt
Allah maʿ Abū Ibrāhīm
qaṭaʿ linā maqārīn
yā ʿazim al-ḥamūleh
yā mfarriḥ hal muḥabbīn

Page 247 (see page 23 above)

Page 251 (see page 73 above)

Page 251

aysh labbasūk ya ghazayyil laylat ḥannūk?
labbasūnī al-aṭālis libs al-mulūk
u aysh hal ghazāl illi ʿand dārnā māriq?
khaṣrū raqīq u būzu fi-l-ʿasal ghāriq
u aysh hal ghazāl illi ʿand dārnā ʿadda?
khaṣrū raqīq u bi-l-kashmīr mishtaddi
u aysh hal ghazāl illi yuʿid walla yinsaddi?
nasabuhū al-shabak u ṣadūh
fi qāʿ al-wādi

Page 261

ḍubbī shunbarik yā bint ḍubbī
yā rayt al-khayr ʿala wajhik yiʿabbī
ḍubbī shunbarik wa-rkhī sanāsil
yā rayt al-khayr ʿala wajhik yirāsil

Page 263

wa-ḥayāt abūyā ma ilbis illā malakah
wa-ḥnā al-mashāyikh sīṭnā fi-l-waraqah
wa-hayāt abūyā mā ilbis illā fṭīreh
wa-ḥnā al-mashāyikh sīṭnā fi-l-dīrī
wa-ḥayāt abūyā mā ilbis illā ikhḍāri
wa-ḥnā al-mashāyikh sīṭnā hal-ʿālī

yā mā aḥlā al-bida wa al-qawl talbisnā
jalālīnā
wa-ḥnā ʿaqqādīn al-shūr fī juwwa ʿalālīnā
yā mā aḥlā al-bida wa-l-qawl talbisnā al-
malakāt
wa-ḥnā ʿaqqādīn al-shūr fi juwwa ruwāqāt

Page 264

takhaddari ya ḥelweh ya zaynah
ya warad juwwa li jnaynah
inḥabak al-lūlū
khalli shalīshik ʿala ṭūlū

la dam baqqah
wala dam barghūth
illā dam bint bikrīyeh
sīṭhā birfaʿ al-ruus

Page 269

ṭallū min al-gharbī
ʿarbān al-ṭarabīnī
slāḥhum heremzī
wa rimāḥhum zīneh

SELECT
BIBLIOGRAPHY

Amir, Ziva 1984. 'The embroidered costume of the women of Tuba – tradition and modernization in a bedouin village', in *Edot: Studies in Ethnography 1*, Jerusalem: The Israel Museum.

Amir, Ziva 1988. *Bethlehem Embroidery: The Evolution and Spread of the Bethlehem-Style Embroidered Chest-Panel*, (in Hebrew). Jerusalem: The Israel Museum.

Ashkenazi, Tovia 1938. *Tribus Semi-Nomades de la Palestine du Nord*. Paris: Geuthner.

Bailey, Clinton 1974. 'Bedouin weddings in Sinai and the Negev', in *Studies in Marriage Customs*. Folklore Research Center, Hebrew University of Jerusalem.

Baldensperger, Philip 1893. 'Woman in the east', in *Palestine Exploration Fund Quarterly*, London.

Baldensperger, Philip 1894. 'Birth, marriage and death among the fellahin of Palestine', in *Palestine Exploration Fund Quarterly*, London.

Baldensperger, Philip 1895. 'Beth-Dejan', in *Palestine Exploration Fund Quarterly*, London.

Baldensperger, Philip 1913. *The Immovable East*. London.

Barbour, Violet 1956. 'Muslim embroideries', in *Traditional Embroideries from the Holy Land and from Norway*, catalogue of fifth 'Craftsman and Designer' exhibition, Oxford.

Bauer, Leonhard 1901. 'Kleidung und Schmuck der Araber Palästinas', in *Zeitschrift des Deutschen Palästina-Vereins*, XXIV, Leipzig.

British Government 1928. *First Palestine Census of Industries 1927*. Jerusalem.

Burckhardt, J. L. 1822. *Travels in Syria and the Holy Land*. London.

Canaan, Tewfiq 1927. *Mohammedan Saints and Sanctuaries in Palestine*, (repr.). Jerusalem: Ariel.

Canaan, Tewfiq 1938–9. 'The decipherment of Arabic talismans', in *Berytus*.

Cohen, Amnon 1973. *Palestine in the 18th Century: Patterns of Government and Administration.* Jerusalem: Hebrew University.

Conder, Claude 1880. *Tent Work in Palestine*. London: Bentley.

Crowfoot, Grace 1936. 'Bethlehem embroidery', in *Embroidery*, December. London.

Crowfoot, Grace 1943. 'Handicrafts in Palestine: Primitive weaving, 1. Plaiting and fingerweaving', in *Palestine Exploration Quarterly*, July–October. London.

Crowfoot, Grace 1944. 'Handicrafts in Palestine: Jerusalem hammock cradles and Hebron rugs', in *Palestine Exploration Quarterly*, January–April. London.

Crowfoot, Grace 1956. 'The embroidery of Ramallah', in *Traditional Embroideries from the Holy Land and from Norway*, catalogue of fifth 'Craftsman and Designer' exhibition, Oxford.

Crowfoot, Grace and Louise Baldensperger 1932. *From Cedar to Hyssop: a Study in the Folklore of Plants in Palestine*. London: Sheldon Press.

Crowfoot, Grace and P. Sutton 1935. 'Ramallah embroidery', in *Embroidery*, March. London.

Dalman, Gustav 1964. *Arbeit und Sitte in Palästina: Band V: Webstoff, Spinnen, Weben, Kleidung*, (repr. of 1937 edn) Hildesheim: Olms.

Davis, Ralph 1967. *Aleppo and Devonshire Square: English Traders in the Levant in the Eighteenth Century*. London: Macmillan.

De Thevenot, J. 1686. *Travels into the Levant*.

Dozy, R. P. A. 1845. *Dictionnaire Detaillé des Noms Des Vêtements chez les Arabes*, (repr.). Beirut: Librairie du Liban

Gilbert, Martin 1979. *The Arab-Israeli Conflict*. London: Weidenfeld.

Goodrich-Freer, A. 1924. *Arabs in Tent and Town*. London: Seeley, Service.

Graham-Brown, Sarah 1980. *Palestinians and their Society 1880–1946*. London: Quartet.

Granott, A. 1952. *The Land System in Palestine*. London: Eyre and Spottiswoode.

Granqvist, Hilma 1931. *Marriage Conditions in a Palestinian Village I*. Helsinki: Societas Scientiarum Fennica.

Granqvist, Hilma 1935. *Marriage Conditions in a Palestinian Village II*. Helsinki: Societas Scientiarum Fennica.

Granqvist, Hilma 1947. *Birth and Childhood among the Arabs: Studies in a Muhammadan Village in Palestine*. Helsinki: Soderstrom.

Granqvist, Hilma 1965. *Muslim Death and Burial: Arab Customs and Traditions Studied in a Village in Jordan*. Helsinki: Societas Scientarum Fennica.

Grant, Elihu 1921. *The People of Palestine*. London: Lippincott.

Himadeh, Said 1938. *Economic Organisation of Palestine*. Beirut: American Press.

Hole, William 1906. *The Life of Jesus of Nazareth*. London: Eyre and Spottiswoode.

Institut du Monde Arabe 1988. *Memoire de Soie: Costumes et Parures de Palestine et de Jordanie. Catalogue de la Collection Widad Kamel Kawar*. Paris.

Issawi, Charles (ed.) 1966. *The Economic History of the Middle East 1800–1914*. University of Chicago Press.

Jaussen, J.-A. 1927. *Coutumes Palestiniennes: 1. Naplouse et son District*. Paris: Geuthner.

Jessup, Henry Harris 1873. *The Women of the Arabs*. New York: Dodd and Mead.

Jones, Christina 1962. *The Ramallah Handicraft Co-operative*, Ramallah, Jordan.

Kawar, Widad 1982. *Costumes Dyed by the Sun: Palestinian Arab National Costumes*. Tokyo.

Kawar, Widad and Katharina Hackstein 'Catalogue de la collection Widad Kawar', in *Institut du Monde Arabe*, 1988: 150–387.

Khalidi, Walid 1984. *Before their Diaspora: A Photographic History of the Palestinians 1876–1948*. Washington DC: Institute for Palestine Studies.

Klein, F. A. 1881. Mittheilungen über Leben, Sitten und Gebrauche der Fellachen in Palästina, *Zeitschrift des Deutschen Palästina-Vereins*, IV. Leipzig.

Lamartine, Alphonse de n.d. *The Holy Land*: London.

Leach, Edmund 1976. *Culture and Communication: the Logic by which Symbols are Connected*. Cambridge University Press.

Lutfiyya, A. M. 1966 *Baytin: A Jordanian Village*. The Hague: Mouton.

Macdonald, Jan 1950–1. 'Palestinian dress', in *Palestine Exploration Fund Quarterly*, London.

Macdonald, Jan n.d. *Palestinian dress (in Fact and Folklore)* (unpublished manuscript in the Museum of Mankind library).

Mansur, Canon A. n.d. *History of Nazareth* (in Arabic). Cairo.

Maundrell, Henry *A Journey from Aleppo to Jerusalem at Easter, AD 1697*. London.

McDowall, David 1987. *The Palestinians*. Minority Rights Group, London.

Mills, E. 1932. *Census of Palestine, 1931: Population of villages, towns and administrative areas*. Jerusalem.

Morris, Benny 1987. *The Birth of the Palestinian Refugee Problem, 1947–1949*. Cambridge University Press.

Naval Intelligence Division 1943. *Palestine and Transjordan*. Geographical Handbook Series, British Admiralty.

Neale, F. A. 1851. *Eight Years in Syria, Palestine and Asia Minor from 1842 to 1850*, 2 Vols. London: Colburn.

Oliphant, Laurence 1887. *Haifa or Life in Modern Palestine*. London: Blackwood.

Owen, Roger 1981. *The Middle East in the World Economy 1800–1914*. London: Methuen.

Pococke, Richard 1745. *Observations on Palestine or the Holy Land, Syria, Mesopotamia, Cyprus and Candia*. London.

Robinson, Edward 1860. *Biblical Researches in Palestine . . . A Journal of Travels in the year 1838*, vols I–III. London.

Rosenfeld, Henry 1957. 'An analysis of marriage and marriage statistics for a Moslem and Christian village', in *International Archives of Ethnography*, XLVIII, no. 1.

Rothstein, Gustav 1910. 'Moslemische Hochzeitsgebrauche in Lifta bei Jerusalem', in *Palästinajahrbuch*, VI. Leipzig.

Ruppin, A. 1916. *Syrien als Wirtschaftsgebiet*. Berlin: Kolonial-Wirtschaftsiches Komitee.

Saussure, Ferdinand de 1974. *Course in General Linguistics*. Glasgow: Collins

Sawwaf, Husni 1938. 'Foreign Trade', in *Himadeh*.

Seger, Karen (ed.) 1981. *Portrait of a Palestinian Village: the Photographs of Hilma Granqvist*. London: Third World Centre for Research and Publishing.

Spoer, H. H. and E. N. Haddad 1927. 'Volkskundliches aus el-Qubebe bei Jerusalem', in *Zeitschrift für Semitistik und verwande Gebiete*, VI. Leipzig.

Stillman, Yedida 1979. *Palestinian Costume and Jewelry*. Albuquerque: University of New Mexico Press.

Thomson, W. M. 1867. *The Land and the Book; or Biblical Illustrations drawn from the Manners and Customs, the Scenes and Scenery of the Holy Land*. London: Nelson.

Tristram, H. B. 1865. *The Land of Israel; A Journal of Travels in Palestine*. London: SPCK.

Ulmer, Friedrich 1918. 'Sudpalästinensische Kopfbedeckungen', in *Zeitschrift des Deutschen Palästina-Vereins*, XLI. Leipzig.

Ulmer, Friedrich 1921. 'Arabische Stickmuster', in *Zeitschrift des Deutschen Palästina-Vereins*, XLIV. Leipzig.

Van de Velde, C. W. M. 1854. *Narrative of a Journey through Syria and Palestine in 1851 and 1852*, 2 vols. London.

Volney, C. F. 1787. *Voyage en Egypte et en Syrie pendant les années 1783, 1784 et 1785*, II. Paris (extract in Issawi, 1966: 213ff).

Warren, Charles 1876. *Underground Jerusalem*. London.

Weakley, E. 1911. 'Report on the Conditions and prospects of British Trade in Syria', in Issawi (ed.), 1966.

Weir, Shelagh 1969. 'The traditional costumes of the Arab women of Palestine', in *Costume*, 3. London.

Weir, Shelagh 1970a. *Palestinian Embroidery*. London: British Museum.

Weir, Shelagh 1970b. *Spinning and Weaving in Palestine*. London: British Museum.

Weir, Shelagh 1973. 'A bridal headdress from southern Palestine', in *Palestine Exploration Quarterly* (January–June). London.

Weir, Shelagh 1976. *The Bedouin: Aspects of the Material Culture of the Bedouin of Jordan*. London: World of Islam Festival Publishing Company.

Weir, Shelagh and Widad Kawar 1975. 'Costumes and wedding customs in Bayt Dajan', in *Palestine Exploration Quarterly*, London.

Weir, Shelagh and Serene Shahid 1988. *Palestinian Embroidery: Cross-stitch Patterns from the Traditional Costumes of the Village Women of Palestine*. London: British Museum.

Wilson, Charles (ed.) 1880–84. *Picturesque Palestine, Sinai and Egypt*, 4 vols. London: Virtue.

Wilson, C. T. 1906. *Peasant Life in the Holy Land*, London.

Winkelhane, Gerd 1988. 'Artisanat du textile et commerce caravanier en Syrie aux XIX et XX siècles' in *Institut du Monde Arabe*, 1988: 118–123.

Index and Glossary

'abā or *'abāyeh* (cloak)
  woman's 166
  man's 14, 15, 17, 27, 33, 40, 48–9, 50, 52, 55, 58, 70
'Aboud 53, 61, 63, 64, 101, 173, 178
Abu Adnan 27
Abu Dis 25, 91
Abū Jwayd bedouin 141
Abu Mishail 32, 34
abu mītayn (fabric) 30, 88, 94, 98, 99, 108, 123
abū quṭbeh (dress) 91, 96, 170
abu rīsheh ('father of feathers') *see* Maria Theresa coins/dollars
Abu Subuh 246
abū wardeh (*malak* or *ikhdāri* fabrics 'with flowers') 29, 31
Acre 24–5, 43, 78
aesthetics 104, 221
age symbolism 61, 63, 64, 104, 105, 109, 148, 176
'Ain Karim 91, 93, 132, 156
'ajami (belt, girdle) 150
Al-Bussah 80, 175
Al-Ghawi (silversmith) 199
Al-Jib half-title page
Al-Malhah 91
Al-Na'ani 108, 117, 118, 122–3
Al-Qubeibeh title page
Al-'Aizeriyeh 14, 18, 91
Al-'Azazmeh bedouin 147, 188
'alam ('banner', back skirt panel) 31, 91
amber necklace 193, 200
Amir, Z. 43 n. 48, 87 n. 11, 12 & 14, 91 n. 19, 107 n. 25, 127 n. 29, 152 n. 35 & 36
amulet 193–4, 201, 202
  see also herz, māskeh
Anabta 40, 92
Anani, Nabil 276
anilin dyes 26, 37, 108
'aqāl (men's head-ropes) 32, 33, 66–8
'Āqir 126
'Arab al-'Aramsheh 87
'Arab al-Hayb 86–7, 162
'Arafat, Yasser 68, 277
'araqiyeh
  (man's cap) 58
  (woman's headdress) 184, 185, 187
'arayjeh (stitch) 107
Artas 25, 34, 47, 49, 51–63, 72, 75, 105, 107, 148, 156, 174, 179, 241–47, 255, 257–61, 265, 271
asāweri (material) 39
'asbeh (headband) 42, 55, 148, 152, 160, 161–3, 166
Ashdod 19, 43, 88, 94, 204, 206
Ashkenazi, T. 87 n. 13
Asian influence 32, 43
aswāreh habbiyāt (bracelet) 199

aswāreh hayayīyeh ('snake' bracelet) 233
aswāreh 'iraḍ ('wide' bracelet) 230
'aṭāfi (fabric) 39
aṭlas (satin) 37–44, 65, 77, 78, 82, 93, 98–100, 148, 176, 184, 188, 213, 219, 235, 257
  sexual significance of 219, 251, 254–7, 265, 267
authenticity 113
'ayb (shame, disgrace) 61, 216

badleh bayḍah (western-style wedding dress) 239
baft (fabric) 43
Bailey, C. 139 n. 31
Baldensperger, L. 25 n. 15
Baldensperger, P. 48 n. 4, 53 n. 11, 55 n. 19, 204 nn. 1 & 4, 206 nn. 9 & 14, 207 nn. 19 & 20
Balfour-Paul, J. 25 n. 15
banamā (fabric) 43
Bani Na'im 184
baqaj (patchwork) 100
bayt al-shām (fabric and dress) 29, 88, 235, 254, 264, 267, 269
Baytin 61 n. 27
bazayl (flannelette) 29
beads, buttons and shells 63, 150–1, 157, 187, 188–90, 193–4, 200–2
Beersheba 26, 43, 193
Beirut 44
Beisan 25
Beit Dagon 209
Beit Dajan 51–2, 63–4, 66, 73–4, 101, 105, 107, 109, 116, 118, 133, 146, 148, 150, 174, 178, 203–70
Beit al-Husan 93
Beit Jala 28, 32, 34, 100, 115, 127, 133, 135, 152, 153, 155–6, 164, 173, 177, 179, 180
Beit Jann 80, 175
Beit Jibrin 110, 184
Bcit Safafah 91
Beit Sahur 127, 179, 180
Beit 'Ula 98
Beit 'Ummar 108, 110, 126, 184
Beitunia 268
belts
  men's 48, 55–6, 58
  women's 35, 36, 113, 150, 272
  see also girdles
benāyiq, sing. *benīqah* (side skirt panels) 116
Bethlehem 6–7, 10, 14, 28, 31–68, 91–100, 118, 120, 127–39, 144, 148, 152–8, 164, 166, 170–99, 263, 265
  influence 44, 95, 105, 109, 133, 156, 225–7, 237
biltajeh (fabric) 30, 88
Bir Zeit 111
bisht (coat)
  woman's 14, 34, 152, 157
  man's 49, 50, 51
blood symbolism 105, 254, 255, 264 (song)
bnūd lūlū (tasselled ties) 117, 223, 233, 267

287